## DATE DUE

| | | | |
|---|---|---|---|
| APR 27 1987 | | | |
| | | | |
| 7-29-92 Ill. | | | |
| | | | |
| | | | |
| | | | |
| | | | |
| | | | |
| | | | |
| | | | |
| | | | |
| | | | |
| | | | |
| | | | |
| | | | |
| | | | |
| | | | |
| | | | |
| | | | |
| | | | |

DEMCO NO. 38-298

# Food Aversion Learning

# Food Aversion Learning

Edited by

**N.W. Milgram, Lester Krames, and Thomas M. Alloway**
*University of Toronto*
*Ontario, Canada*

**PLENUM PRESS • NEW YORK AND LONDON**

Library of Congress Cataloging in Publication Data

Main entry under title:

Food aversion learning.

Includes bibliographies and index.
1. Conditioned response. 2. Aversive stimuli. 3. Avoidance (Psychology) 4. Food.
I. Milgram, Norton William. II. Krames, Lester. III. Alloway, Thomas.
QP416.F66                                  156'.3'1526                                  77-21965
ISBN 0-306-31040-6

© 1977 Plenum Press, New York
A Division of Plenum Publishing Corporation
227 West 17th Street, New York, N.Y. 10011

Printed in the United States of America

# Contributors

**John H. Ashe**            University of California, Irvine, California

**J. Bureš**                Institute of Physiology, Czechoslovak
                            Academy of Sciences, Prague,
                            Czechoslovakia

**O. Burešová**             Institute of Physiology, Czechoslovak
                            Academy of Sciences, Prague,
                            Czechoslovakia

**Howard Cappell**          Addiction Research Foundation, Toronto,
                            Ontario, Canada

**Mauro Caudarella**        Department of Psychology, University of
                            Toronto, Toronto, Ontario, Canada

**Janet D. Coil**           Departments of Psychiatry and Psychology,
                            Mental Retardation Research Center,
                            University of California, Los Angeles,
                            California

**John Garcia**             Departments of Psychiatry and Psychology,
                            Mental Retardation Research Center,
                            University of California, Los Angeles,
                            California

**Walter G. Hankins**       Departments of Psychiatry and Psychology,
                            Mental Retardation Research Center,
                            University of California, Los Angeles,
                            California

**James W. Kalat**        Department of Psychology, North Carolina State University, Raleigh, North Carolina

**Lester Krames**        Department of Psychology, University of Toronto, Toronto, Ontario, Canada

**A. E. LeBlanc**        Addiction Research Foundation, Toronto, Ontario, Canada

**N. W. Milgram**        Department of Psychology, University of Toronto, Toronto, Ontario, Canada

**Marvin Nachman**        University of California, Riverside, California

**Joan Rauschenberger**        University of California, Riverside, California

**Sam Revusky**        Memorial University of Newfoundland, St. John's, Newfoundland, Canada

# Preface

During the past 10 years, the study of learned aversions to foods has become one of the most "popular" areas of research in animal psychology. Learned aversions to foods are typically produced in the laboratory by first allowing an animal to eat (or drink) some distinctively novel substance and then making the animal "ill" in some way, most frequently by either giving it an injection of some "illness"-producing drug such as lithium chloride or by exposing it to a toxic dose of radiation. When an animal that has been treated in this way is subsequently given another opportunity to ingest the same or a similar substance, one usually observes that it will either totally avoid ingesting the substance or that it will consume less of it than a control animal that was not made ill after previously consuming the same substance.

This form of learning has attracted the interest of many researchers because there are two apparently striking differences in the acquisition of food aversions and the acquisition of other types of associative learning. First, a single pairing of food with "illness" is often sufficient to produce a strong aversion. Although other examples of one-trial learning have been reported, such reports are rare enough to attract attention to a learning situation in which one-trial acquisition is frequently observed. Second, and perhaps more importantly, food aversions can often be demonstrated even though several hours have elapsed between the ingestion of food and the inception of "illness." If the food is considered to be analogous to a conditioned stimulus (CS) and the "illness" to be analogous to an unconditioned stimulus (UCS) in classical conditioning, then acquisition of a learned association when the CS–UCS interval is several hours long is most remarkable. In "typical" classical conditioning situations, optimal CS–UCS intervals are a matter of a few seconds or less; and no conditioning whatever is ordinarily observed with CS–UCS intervals of even a few minutes' duration.

Another striking characteristic of food aversion learning is the phenomenon which has been variously labeled "belongingness," "preparedness," or "stimulus relevance." Thus, single-trial acquisition and the acquisition of aversions when long CS–UCS intervals are employed are not general phenomena. Rather, they are observed only when the animal has the opportunity to associate the "right kind" of CS with the "right kind" of UCS. Usually, the UCS must involve the induction of toxicosis. Other forms of aversive stimulation such as foot shock may induce food aversions, but only after several trials and never with long CS–UCS intervals. However, the effectiveness of toxicosis in inducing food aversions does not mean that toxicosis is generally a more effective UCS than foot shock. Foot shock is much more effective than toxicosis in inducing avoidance of distinctive places. What the "right kind" of CS is depends upon species. Rats are particularly prone to associate tastes with toxicosis. In contrast, many kinds of birds seem predisposed to associate the visual characteristics of food with toxicosis. In general, it appears that these differing predispositions are highly correlated with the fact that different kinds of animals use different sensory modalities in the selection of food. Animals are usually predisposed to associate their dominant "food-locating" modality with toxicosis. The fact that animals are not equally "prepared" to associate any kind of CS with any kind of UCS in the acquisition of food aversions is theoretically important, because food aversion learning provides an important counterexample to the doctrine that stimuli from all sensory modalities should be equally associable.

As a consequence of these discoveries, a number of students of animal learning have begun to doubt that learning can be conceived of as a unitary process. It has been argued by some that learning over long delays and the fact that animals are prepared to associate certain stimuli but not others with toxicosis set food aversion apart as a phenomenon that is conceptually distinct from ordinary classical and instrumental conditioning.

Another reason why the study of food aversion learning appeals to so many animal psychologists is the fact that it is so obviously biologically adaptive. Learned food aversions help to insure that animals will in future avoid eating foods which have previously been associated with "illness." In this connection, it is not surprising that food aversion learning appears to be ubiquitous. All species that have been studied have manifested food aversion learning in one form or another.

In this volume, we have attempted to assemble in a concise format a theoretical overview of food aversion learning and reviews of the majority of important empirical studies. We begin with two somewhat contrasting theoretical treatments of the subject by Revusky and Kalat. Revusky argues that food aversion learning can be incorporated into a general process theory of learning; Kalat questions this possibility. Chapter 3 by

Nachman and Rauchenberger and Chapter 4 by Cappell and LeBlanc deal with problems related to the role of the CS and UCS, respectively. In Chapter 5, Milgram, Caudarella, and Krames examine the effect of toxicosis on a noningestive response, interspecific aggression. In Chapter 6, Garcia, Hankins, and Coil consider the effects of other kinds of UCSs, particularly those which can be used to produce acquired food preferences. Finally, in the last chapter, Bureš and Burešová review the extensive physiological literature pertinent to the phenomenon of food aversion learning.

N. W. Milgram
Lester Krames
T. M. Alloway

# Contents

**Chapter 2**
**Biological Significance of Food Aversion Learning** ............. 73
*James W. Kalat*

**Chapter 3**
**Stimulus Characteristics in Food Aversion Learning** ........... 105
*Marvin Nachman, Joan Rauschenberger, and John H. Ashe*

## Chapter 4
**Gustatory Avoidance Conditioning by Drugs of Abuse:**
**Relationships to General Issues in Research on Drug Dependence** **133**

*Howard Cappell and A. E. LeBlanc*

## Chapter 5
**Suppression of Interspecific Aggression Using Toxic Reinforcers** . **169**

*N. W. Milgram, Mauro Caudarella, and Lester Krames*

**Chapter 6**
**Koalas, Men, and Other Conditioned Gastronomes** ............ **195**

*John Garcia, Walter G. Hankins, and Janet D. Coil*

**Chapter 7**
**Physiological Mechanisms of Conditioned Food Aversion** ....... **219**

*J. Bureš and O. Burešová*

# Learning as a General Process with an Emphasis on Data from Feeding Experiments

**1**

**Sam Revusky**

General process approaches to learning presuppose that there are learning processes governed by principles general enough to apply to many species in wide varieties of learning situations. A parade example of a general process approach in action is B. F. Skinner's teaching-machine method. This is a technology of teaching verbal materials to humans largely based on principles derived from conditioning repetitive feeding behaviors in rats and pigeons. Two leaps of faith are implicit: (1) that one can validly extrapolate from pigeons and rats to humans; (2) that one can validly extrapolate from teaching repetitive feeding behaviors to teaching verbal materials. Although Skinner's approach is an extreme example, most experimental psychologists during the last century have considered learning to be the study of general processes which underlie a great diversity of phenomena.

The last 25 years have seen a steady increase in attacks upon the general process approach. One set of attacks has come from minitheorists.

**Sam Revusky** • Memorial University of Newfoundland, St. John's, Newfoundland, Canada.

These students of learning typically believe in the general process approach in principle, but feel that the only practical methodology, at least for the time being, is to construct theories limited to narrow situations and effects. A second set of attacks strikes closer to the conceptual core of general process approaches. It has come from certain ethologists and ethologically oriented psychologists who have always felt that general process approaches to learning were useless. These critics will be called neoevolutionists here because it is a convenient label, although a major theme of this chapter will be that they do not offer the best application of evolutionary theory to the study of learning. Their theme is that learning must be analyzed in a very specific manner with the main emphasis on species-specific and situation-specific factors rather than on general principles. Seeming to validate their attacks upon general process approaches has been a variety of recently discovered effects which seem to contradict traditional theories. These include the tendency of learned operant behaviors to drift, in certain cases, toward instinctive behaviors in apparent violation of the law of effect (Breland and Breland, 1961), long-delay flavor aversions (Garcia, McGowan, and Green, 1972), and the autoshaping effect (Jenkins, 1973; Moore, 1973).

Thus, there is a widespread feeling that general process approaches are too broad and vague to be of any real use in the detailed analysis of any particular learning situation and that a more empirical strategy would be better. It would be surprising if the hostility toward general process approaches did not intensify over the next decade or so. For experimental data are increasingly being gathered and interpreted with a view not only to discrediting traditional general process learning theories but the general process approach itself.

Although the attacks against traditional general process theories have substantial validity, a retreat at the present to an extremely empirical approach to learning would be a reversal of the usual historical sequence. Empirical approaches tend to be more useful while a scientific field is in its infancy, while more highly organized theoretical approaches gain ascendancy as a field becomes more advanced. Part of the reason for the usual historical sequence is that with little information, one can simply remember all of it; more theoretical approaches become necessary when a large body of information must be integrated. The psychology of learning ought to be past the empirical stage because it already contains large masses of data. Although advocates of neoevolutionary approaches may claim that most of these data are useless, I do not entirely agree and do not feel that a highly empirical strategy is practical at this time. Its main effect will be the encouragement of thoughtless experimentation and the creation of narrow theories that hardly extend beyond the data upon which they are based.

This chapter is an attempt to sell my point of view. In Section 1, the basic assumptions of most traditional learning theories will be shown to be invalid. In Section 2, the presumed deficiencies of the neoevolutionary approach will be explained. In Section 3, evidence in favor of general process learning will be presented. In Section 4, a practical general process approach in terms of learning as an adaptation to causal relationships will be presented.

## 1. Deficiencies of Traditional Learning Theories

The main objection to the traditional study of animal learning is that people have been working on it for over 75 years and it is still almost in a state of chaos. Just recently, an eminent learning theorist (me) was capable of writing that "the factors which can supply coherence to learning are . . . ephemeral . . . and there is remarkably little agreement about the nature of the learning process" (Revusky, 1975). No other basic biological process has had so much attention devoted to it, as evidenced by countless volumes of learning-related journals, with so little in the way of generally accepted basic concepts. No wonder its critics would like to call a halt to such a wasteful enterprise.

The reason I nevertheless remain optimistic about the possibility of a successful general process approach to learning is that I think traditional work in animal learning has been based on invalid assumptions. These are behaviorism and *tabula rasa* theory. The incorrect assumptions contained in these theories have resulted in an emphasis upon trivial distinctions, as well as upon trivial generalizations. Presumably, a general process approach based on more valid assumptions would not share these shortcomings, which will be explained in more detail below.

### 1.1. Behaviorism

Behaviorism began as a rebellion against the metaphysical doctrine of mind and treated learning as a change in behavior rather than as the acquisition of knowledge or skill. This position was long considered virtually synonymous with a proper scientific attitude by nearly all animal-learning psychologists. Nowadays behaviorism is often defined so loosely that any biological change in the animal which occurs in the course of learning is defined as a change in behavior. By such a definition, behaviorism is merely an affirmation that the usual scientific method is applicable to psychology. Since such a loosely defined behaviorism is not a specific scientific theory, there can be no disagreement with it. But the behaviorism which has strongly influenced traditional theories of learning includes specific scientific assumptions which I believe to be ill-advised. I will divide these assumptions into two types and will deal with each in order.

### 1.1.1. Classical Behaviorism

According to classical behaviorism, there is no learning without a change in behavior; behavior is defined as a response which is observable —at least in principle. This literally means that the change in overt behavior which occurs in either Pavlovian conditioning or in instrumental learning is what has been learned; there is no underlying learning process which controls the behavior. Of course, nobody ever denied that in practice some learned behavior is unobservable. But this unobservable behavior was supposed to consist of glandular and muscular responses that could be observed were it not for as yet unsolved technical problems. Moreover, such covert responses were assumed to be learned in the same way as readily observable behaviors. For example, Skinner (1957) wrote a book in which it was supposed that the rules which govern covert verbal behavior are the same as those which govern simple overt instrumental behavior.

Mackintosh (1974) has recently summarized evidence disproving the theory that apparent instances of learning without an overt behavioral change must depend on tiny glandular or muscular reactions. The single result which best illustrates this type of evidence was obtained by Cousins, Zamble, Tait, and Suboski (1971). They excluded any important role in learning for glandular reactions by using the sensory preconditioning (SPC) procedure to teach rats that a tone would be followed by a flash of light; it is unlikely that tones and lights produce strong glandular reactions. They excluded any role for muscular reactions (such as those of the investigatory response) during SPC by curarizing the rats so that no muscular reactions were possible. The outline of the experiment was as follows. During SPC, a combination of a tone followed by a light were repeatedly administered while the rats were curarized. Later, while the rats were no longer curarized, the light was paired with shock to produce fear of the light. Finally, in a test phase in which the tone was presented by itself, the rats exhibited fear of the tone. Since the tone had never been directly paired with the shock, the fear of the tone must have been mediated by the tone–light association learned during SPC while the rats were paralyzed.

### 1.1.2. Neobehaviorism

The neobehavioristic position, as defined here, presupposes that learning can occur in the absence of muscular or glandular responses.

Thus, it is admitted that a process of association or absorption of information which does not depend on muscular or glandular responses may underlie learned changes in behavior; presumably, this process occurs in the nervous system. The theory itself is that any such underlying process of association follows the same laws as the laws determined for overt changes in learned behavior.

Neobehaviorism is an obvious attempt to retain as much as possible of classical behaviorism in the face of its experimental disproof. The underlying learning process is treated as an interiorized version of the process by which overt changes in behavior occur. The strangeness of this doctrine can be illustrated by pretending that the study of mammalian respiration had developed in the same way as a neobehavioristic analysis of learning. It would be theorized that each mammalian cell contained a miniature set of lungs to absorb oxygen from the blood. Similarly, each cell would contain a miniature mouth and teeth to permit absorption of nutrients from the blood. Obviously, of course, such a theory would be wrong. W. K. Honig (unpub. ms.) has expressed the objections to this approach so eloquently that I cannot do any better than quote him directly:

> It may be attractive to think that behavioristic principles can account for nonbehavioral activity, but it is gratuitous to assume that the empirical paradigm for behavior should be incorporated, somehow, into the functioning of the nervous system. . . . What separates the sciences are discontinuities in mechanism—those boundaries at which a set of facts *cannot* be explained by reference to terms of processes based upon the paradigm within which these facts were gathered and organized. I have called the postulation of the little theoretical stimuli and responses the creation of a "behaviorunculus" with which behaviorists replaced the "homunculus"—the little man inside the big man—that they were trying to get rid of. The role of behavior, little or big, overt or covert, in the explanation of intellective processes has to be established by observation and not postulation.

Honig's objections in this excerpt are both to classical behaviorism and neobehaviorism, but I have included them in this section on neobehaviorism, because classical behaviorism has already been experimentally disproven. His snarky references to "homunculus" and "behaviorunculus" point up a parallel between a trap the behaviorists were trying to avoid and a trap they fell into themselves. "Homunculus" is a pejorative term used by behaviorists to refer to the mentalistic proclivity for naming an internal process in lieu of offering a substantive explanation. "Sensorium" is an example of a homunculus. It was a mentalistic term for an internal locus of sensations which was postulated to have exactly the same characteristics as the person whose sensations were to be explained. Honig points out that although such devices were anathema to behaviorists, they ended up with a remarkably similar methodology. A behaviorunculus is a system inside the animal with exactly the same properties as the overt response system to be explained.

The present denial of behaviorunculus theory is not a denial that the learning psychologist may have to continue using behavioral evidence to infer the underlying course of associative learning at least until there is a remarkable neurophysiological breakthrough. But behavioral evidence can be used for methodological reasons without acceptance of the baseless *a priori* assumptions of the behaviorunculus model.

## 1.2. Tabula Rasa

Classical behaviorism can be described as the postulation of conditioning mechanisms which result in the type of learning to be expected from the *tabula rasa* model of the mind. *Tabula rasa* is the doctrine that the mind is like a blank slate written upon by experience. Although this doctrine seemed to be confirmed by many observations, it originated in metaphysics and, like most metaphysical doctrines, has a strong element of wishful thinking.

The ideological motive of the British empiricists, who were early and persuasive advocates of *tabula rasa* psychology, was to justify dependence upon reason instead of authority as a guide to human activity. It was tacitly supposed that for reason to be a viable objective guide, it must always lead to unequivocal conclusions. If different minds were to come to different conclusions as a result of identical past experiences, then the mind would not be an objective instrument and reason would not be an unerring guide to action. By postulating that the mind is an instrument which translates sequences of sense impressions into conclusions in a straightforward manner, the *tabula rasa* doctrine implies that all minds uncorrupted by authority will come to the same conclusion as a result of the same past experiences. The mind makes impressions which objectively reflect the outside world, just as soft wax makes impressions which objectively reflect the object to be copied.

The most important corollary of the *tabula rasa* doctrine is clearly false and yet it was so widely accepted for so long that it rarely was seriously discussed. In fact, it did not even have an explicit label until recently when Garcia, McGowan, and Green (1972) called it the "equivalence of stimuli." This is the theory that the propensity of a cue to become conditioned ("salience") is independent of the consequences to which the cue is to become conditioned. As most readers of this volume already know, Garcia and Koelling (1966) disproved this theory for the rat by showing that the same taste cue which was more salient than an audiovisual cue in a food aversion learning situation was less salient than the same audiovisual cue in a shock avoidance situation. "Equivalence of stimuli" has also been disproven in other situations (for instance, Foree and Lo-Lordo, 1973). In fact, Thorndike (1911) supplied suggestive evidence against this doctrine early in his career. It is a remarkable demonstration of the important role of *tabula rasa* preconceptions in the development of contemporary learning theories that Thorndike's evidence was largely ignored for the better part of a century.

## 1.3. Effects of the Falsity of Traditional Assumptions

Because traditional general process theories of learning have been based on two false assumptions, behaviorism and *tabula rasa,* they were false. As I try to describe a general process approach to learning which does not incorporate these fallacies, I will point out specific areas in which they have led us astray.

The fundamental behavioristic error was a failure to develop abstract formulations of the underlying learning process which ignore unimportant behavioral distinctions. An example with which I have become very familiar is that of association over a delay (Revusky, 1971). It seems clear to me that all instances of association between two events separated by a delay ought to involve at least some common underlying process. But behaviorists divided this single problem into at least three problems to be explained through different theories: (1) delayed reward learning, in which the delay was between a response and a reward (or punishment); (2) delayed reaction learning, in which the delay was between a cue and the opportunity to respond; and (3) the effects of an interstimulus interval, in which the delay was between a Pavlovian conditioned stimulus (CS) and an unconditioned stimulus(UCS).

Although a detailed analysis of the reasons for this division of one problem into three would require an entire chapter, the main reason it occurred was because stimuli, responses, and rewards were defined as different types of events due to their different roles in a learning paradigm. In such a theoretical context, it seemed superficial to treat, for instance, a delay between a stimulus and a response as similar to a delay between a response and a reward. A particularly difficult stumbling block was the frequent definition of learning as the acquisition of stimulus–response connections, in which the role of the reward was to stamp in this connection. In such a framework, there was no association between the response and the reward and hence it was unreasonable to consider delays between stimuli and responses as similar to delays between responses and rewards. In stimulus–response delays, the delay was between two elements of an association. In response–reward delays, there was no delay between the elements of the association; the delay was between the associated elements and the reward which stamped in the association.

It is true that generalizations were made within the contexts of traditional learning theories, but I agree with Rozin and Kalat (1972), Garcia, McGowan, and Green (1972), and Hinde (1973) that these often were superficial. Where I disagree is with any implication that this shows the general process approach to be invalid. It will be shown in Section 4 that many traditional generalizations become less superficial when placed in a new general process context.

## 2. Neoevolutionary Learning Theories

Neoevolutionary theorists hope to organize data about learning in terms of evolutionary adaptation to particular environments. For instance, Rozin and Kalat (1972) have proposed "that learning and memory are situation-specific adaptations which have evolved as efficient solutions to particular types of environmental challenges." They clearly feel that general principles of learning are not important for the evolutionary analysis of learning. Other neoevolutionary learning theorists share this belief. I disagree almost entirely. While it may be that there has been an underemphasis on species-specific and situation-specific factors in the animal-learning literature, the main emphasis must continue to be on broad general principles of learning.

The precedent from the use of evolutionary theory in biology is that to understand what is specific, one must have knowledge of what is general. Evolutionary adaptation involves changes in bodily organs and/or physiological processes. To explain a particular adaptive change in an incisive fashion, one must understand the organ or process which is changed and this necessarily involves dealing with matters which are not species-specific or situation-specific. For instance, an analysis of the capacity of the desert rat to urinate almost a semisolid is bound to be superficial if it is not based upon the available general knowledge of kidney function. It may be that the biologist knows his general processes so well that he can occasionally forget that his study of diversity is in terms of general processes.

### 2.1. The Adaptive Complex

Of course, neoevolutionists are aware that scientific facts must be organized. They do not propose simply to gather wondrous instances of behavior and prattle about the wisdom of nature. The specific concept which is generally proposed to take the place of general principles of learning may be called an *adaptive biological complex*. Such a complex supplies a framework for understanding how a variety of biological and environmental factors interact in a specific situation. Hinde (1973), for example, has briefly indicated how respiration is understood in terms of such an adaptive complex.

> Frogs may breathe through skin, oral cavity, or lungs, or through combinations of these, in accordance with the different media in which they live, and these mechanisms are associated with a wide variety of other adaptations, such as the position of the external nares on the head permitting them to breathe air when nearly submerged, and the function of the hyoid apparatus as a respiratory pump. The significance of each character can be seen only in relation to others, and evolutionary change in one is likely to have repercussions through the whole complex.

An explanation of learning in terms of such an adaptive complex would be superficial. The types of situation-specific interactions which Hinde has described for respiration supply details about how respiration works in particular situations, but they cannot provide the basis for a general understanding of respiration. Rather the interactions which Hinde has described must be understood in terms of general biological principles. For instance, one does not understand lungs in terms of the specific adaptive complex in which they are imbedded, but in terms of what is common to their structure and function in many species. Although physiology textbooks may deal with how lung function can vary under different conditions, their main emphasis is properly on general principles of lung action. The study of adaptive complexes is possible mainly because of the availability of information about a variety of general principles. It follows that a study of learning based nearly entirely on its roles in specific interactions without an emphasis on general principles would be very superficial; as superficial as a similar study of respiration. There is no denial here that the study of how learning participates in specific adaptive complexes has a legitimate role, but there is a denial that this study would be very fruitful in the absence of a knowledge of learning as a general process.

My impression is that most neoevolutionary learning theorists are fully aware that the study of biological process in an adaptive complex depends upon general principles but feel that this precedent does not apply to learning. Most biological traits and physiological processes are presently understood in terms of known anatomical and chemical substrates. This is not true of learning at the present time. Thus, it could be argued that learning ought not to be studied as a primary biological process, but as a resultant of the interaction of "true" biological processes in an adaptive complex. In Sections 3 and 4, I hope to supply evidence against such an argument.

## 2.2. Are General Laws of Learning Unimportant?

An alternative to the view that learning is not a general process also fits into contemporary neoevolutionary learning theory. This is the belief that learning is a general biological process, but that it is so obvious and trivial that it ought to be analyzed in some other way. An analogy might be the size of an animal or of its organs. Clearly this is a biological trait subject to evolutionary selection, but one will not find chapters on size as a topic in general biology textbooks. One can casually note that the size of an animal or of an organ has changed as a result of evolutionary pressures without detailed discussion of general principles relevant to size. One gets the impression of a similar casual attitude toward learning from a statement by K. Lorenz about Skinner's operant conditioning (Evans, 1974):

> But practically *all* organisms with a higher developed nervous system have a learning apparatus which feeds back the results of successive behavior to antecedent behavior. The learning apparatus is pretty much the same in cephalopods, in crustaceans, in insects, and in vertebrates. If you study nothing but this learning apparatus, you fail to consider the things that are different among species . . . The Skinnerian has no right to comment on innate behavior or on aggression, because he cuts it from consideration.

It is amusing that in a very literal sense, Lorenz seems to have a stronger belief in general process learning than, say, Clark Hull, who never claimed that insect learning and vertebrate learning were "pretty much the same." Of course, the difference is that Lorenz considers the general process to be unimportant, in contrast to Hull.

Rozin and Kalat (1972) really have the same opinion as Lorenz, but their emphasis is such as to imply a wide variety of learning mechanisms:

> Biologically speaking, we should expect a variety of different mechanisms or parameters of learning in different situations, rather than a uniform set of properties in all situations. There might indeed be some general laws of learning resulting from basic constraints and features of the nervous system, and perhaps reflecting general principles of causality in the physical world. However, if we look at learning within an adaptive evolutionary framework, we would seek not only to uncover some of the common elements among the behaviors we study, but also to explore the plasticity of the mechanisms themselves, as they are shaped through selection to deal with particular types of problems.

I agree with every single statement by Rozin and Kalat in the above excerpt, but disagree with their general attitude. They denigrate general laws of learning, despite occasional lip service to the legitimacy of studying them by omitting any reference to them in a paper setting forth a program for the study of learning. Rozin and Kalat and other neoevolutionary learning theorists aggrandize minor science, the study of the particular, at the expense of extremely important science, the study of the general. Evidence that this denigration of general process learning is not justified will be deferred until later. In Section 3, I will try to show that there are nontrivial general laws of learning. In Section 4, I will show how "laws of learning which reflect general principles of causality" are a practical framework for the study of learning.

## 2.3. Traditional Preconceptions in Neoevolutionary Theory

The basic evidence used against general process learning seems to be lists of phenomena which do not fit into a known general process framework. Critics who use such "evidence," particularly Hinde (1973), do not seem disturbed be the fact that few of these phenomena can be explained by means of any other reasonably rigorous approach.

There is a natural tendency to pay more attention to exciting new phenomena which seem to contraindicate a general process approach than to those humdrum old phenomena which fit in with it. The unusual is newsworthy and it is entirely proper that we pay great attention to it, but this ought not to blind us to the basic pattern of the mass of facts. Although it is news when a man bites a dog and not news when dog bites a man, one ought not to conclude from perusal of the newspapers that men bite dogs more often than dogs bite men.

The illusion among those who overemphasize unusual learning effects is much like the size–weight illusion. If a person lifts objects of the same weight but varying sizes, his estimate of the weight of each object will be an inverse function of its size. The apparent reason is that a person's expectation of the weight of an object before lifting depends upon its size, and he tenses his muscles according to his expectation; if the actual weight is lighter than expected, he tends to underestimate the weight because he is prepared for a heavier weight. The net result is that a person's conclusion about the weight of an object is likely to err in the direction opposite from his initial expectation.

This is how the contemporary emphasis on specific factors in learning parallels the size–weight illusion: The *tabula rasa* model of learning is strongly ingrained in Western culture. It causes an expectation that learning will be identical across different species and different situations. When facts contrary to this expectation are uncovered, they loom very large and lead to the conclusion that there are few general properties of learning. This conclusion is opposite to initial expectations in the same way that an estimate of weight is opposite to initial expectations.

The implicit acceptance of the *tabula rasa* model by those who would count themselves as its enemies is illustrated by the use of the term "constraints on learning" almost as a rallying cry among neoevolutionary learning theorists. "Constraints on learning" refers to species-specific and situation-specific deviations from the *tabula rasa* model. The term is odd.

We do not refer to the adaptation of kidney function in the desert rat as a constraint on kidney function. We expect differences in kidneys among species. We refer to differences in learning as constraints because we begin with the assumption that learning is the same under all conditions and hence suppose that any apparent differences in learning must be due to factors extraneous to learning itself: constraints. This illustrates how critics of general process learning have started with an unrealistic and extreme *tabula rasa* model and, when it does not hold up, conclude that there are no nontrivial general properties of the learning process. Admittedly, it may be pettifogging to make so much of a vagary of linguistic usage, yet it illustrates the origins of the present overreaction against general process learning.

## 2.4. Evolutionary Principles and Prediction

On the relatively few occasions when predictions were made about learning on the basis of evolutionary considerations, the record of success was about as poor as that of traditional learning theories. A decade or so ago, it was popular among neoevolutionary thinkers to deplore the emphasis on rats in animal learning because the white rat was supposed to have degenerated in the course of its adaptation to the laboratory environment. Lockard (1968), for instance, claimed that the albino rat was an indefensible choice for the study of "dietary and taste preferences (*albinus* may now eat whatever does not bite back)." In view of the many food aversion studies with rats which have since appeared, it is hard to imagine how Lockard could have been more incorrect. When first confronted with this new evidence, a number of neoevolutionary theorists decided that the rat was unusually skillful at food selection because it was a scavenger. According to this new armchair theory, carnivores ought not to develop food aversions because they have no biological need for them; they can simply select food on the basis of the fact that animals which move are probably healthy and safe to eat. This also is incorrect, since Gustavson and Garcia (1974) are now busy developing a technology of controlling the carnivorous habits of wild coyotes by exposing them to poisoned lamb meat. The point is that neoevolutionists are badly misguided when they underestimate the generality of the learning process, and a number of them refuse to learn from experience.

The work of Wilcoxon, Dragoin, and Kral (1971) shows how knowledge of a general process allows the theory of evolution to be used effectively. It seemed likely to them that birds would make far better use of visual cues for feeding than rats, particularly when they are up in the air. They confirmed this expectation by using their general knowledge of food aversion learning to create a situation in which an aversion learning experience was to be equated for quail and rats as closely as possible. Quail learned aversions to colored water on the basis of later sickness, while rats did not. Furthermore, an overshadowing procedure, originally developed by Pavlov (1927) for use with dogs, was used to show that the color cue was far more salient for the quail than a taste cue. This illustrates how the study of a specific adaptation makes sense in terms of general process considerations. However, even the type of situation pioneered by Wilcoxon and his co-workers illustrates how limited evolutionary considerations are as a basis for prediction. Both guinea pigs (Braveman, 1974, 1975) and codfish (Mackay, 1977) can use visual cues for feeding far more effectively than rats. Nobody really knows why, although there are bound to be a plethora of *ex post facto* evolutionary explanations.

## 3. Food Aversion Learning Governed by a General Process

Although there are a number of instances of learning which contradict traditional preconceptions, none has seemed to pose as severe a threat to the traditional wisdom as food aversion learning. In most of the familiar animal learning experiments, associative learning between events separated by delays of even a minute or so requires many trials; powerful food aversions develop when a single instance of feeding is followed many hours later by sickness. If food aversion learning can reasonably be shown to fall within the same theoretical context as these other types of learning, then the strongest single objection to a general process approach will have been removed.

There are biological precedents for putting apparently different things in the same category. As a crude example, consider Chihuahuas and Great Danes. Despite the great differences in their sizes and appearances, they are both considered dogs because they have important properties in common which mark them as dogs. The same principle applies to the differences between food aversion learning and more conventionally studied forms of learning. There are so many important similarities between food aversion learning and other types of learning as to mandate that learning be studied as a single process.

### 3.1. Parametric Effects

Revusky and Garcia (1970, pp. 5–16) have summarized the evidence that learned food aversions are affected by the various parameters of learning in much the same way as other behaviors with two exceptions: (1) they occur with long delays of punishment and (2) the learning is so rapid that parametric effects are often difficult to detect due to ceiling effects. When other parametric effects are teased out by slowing up the learning in some way, they are shown to be much like those studied in traditional learning experiments. For instance, the aversions become more pronounced with increases either in the intensity of the taste stimulation or of the sickness. They develop in the course of conditioning trials and extinguish in the course of extinction trials. Also, preferences can be increased by a physiological aftereffect which is rewarding; for instance, by repletion of a thiamine deficiency after consumption of flavored water.

Revusky and Garcia (1970) emphasized the parametric similarities between food aversion learning and other types of learning because at the time they wrote their chapter, it was necessary to convince legions of doubters that food aversions produced by sickness were learned. However, the present general process position is far too extreme to be strongly supported by the mere existence of parametric similarities. If there were a variety of different learning mechanisms, it would be reasonable to conjecture that they might develop parametric similarities through similar evolutionary pressures. For instance, it would be adaptive both for food aversion learning to become more marked with more intense sickness and for fear conditioning to become more marked with more intense shock even if each depended on a different mechanism. Thus, to make a strong argument for general process learning only on the basis of parametric similarities in different learning situations would be very superficial. In my early writings, I was not fully aware of this point; however, the influence of neoevolutionary learning theory has made me aware of it.

Although the parametric similarities between different types of learning are not strong evidence for a general process, strong evidence will be supplied later. Once it is established that there is a general learning process, parametric similarities must be considered to be due to this general process. To admit that there is a general learning process and still claim that similar parametric effects evolved independently would be very unreasonable.

## 3.2. Relative Cue Validities

This subsection will deal with experiments in which a number of potential cues precede a single aftereffect. It will be shown that animals deal with such experiences in a similar way, regardless of whether they occur in conventional learning situations or in food aversion learning. We will begin with conventional learning situations.

If an animal is subjected to a number of external cues prior to shock (or some other aftereffect), the more valid cues tend to become selectively associated with the shock. In effect, the animal compares all the cues which precede the shock and selects out those most likely to have caused the shock (Wagner, 1969). The process responsible for this effect has been called concurrent interference by Revusky (1971). It is as though cues compete to become associated with the shock and the stronger associations tend to drown out the weaker associations. Rescorla and Wagner (1972) have independently dealt with this same process, but have conceptualized it in a slightly different way. According to them, every UCS has some limited capacity to condition cues; as some cues become conditioned, they use up the conditioning capacity of the UCS and thus prevent other cues from becoming conditioned by the same UCS. Although I would cavil with certain details of Rescorla and Wagner's formulation, it has great heuristical and predictive power.

One type of concurrent interference is the blocking effect popularized by Kamin (1969). An example of it is shown in Table 1 together with a control procedure. In the first phase, rats assigned to the blocking procedure are subjected to noise paired with shock on a number of occasions. During the second phase, the noise and a light are presented together and followed by shock. During a final test phase, the light is presented to determine the strength of the fear reaction it produces. The fear reaction to the light is hardly detectable and the reason is that the prior noise–shock association ''blocked'' the light–shock association. This is evidenced by a control procedure shown in Table 1 in which there is no first phase and the rat exhibits pronounced fear of the light during the test.

A second example of concurrent interference is the reduction of interference by familiarity. It is well established that repeated presentation of a cue in the absence of any aftereffect makes that cue difficult to condition in the future (Lubow, 1973). Since, according to the principle of concurrent interference, the interference produced by any cue is directly related to how strongly it becomes conditioned itself, a reference cue will become more strongly conditioned if it is in compound with a familiar cue than if it is in compound with a novel cue. In other words, if a light–noise compound

*Table 1.* Blocking Procedure Compared with a Control Procedure

|  | Blocking | Control |
|---|---|---|
| Phase 1 | Noise→shock (repeatedly) | Nothing specific is done |
| Phase 2 | Compound noise–light→shock (both groups) | |
| Result of test | Little fear of light | Substantial fear of light |

precedes shock, the resulting fear of the light will be greater if the noise is familiar than if the noise is novel. Of course, this is adaptive. If the noise is familiar, it has previously occurred in the absence of the shock and hence is unlikely to suddenly have become the cause of the shock; this implicates the light more strongly by a process of elimination. If the noise is novel, both the noise and light are about equally likely to be responsible for the shock and hence the rat can be less certain that the light is the cause. Carr (1974) has shown that this is how rats actually behave.

The blocking effect and the reduction in interference produced by familiarity each occur in food aversion learning (Revusky, 1971; Revusky and Garcia, 1970; Revusky, Parker, and Coombes, in press). The blocking effect will be used as an example here because there is some controversy about it (Kalat and Rozin, 1972). The treatment used by Revusky (1971) which corresponded to the Phase 1 treatment for the blocking rats in Table 1 was to allow rats to drink coffee prior to toxicosis on a number of occasions in order to produce a strong coffee–toxicosis association. During Phase 2, the rats first drank novel saccharin solution, then were exposed to the coffee, and finally were made sick. The resulting aversion to saccharin solution was considerably milder than among control groups, indicating that the prior coffee–toxicosis association blocked the saccharin–toxicosis association. Thus, in intuitive language, an animal which drinks both saccharin solution and coffee prior to sickness does not develop a strong aversion to the saccharin if it already knows that the sickness is produced by coffee.

That the blocking effect can be obtained in flavor aversion learning has been confirmed by Kalat and Rozin (1972) and by Best, Best, and Rudy (1975). However, Kalat and Rozin (1972) have been more impressed by the fact, which I do not dispute, that it is more difficult to obtain blocking in food aversion learning than under Kamin's original conditions. They explain this in terms of their theory that food aversion learning is more primitive than other types of learning. According to them, food aversion learning readily produces simple associations but does not easily produce the integration of complex information which occurs in the blocking effect. However, the difficulty in demonstrating blocking in food aversion learning can be more parsimoniously attributed to a methodological shortcoming: in order for an animal to be strongly stimulated by a flavor, it must do some eating or drinking (except under unusual conditions). Thus, if a rat is exposed to saccharin solution and aversive coffee solution in sequence prior to sickness, it will avoid the coffee and obtain little stimulation from it; as a result, the coffee flavor will not be sampled enough for it to block the saccharin–toxicosis association as effectively as it otherwise might. There probably is also an additional factor which gives the impression that blocking is less pronounced in food aversion learning than in conventional experiments. Kamin's (1969) original demonstration of blocking also included an element of overshadowing, which exaggerated the blocking effect.

Luongo (1976) has recently supplied definitive evidence that Kalat and Rozin (1972) are incorrect in their claim that integration of complex information is markedly inferior in the food aversion learning situation. Consider the following logical problem. A man learns that he gets sick after drinking a solution containing both cinnamon and saccharin. After drinking a solution containing both oil of wintergreen and saccharin, he does not get sick. Obviously, if such a man is clever, he is likely to decide that the cinnamon makes him sick and that the saccharin does not make him sick. As a control situation, consider a man who gets sick half the time after he drinks cinnamon–saccharin solution and also gets sick half the time after he drinks wintergreen–saccharin solution. It would be reasonable of the man to conclude that the saccharin probably makes him sick. This is exactly the procedure to which Luongo subjected rats. In a test for saccharin preference, he found that those rats for which cinnamon was perfectly correlated with later sickness developed a far weaker aversion to saccharin than the controls. Luongo's experiment had been modeled on a similar experiment by Wagner, Logan, Haberlandt, and Price (1968) which utilized external cues and shock. The results of both experiments agreed despite the situational differences between them.

Not only are food aversion learning and other types of learning similar in their integration of complex information, they also share a similar limitation and this further suggests that a common mechanism underlies both types of learning. We have seen that when an animal is presented with two cues prior to an aftereffect, the animal's history with one cue is a determinant of how strongly the other cue will become conditioned. Consider the blocking effect outlined in Table 1 as a specific example. When a compound light–noise is paired with shock, the fact that the noise has been paired with shock in the past prevents the light from becoming strongly associated with shock. However, although it would seem equally adaptive, future experience does not produce blocking in the same way past experience does. If future experience were to produce blocking, the blocking effect would still occur if Phase 1 and Phase 2 in Table 1 were interchanged. Thus, an animal conditioned to fear both a noise and a light through pairing of the noise–light compound with shock could have its fear to the light reduced by later pairings of the noise with shock. Although the evidence is much more meager than desirable, it seems unlikely that this sort of retrospective use of information occurs either in conventional learning experiments (Kamin, 1969; Rizley and Rescorla, 1972) or in food aversion learning (Kalat and Rozin, 1972; Revusky, Parker, and Coombes, in press).

These close similarities between food aversion learning and other types of learning in how information is integrated strongly suggest that these are not separate mechanisms which evolved independently. The parade example in biology of how different processes can evolve independently toward a similar function is flying in birds and in bats. But these two types of flying are not similar in detail. A better analogy to the present similarities seems to be respiration in dogs and in cats.

## 3.3. Conditioned Inhibition

Best (1975) and Taukulis and Revusky (1975) have shown that conditioned inhibition occurs in food aversion learning in almost precisely the same way it occurs in conventional learning situations. A conditioned inhibitor is a cue which guarantees that a UCS will not occur when it otherwise might be expected to occur. For instance, if a tone is followed by shock, but a light–tone compound is never followed by shock, the light becomes a conditioned inhibitor (safety signal). A very rigorous control procedure for conditioned inhibition is latent inhibition; here the animal is also made familiar with a cue, but because the UCS never occurs in the experimental situation, the cue does not become a guarantee that an expected UCS will not occur (Reiss and Wagner, 1972).

Taukulis and Revusky (1975) made the smell of amyl acetate into a conditioned inhibitor of sickness: if the rats drank saccharin solution alone, they were made sick by injection of lithium afterward; but if the smell of amyl acetate was present while they drank saccharin solution, the rats were not made sick. Control latent-inhibition rats were made familiar with amyl acetate, but were not subjected to sickness at any time; thus, the smell of amyl acetate did not signal safety from an otherwise expected sickness. After this training phase, the experimental rats exhibited conditioned inhibition in comparison to the controls according to each of three tests as follows.

### 3.3.1. Summation Test

In this test, the conditioned inhibitor is shown to counteract a reaction to a positively conditioned cue, called an excitor. Thus, both groups of rats were made sick after drinking water flavored with hydrochloric acid, so that the sour taste of acid would become an excitor. After recovery, they were tested by being allowed to drink water flavored with hydrochloric acid in the presence of the smell of amyl acetate. Figure 1 shows the amount consumed by each group on the hydrochloric acid training day and on each of three test days during which the smell of amyl acetate and the hydrochloric acid solution were presented together. It is obvious that when

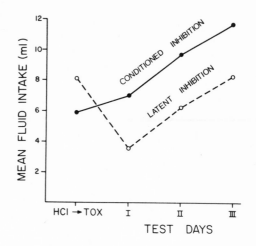

**Figure 1.** Mean intake of hydrochloric acid for two groups. In one group, the odor of amyl acetate was a conditioned inhibitor and in the second group, it was a latent inhibitor. On the treatment day, the HCl solution was presented alone prior to toxicosis. On the test days, the same solution was consumed in the presence of the odor of amyl acetate.

the smell of amyl acetate was a conditioned inhibitor, it reduced the tendency to avoid drinking, just as a conditioned inhibitor in a shock situation reduces the tendency to act fearful in the presence of a CS associated with shock.

### 3.3.2. Enhancement of Conditioning Test

Here both groups were allowed to drink salt (NaCl) solution in the presence of amyl acetate and then were made sick. The test was the opportunity to drink salt solution in the absence of the amyl acetate. It was found that when the smell of amyl acetate was a conditioned inhibitor, there was a stronger aversion to the salt solution than when amyl acetate had simply been made familiar. This parallels an effect obtained by Rescorla (1971) in a shock situation which is predictable from the model of compound conditioning proposed by Rescorla and Wagner (1972). Unlike most learning effects, this effect does not obviously make intuitive sense. Some readers may feel that the rat acts as if it thinks a substance which can produce sickness even in the presence of a safety signal must be exceedingly harmful.

### 3.3.3. Retardation of Learning Test

In this test, both groups were repeatedly made sick after being subjected to the amyl acetate smell while drinking tap water. It was found that the conditioned-inhibition group developed an aversion to drinking tap water in the presence of the amyl acetate smell more slowly than the latent-inhibition group (Figure 2). This agrees with the findings in conventional

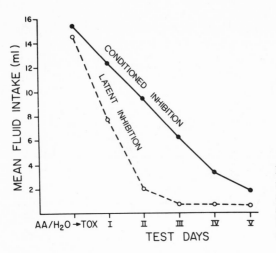

**Figure 2.** Development of an aversion to drinking in the presence of amyl acetate. For one group, amyl acetate was a conditioned inhibitor; for the other group, it was a latent inhibitor.

experiments that a conditioned inhibitor is extraordinarily resistant to later excitatory conditioning (Pavlov, 1927).

It is hard to see how the differences between conditioned inhibition and latent inhibition reported here and shown in Figures 1 and 2 are specifically adaptive in the feeding situation; both types of experiences are strong evidence that a substance is safe. It may be speculated that conditioned inhibition is highly adaptive for dealing with external dangers signaled by external cues. If so, that it carries over to the feeding situation suggests that the learning process is not nearly as specialized for specific situations as neoevolutionary learning theorists claim.

### 3.4. Sensory Preconditioning

Probably the strongest single bit of evidence for general process learning is Lavin's (1976) discovery that sensory preconditioning (SPC) occurs in the food aversion situation in a manner almost identical to its occurrence in conventional learning situations. Before describing the effect in detail, I will outline why I think it is such strong evidence.

The parametric rules which govern SPC in food aversion learning are similar in detail to those which govern SPC in other situations. Furthermore, SPC is not biologically adaptive for the animal in the regulation of food intake; indeed, it probably is mildly maladaptive. From these facts, to be validated in detail below, a counterpart of the classical evolutionary argument about vestigial organs follows. For instance, the occurrence of a nonfunctional vestigial tail in human embryonic development suggests that humans are related to species in which a functional tail is present. Similarly, the occurrence of nonfunctional SPC in food aversion learning suggests that food aversion learning is related to learning in which SPC is adaptive.

Table 2 compares an example of SPC in a feeding situation with SPC in a fear learning situation. In the feeding situation, the rat is trained to drink from two spouts in sequence prior to the experiment proper. During the SPC phase, it drinks saccharin solution prior to coffee solution on a number of occasions. During a training phase, the rat drinks coffee prior to induction of sickness on a number of occasions. A later preference test shows that rats subjected to SPC exhibit an aversion to saccharin solution relative to controls for which vinegar solution was substituted for coffee either in the SPC phase or in the training phase (Lavin, 1976). It is obvious from Table 2 that the SPC effect in food aversion learning is paradigmatically similar to that which occurs in conventional fear conditioning (such as conditioned suppression).

Using the example in Table 2, it will now be shown why SPC is maladaptive for the feeding situation through a comparison of what rational rats ought to do with what real rats actually do. During the sac→cof SPC phase, a rational rat would learn that it can drink both saccharin solution and coffee without getting sick; real rats seem to learn the same thing, since they habituate to both tastes so that they do not form aversions to them as readily as they would if the tastes were novel (Revusky and Garcia, 1970). During the cof→tox training phase, rational rats ought to change their minds about the harmlessness of coffee and develop an aversion to it; this is also what real rats do. The difference between rational rats and real rats becomes apparent in their later preferences for saccharin solution. Rational rats ought to decide that saccharin solution is very good for them; coffee solution consumed alone makes them sick, but if they consume saccharin

**Table 2.** *Sensory Preconditioning in Feeding and in Fear Learning*

| Phase | Feeding | Fear learning |
|---|---|---|
| Pretraining (SPC) | Sac→cof | Tone→light |
| Training | Cof→tox | Light→shock |
| Test Result | Aversion to sac | Fear of tone |

solution prior to the coffee, they do not get sick. Hence the net result of the SPC procedure in rational rats ought to be an increased preference for saccharin solution. Since SPC produces an aversion to saccharin solution in real rats, it seems clear that SPC is maladaptive in the feeding situation.

The question may arise as to whether SPC ever is adaptive. The supposition here is that it is adaptive for dealing with external stimuli. Presumably, if a sound and a visual stimulus are paired in a biological environment, they are likely to mean that the same animal caused both. If pain follows one of these stimuli, it would be reasonable to become fearful of the other because both are indicators of the same unfriendly animal. Admittedly, this consideration is not rigorous proof that SPC is adaptive outside of the feeding situation. Some may regard SPC as not specifically adaptive in itself but as an epiphenomenon caused by the nature of the associative learning process. But even if this is so, the case for a nontrivial relationship between food aversion learning and other types of learning still seems strong. It is hard to imagine how different associative mechanisms might result in the same epiphenomenon.

Lavin (1976) also showed that SPC in the feeding situation is affected by parameters of learning in almost the same way as it is affected in traditional learning situations. For instance, if the two flavors are paired in the reverse of the order shown in Table 2 during the SPC phase, there is no noticeable effect (Figure 3). In other words, cof→sac followed by cof→tox does not yield SPC; sac→cof followed by cof→tox does yield SPC. This parallels exactly what happens in conventional SPC experiments. Indeed, there is more to the parallel. Lavin varied the delay between presentation

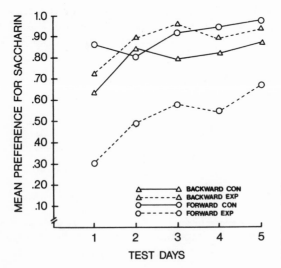

Figure 3. The results of a forward sensory preconditioning procedure, a backward procedure, and two control procedures. Data courtesy of M. Lavin.

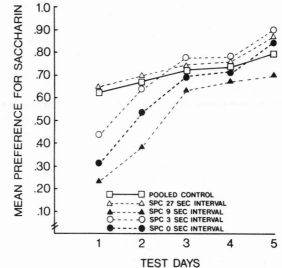

**Figure 4.** The sensory preconditioning effect as a function of the delay between the consumption of coffee and saccharin solutions during the SPC pairings. Data courtesy of M. Lavin.

of the two flavored solutions in the SPC phase. There was a clear SPC effect when there was a 9-s delay between removal of the saccharin spout and presentation of the coffee spout, but no conditioning with a 27-s delay (Figure 4). This is remarkably similar to the exact delay gradient obtained in conventional SPC experiments.

## 3.5. The Delay Problem

The one characteristic of food aversion learning which seems unique is its occurrence despite a delay of hours between feeding and toxicosis. Nevertheless, I feel that even this characteristic is best understood in terms of general learning processes and have written a chapter about as long as the present chapter to support my position (Revusky, 1971). Here only a brief, crude summary of this earlier analysis will be included. Because this summary contains logical gaps, the reader with a specialized interest in the delay problem is referred to my earlier chapter as well as to various papers by Lett (1973, 1974, 1975, in press).

### 3.5.1. Interference Theory

In delay learning experiments, an animal is expected to associate between two events which are separated by a delay. The assumption at the core of traditional analyses of delay learning, expressed in lay language, is that the animal does not remember the first event at the time the second event occurs when the delay is over a few seconds. Any instance of apparent association over longer delays was explained in terms of presumed mediating events that bridge the temporal gap; lingering stimulus traces, mediating motor reactions, and secondary reinforcement were frequently invoked. However, animals may have failed to learn traditional delay problems simply because these problems were logically insoluble. Long ago, William James described the world of an infant as a buzzing booming confusion, and the same applies to animals in artificial situations. In the traditional delay problems, animals were placed in this confusion and asked to associate between two events which were separated by a delay; even with perfect memories, they should not have been expected to learn. Consider, for example, a rat in a Skinner Box which depresses a lever and the lever is then withdrawn; an hour later, the rat is rewarded with food. An active rat in a new environment is bound to emit many behaviors during the hour delay of reward. No matter how well the rat might remember the earlier lever depression at the time of reward, it would be unreasonable for it to attribute the reward to depression of the lever an hour earlier when there are so many other potential causes. Thus, traditional delay experiments do not show that animals cannot remember; they show that animals cannot solve insoluble problems.

For this reason, Revusky (1971) felt it would be better to disregard traditional approaches to delay learning and start over. He began with the assumption that animals remember quite well and that the detrimental effects of delays on learning are mainly a result of interference by uncontrolled events which occur during the delay. The interference process which tends to prevent delay learning is the same as that permitting selective association of the more valid cues with an aftereffect (Section 3.2. of this chapter). Specifically, the learning of an association between two reference events selected by an experimenter (such as depression of a lever and reward) can, presumably, be hindered by two types of interfering associations: (1) associations of the earlier reference event with extraneous events which occur during the delay and (2) associations of events which occur during the delay with the later reference event. There is much more evidence for the second of these sources of interference than for the first (Lavin, 1976; Revusky, 1971).

The preceding considerations by themselves suggest that long-delay food aversion learning ought not to occur. There ought to be interfering associations between the feeding cues and the many uncontrolled events which occur during the delay. There also ought to be interfering associations between the events which occur during the delay and toxicosis. Thus, it is a dilemma that long-delay food aversions actually occur. This dilemma cannot be resolved by denying that an interference process exists because there is too much independent evidence for such a process (Rescorla and Wagner, 1972; Revusky, 1971). Instead, there must be a factor in the feeding situation that circumvents the usual interference process. This factor is a principle of selective association, called stimulus relevance (Capretta, 1961; Garcia, McGowan, and Green, 1972), which insures that associations between feeding stimuli and toxicosis will be far stronger than interfering associations.

The classical demonstration of stimulus relevance was by Garcia and Koelling (1966). They showed that rats are far more likely to associate between taste stimuli and toxicosis than between external stimuli and toxicosis. However, when the aftereffect was changed from toxicosis to painful electrical shock, the external stimuli became more salient than the taste stimuli. A variety of replications and extensions of this basic finding show that stimulus relevance must be regarded as a fact. However, its exact nature is not yet entirely clear and, to avoid a long digression, it will be described here in a way which is only approximately true.

Events can be placed in two classes, internal and external. Internal events include feeding stimuli and physiological aftereffects. External events include auditory, visual, and proprioceptive stimuli, as well as aftereffects which seem to emanate directly from the external environment. The stimulus relevance principle is that associations are learned more readily if both events are of the same class than if each event is in a different class. It can reasonably be assumed that the vast majority of salient events in the buzzing booming confusion of experience are in the external class. As a result, the long delay between ingestion and toxicosis includes relatively few events capable of producing interference by becoming associated either with the feeding stimuli or with the toxicosis. In short, long-delay food aversions occur for two reasons: (1) the feeding stimuli and toxicosis have high associative strength relative to each other and (2) feeding stimuli and toxicosis each have low associative strength relative to the vast majority of the uncontrolled events that occur during the delay.

It must be admitted that this interference approach to long-delay learning is no more precise and testable than traditional interference theories. To test it rigorously, it first would be necessary to identify all the extraneous events that occur during a delay; then it would be necessary to show that associations of these extraneous events with reference events are responsible for the decrement in learning produced by a delay. However, a partial test of the theory was successful. In the interval between consumption of a reference solution and toxicosis, Revusky (1971) allowed rats to drink a different flavored solution so as to produce interference. The associative strength of the second solution was varied in different ways in different experiments. It was always found that the stronger the association of the interfering flavor with toxicosis, the greater the interference with the reference association. Some of these experiments have been mentioned in Section 3.2. because they also demonstrate how the animal selects the most valid flavor cue for association with toxicosis.

### 3.5.2. Extension to Conventional Learning Experiments

Because the interference analysis of long-delay learning is an extreme general process approach, it has implications far beyond the food aversion learning context in which it was originally developed. It permitted reinterpretation of two well-substantiated effects as instances of long-delay learning. On the basis of this reinterpretation, it was possible to produce exciting new instances of long-delay learning which disproved the traditional assumptions. First, the two effects reinterpreted in terms of long-delay learning will be described.

*a. Alternate Reward in a Runway.* Tyler, Wortz, and Bitterman (1953) rewarded rats in a runway on odd trials, but not on even trials. The rats gradually began to run more slowly on even trials than on odd trials, indicating that during any trial, they could use the reward outcome of the preceding trial as a cue for whether reward would be obtained. A reward on the preceding trial indicated that reward would not be obtained on the present trial and a failure to receive reward on the preceding trial indicated that reward would be obtained. Capaldi (1967, 1971) has replicated this basic effect in a large number of ways and it is very robust when the intertrial interval is many minutes long.

*b. Response Alternation in a T-Maze.* Petrinovich and Bolles (1957) rewarded rats in a T-maze only if the rats ran in the direction opposite to that of the preceding run. The rats performed this discrimination with delays of up to several hours. Thus, the rats learned that if the previous run had been to the left, only a run to the right would be rewarded and vice versa. Petrinovich, Bradford, and McGaugh (1965) found this effect robust enough to use in a study of drugs which affect memory.

Both of these instances of long-delay learning may be called *intertrial associations*. This term is used here to emphasize the absence of the animal from the apparatus during the delay over which association was to occur. As will be explained below, this absence from the apparatus permits an analysis of long-delay intertrial associations which corresponds to the analysis of long-delay food aversions in terms of stimulus relevance.

It will be recalled that according to the stimulus relevance principle, events could be placed in two classes, internal and external, and that association between a pair of events is facilitated if both are in the same class. It is assumed here that an analogous principle, called *situational relevance,* is responsible for long-delay intertrial associations; here events are classified according to the environmental situation in which they occur. Presumably, animals are much more likely to associate between two events that occur in the same environment than two events that occur in different environments. Although it is interesting to speculate on what causes situational relevance, it is not important for the purpose of the present chapter.

Situational relevance weakens the strength of the two types of extraneous associations that might otherwise interfere with the intertrial association. These are (1) associations of cues that occur inside the apparatus with aftereffects that may occur outside of the apparatus during the intertrial interval, and (2) associations of cues that may occur outside of the apparatus with aftereffects occurring when the animal has been returned to the apparatus. Thus situational relevance prevents interference in much the same way in which stimulus relevance prevents interference produced by (1) associations between feeding stimuli and events of the delay and (2) associations between events of the delay and toxicosis.

### 3.5.3. Intertrial Association Experiments Suggested by Interference Theory

The interference approach suggests that the occurrence of long-delay learning in intertrial association experiments depends on the absence of the animal from the apparatus during the delay. However, both of the early intertrial association procedures utilized unusual cues which may have been more salient than the auditory and visual cues used in traditional experiments. Conceivably, for instance, the salience of the difference between nonreward and reward in the alternate reward procedure may have been unusually great: nonreward is known to produce a strong emotional reaction of frustration (Amsel, 1967) and probably reward produces an emotional reaction of the opposite type (Solomon and Corbit, 1974). Amplification of the cue salience of nonreward and reward by these reactions might be responsible for long-delay alternate reward learning. If so, the rat's absence from the apparatus during the delay might be irrelevant.

Since it was necessary to exclude such possible alternative explanations of long-delay intertrial associations, interference theory led to the development of new procedures for intertrial association experiments. For convenience, these new procedures can be placed in two categories: (1) delayed reaction experiments, in which the delay is between a cue and the next opportunity to respond and (2) delayed reward learning, in which the delay is between a response and a reward.

*a. Delayed Reaction Experiments.* Pschirrer (1972) showed that rats could use two different types of food rewards, chow pellets and milk, as differential discriminative stimuli for intertrial associations. Thus, the difference between the emotional reactions produced by reward and non-reward could not be responsible for the ability of rats to adjust to reward on alternate trials in a runway.

Pschirrer began by modifying Tyler, Wortz, and Bitterman's (1953) alternate reward procedure. Instead of the cycle of rewarded and un-rewarded runway trials indefinitely, he utilized a repeating cycle of three runway trials; the first trial was rewarded with milk, the second trial was rewarded with chow pellets, and the third trial was unrewarded. In this milk→pellets→nonreward cycle, the cue functions of chow pellets and nonreward in the cycle were identical to the respective functions of reward and nonreward in the alternate reward cycle: pellets indicated that reward would not be obtained on the following trial, while nonreward indicated that reward (milk) would be obtained on the following trial. The innovation in Pschirrer's procedure was in the cue function of the milk reward: it indicated that reward (pellets) would be obtained on the following trial. Thus, the cue function of the milk reward was opposite to that of the pellet reward, which indicated that no reward would be obtained on the following trial. (Of course, Pschirrer interchanged the sequence of milk and pellets for half the rats.)

With an intertrial interval of 15 min, Pschirrer's rats learned to run equally quickly on each of the rewarded trials and more slowly on the unrewarded trials. Thus, they successfully learned that the milk reward was followed by another reward on the next trial and that the pellet reward was followed by nonreward. If the emotional aftereffect of reward was an important factor in the discrimination, there would have been gener-alization of the milk cue with the pellet cue. Pschirrer (1972) explained how details of his results indicate the absence of such generalization, but his argument will not be summarized here because it is too complex. In addition, Pschirrer's results contradicted the theory that rats in alternate reward trials run faster after nonreward solely due to an activating aftereffect of frustration; for if that were true, why did Pschirrer's rats run just as quickly after milk rewards?

The next step was to show that response selection in a T-maze could be made to depend upon the type of food reward obtained on the preceding trial, just as Petrinovich and Bolles (1957) had shown that response selec-tion could depend upon the response emitted on the preceding trial. Thus in Pschirrer's second experiment, the right goalbox of a T-maze contained reward if the preceding reward had been milk and the left goalbox con-tained reward if the preceding reward had been pellets (or vice versa). Otherwise, the sequence of correct responses was quasi-random. After about 700 trials with an intertrial interval of over 3 min, the rats were correct on over 80% of the trials.

Revusky (1974) modified Pschirrer's (1972) runway experiment by using cues that are more conventional than different types of food reward. The rats learned that reward would be obtained if the preceding trial had terminated in a black goalbox, but not if it had terminated in a white goalbox (or vice versa). More specifically, the goalboxes of the runway were removable so that a wide, black, wooden goalbox could be used on half the trials and a narrow, white, plastic goalbox could be used on the remaining trials. There were nine trials per day with a minimum intertrial interval of 4 min. The sequence of black and white trials was quasi-random and different for each rat, so that olfactory cues from other rats would not be useful for prediction. The reward outcomes of the preceding trial also were not useful for prediction because the sequence was so arranged that half the rewarded trials were preceded by reward, while the other half were preceded by nonreward; the same was true for the nonrewarded trials. Furthermore, half of each rat's rewards were received in the black goalbox and the other half were received in the white goalbox; the same was true for failures to receive reward. Consequently, the only possible cue for reward or nonreward was the type of goalbox on the preceding trial.

Figure 5 shows mean running speeds on rewarded and unrewarded trials in the course of the experiment. The learning was very slow, not being apparent until over 300 trials, but eventually each of the four rats learned the discrimination. The slow learning, by the way, need not be attributed to the 4-min delay over which association occurred. The intertrial association procedure necessarily involves handling the rat at the beginning and at the end of the intertrial interval. This distracting experience alone might explain why learning was slower than in other black–white discrimination experiments. The repeated handling, however, also has an advantage: it excludes any reasonable possibility that the rats could have maintained a muscular set to mediate the long-delay association (Spence, 1956). Thus, it is clear that by means of the intertrial association procedure, rats can be made to associate directly between conventional cues and consequences which occur minutes later.

*b. Delayed Reward Learning.* The occurrence of long-delay intertrial associations is not limited to the delayed reaction paradigm, in which the delay is between a cue and the next opportunity to respond. It will be shown below that intertrial associations also occur when there is a long delay between a response and a reward. This supports the assertion in Section 1.3 that the same associative processes govern delay learning in both situations.

The obvious way to adapt the intertrial association procedure to yield delayed reward learning would lead to ambiguous results. Suppose, for example, that a rat is allowed to select one of two goalboxes in a T-maze and then is immediately removed from the apparatus without being rewarded; if it selects the correct goalbox, it is returned there after a delay and rewarded. According to an analysis in terms of interference and situational relevance, the rat would learn because the events occurring outside of the apparatus would not enter into strong interfering associations with events that occur inside the apparatus. However, learning with such a procedure could also be attributed to secondary reinforcement. The correct goalbox is bound to become secondarily reinforcing because the rat is rewarded in it, and, of course, the rat prefers a secondarily reinforcing goalbox to one which is not secondarily reinforcing.

Lett (1973, 1974, 1975) avoided this secondary reinforcement artifact in a unique way: when a rat made the correct response, she rewarded it in the startbox after a delay spent outside of the apparatus. Since the startbox also functioned as a goalbox, no separate goalbox was needed; the rat had a choice of entering one of two endboxes and if it selected the correct endbox, it was later rewarded in the startbox. The correct endbox could not become secondarily rewarding except through association over a delay

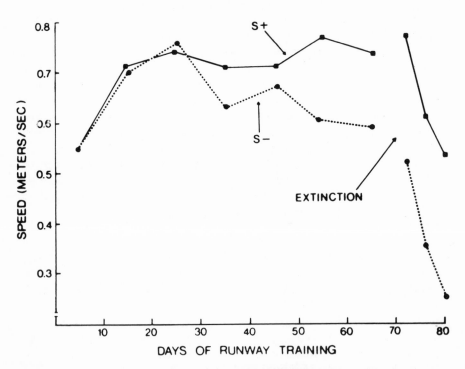

**Figure 5.** Mean running speeds on rewarded (S+) and on unrewarded (S−) trials when the cue was the type of goalbox on the preceding trial over 4 min earlier.

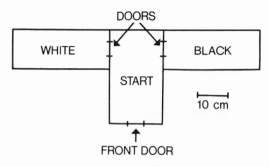

**Figure 6.** The simplified T-maze used by B. T. Lett; a gray wooden startbox flanked by two endboxes opposite in color.

because the rat was never fed in it. Figure 6 shows the simplified T-maze which Lett used; each of two endboxes could be entered directly from the startbox. The white endbox was always on the left and the black endbox was always on the right, so that the rats could use both visual and positional cues.

Lett subjected rats to one trial per day with a very simple procedure. The rat was placed head first in the startbox and could enter either endbox through one-way doors. Immediately after it entered an endbox, the rat was returned to its home cage. After a delay, it was returned to the startbox; the side doors to the endboxes were now locked. If the rat had previously selected the correct endbox (left-white for half the rats and right-black for the other half), it found a small cup containing 2.5 ml of 25% weight/volume sucrose solution. If the rat had previously selected the incorrect endbox, it was confined in the empty startbox for one minute and then was returned to its home cage.

Figure 7 shows the results of two experiments (Lett, 1975) in which groups of 11 or 12 rats were trained with reward delayed either by 1, 20, or 60 min. Each of the five groups in Figure 7 learned, but neither experiment yielded a statistically significant delay gradient. The absence of a significant delay gradient is reminiscent of McLaurin's (1964) early failure to obtain a delay gradient for saccharin aversions induced by radiation sickness when the delays ranged from 3 to 180 min. Smith and Roll (1967) were later to show that McLaurin's range of delays was too small to yield a gradient under his experimental conditions; the minimum delay that noticeably interfered with aversion learning was greater than 6 h. If it turns out that Lett's failure to obtain a delay gradient is also due to too small a range of delays, then her procedure ought to yield learning with delays of at least several hours.

In the procedure Lett used to obtain the data in Figure 7, a rat was returned to its home cage immediately after it entered an endbox. The

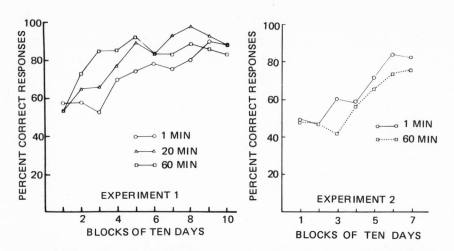

Figure 7. Percentage of correct responses in blocks of 10 days with various delays of reward. Data courtesy of B. T. Lett. Experiment 1, left; Experiment 2, right: see text for details.

purpose of this immediate removal from the endbox was to minimize the number of delay events in the endbox which would follow the rat's response. Such delay events were expected to enter into associations that would interfere with development of an association between the response and the reward. The theoretical reasoning underlying this expectation involved both situational relevance and interference. According to the situational relevance principle, delay events in the endboxes are likely to enter into association with the response and the reward because they occur in the same apparatus. According to interference theory, these extraneous associations ought to hinder development of the association between the response and the reward. Hence, the longer the animal remains in the endbox after a response, the poorer learning ought to be.

Lett (1975) tested this analysis in her next experiment. Three groups of 10 or 11 rats each were trained in the two-choice task used in the preceding experiment with a 2-min delay of reward. The groups differed only in how long they remained in the endbox after a response. Group Stay-0 was removed to the home cage immediately after entry into an endbox, Group Stay-15 was removed 15 s after entry, and Group Stay-60 was removed 60 s afterward. The groups were returned from the home cage to the startbox 120 s after they had first entered an endbox; thus, the time spent in the home cage was 120 s for Group Stay-0, 105 s in Group Stay-15, and 60 s in Group Stay-60. If the rat had previously selected the correct endbox, it was rewarded with 2.5 ml of 25% sucrose solution. However, if it had previously selected the incorrect endbox, the method was different from that of the earlier experiments. The rat simply was subjected to another trial in which it could select one of the two endboxes; the procedure was identical with that of the preceding trial in all respects. The day's training did not end until the correct response was made, no matter how many incorrect responses there were. In earlier experiments, Lett (1973, 1974) and Denny (1974) had successfully used this procedure of running an animal each day until it was correct.

Figure 8 shows the percentage of correct responses on the first trial of each day in blocks of ten days for each group. The longer the animals were left in the endbox during the delay, the poorer was their performance. The only known theory which can account for this finding is the present interference theory.

### 3.5.4. Some Metatheoretical Comments

The preceding analysis of delay learning illustrates the lack of attention to details which neoevolutionists find objectionable in general process approaches. Stimulus relevance and situational relevance were described as similar parallel processes simply because both produced selective association which could overcome interference. The possibility of real differences between these processes was ignored. It was this blurring of distinctions which made it possible to extrapolate from food aversions to intertrial associations. The net result was a discovery which disproved nearly every traditional approach to delay learning: learning with a one-hour delay of reward in the absence of any source of indirect temporal contiguity (Figure 7). The point is that blurring of distinctions permits

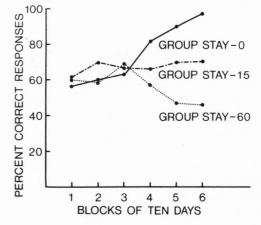

**Figure 8.** Percentage of correct responses during each block of 10 days for groups which differed in the amount of time they were allowed to stay in the endbox prior to return to the home cage. Data courtesy of B. T. Lett.

abstract analyses and generalizations beyond the immediate data. Thus, it is often a scientific virtue. This is why I consider the extreme emphasis on the specific by neoevolutionary learning theorists to be an unfortunate overreaction to traditional approaches. Admittedly, there are dangers in abstract analyses and the ideal scientist working at one level of analysis ought to be able to keep the other level in mind.

Of course, the study of abstract principles should not depend on denial of the specific. In fact, the present abstract analysis of delay learning would have been impossible without wholehearted acceptance of the existence of situation-specific adaptations in learning. Stimulus relevance, upon which the interference analysis of food aversions depends, is a specialized adaptation for the feeding situation. It permits occurrence of biologically adaptive associations between feeding stimuli and those important physiological aftereffects which may not begin for hours. The difference between the present analysis and that advocated by neoevolutionary learning theorists is as follows. In the present analysis, the situation-specific adaptation was understood in the context of its interaction with general processes. Neoevolutionary learning theorists seem to advocate analysis of situation-specific adaptations in terms of their roles in adaptive complexes (Section 1.1).

In passing, it is emphasized that the exposition of delay learning in this chapter is meant as an example of a general process approach in action. It does not include everything known about delay learning. Insights into delay learning not afforded by the present interference theory are obtainable from the learned safety theory of Kalat and Rozin (1973) and the memory theory of Lett (in press).

### 3.6. Crossvalidation: General Processes Explain Another Anomaly

Although the very occurrence of food aversion learning has been considered evidence for the bankruptcy of any general approach to learning, this is simply not so. The details of food aversion learning are elucidated by consideration of data from traditional learning experiments. Further, the analysis of learning in traditional situations is elucidated by consideration of food aversion learning. Below, it will be shown that much the same is true of another set of findings which also once seemed to contraindicate a general process approach to learning.

The universal belief among learning theorists of a decade ago was that motor learning in feeding situations was instrumental: that it occurred because it preceded food reward. Intertwined with this belief were two assumptions: (1) that any arbitrary response of a hungry animal which preceded food reward would increase in strength; and (2) that traditional studies of food-rewarded motor learning used responses which had been arbitrarily selected by the experimenter. Both of these assumptions were central to the learning methodologies of the last few decades and both were shown to be largely incorrect.

The Brelands (1961) showed that continued response-contingent food reward does not always continue to strengthen an arbitrary motor response of a hungry animal. Animals trained to emit an arbitrary response through operant conditioning with food reward sometimes gradually switched to an instinctive behavior connected with feeding even when this reduced the frequency of reward. This effect is called instinctive drift.

Brown and Jenkins (1968) showed at least one motor response seemingly maintained by contingent presentation of food reward was neither an arbitrary response nor maintained by contingent reward. Their procedure, called autoshaping, was simply to subject experimentally naive pigeons to pairings in which illumination of a key preceded reward. The pigeons began to peck at the key, although the birds had never been rewarded for approximating pecks to the key. A variety of follow-up procedures showed that development of autoshaping does not depend on adventitious pairing of the pecking response with the reward (Jenkins, 1973). The Williamses (1969) showed that maintenance of key pecking after its initial development by the autoshaping technique also does not depend on the contingency of the peck with the reward. They changed the original autoshaping procedure so that reward was dispensed after illumination of the key only if there had not been a peck to the key; the pigeons still continued to peck. Thus, pairing of the illumination of the key with food reward was adequate both to produce pecking and to maintain it in strength without any instances in which pecking was followed by reward. Students of operant behavior had long claimed that the pecking response was an arbitrary operant developed and maintained by means of contingent reward. The autoshaping experiments showed that pecking at the key developed spontaneously when illumination of the key became a cue for reward.

Although these findings contradicted the general process theories of the time, they did not contradict the earlier general process approach of Pavlov. Moore (1973) has shown in detail how these effects can be accounted for in terms of Pavlov's (1932) stimulus substitution theory that animals tend to behave toward a CS in much the same way they behave toward a UCS. For instance, when illumination of a light bulb precedes feeding, dogs begin to act as if they were trying to eat the light bulb. Pavlov attributed the learning of motor responses to this tendency to redirect goal responses toward CSs. According to Moore (1973), the autoshaping effect is similar: pigeons direct pecks toward the illuminated disc which is a CS for food in much the same way that they peck at the food itself. It appears that Pavlovian reactions directed toward a CS also occur in stickleback fish (Sevenster, 1973) and that instinctive drift in mammals depends upon related mechanisms.

The point made here is that these effects, which are similar in mammals, birds, and fish, require analysis in terms of general processes. This cross-validates the corresponding point made about learned food aversions. Further discussion of instinctive drift and autoshaping is outside of the scope of this chapter.

## 4. The Epistemic Part of the General Learning Process

Although learning is certainly a biological process, at the present time it cannot be meaningfully described in the way other biological processes are described. Consider mammalian respiration as an example. Its analysis depends on the fact that all mammals have evolved in similar gaseous environments and have similar blood–lung systems. Thus, mammalian respiration can be described in terms of nearly incontrovertible facts about anatomy, chemistry, and physics. These give the subject matter a structure that is rigorous and not arbitrary. For the foreseeable future, learning will not be explicable in terms of similar solid information.

Despite the lack of solid biological information about its underlying mechanism, the material in Section 3 shows that learning is a general process. One aspect of learning will now be discussed in general terms; it may be called the epistemic process. It involves the acquisition of knowledge, rather than the development of behavior based upon that knowledge. It usually is possible to infer from an animal's behavior the information which it has learned without explaining acquisition of the behavior itself. For instance, from the salivation of a dog to a CS previously paired with a food UCS, we can infer that the dog has learned the CS–UCS association without having to explain why it salivates. Similarly, if a pigeon learns to peck at a green key but not at a red key as a result of discrimination training, we can infer that it has learned the different relationships of the two keys to reward without having to explain why it pecks.

In Sections 1.1 and 1.3, some of the advantages of focusing on the acquisition of knowledge rather than the development of behavior were discussed. There is also a very pragmatic advantage: Jenkins (1973) and Moore (1973) have shown that the process of response acquisition is not nearly as well understood as people once thought. I expect the understanding of response acquisition to develop and change rapidly in the next decade. In contrast, I think that there can be far less dispute about the very broad principles by which animals acquire knowledge.

Epistemic learning is the prediction of the future on the basis of past experience. Of particular concern here will be associative learning, in which an animal learns to predict the consequences which follow prior events. The epistemic process is remarkably similar in different situations and among different species because the rules by which the future can be predicted are remarkably uniform. Thus, the epistemic mechanism can be considered a biological adaptation to the causal nature of environments in much the same way that the lungs–blood system is an adaptation to the gaseous nature of the atmosphere.

The learning process in animals is analogous to the process of logical deduction of humans in that the function of both is to uncover causal relationships. Both processes are very fallible because causal relationships are usually uncertain. For instance, a person who gets sick on different occasions after drinking brandy and soda, Pernod and soda, bourbon and soda, and scotch and soda may incorrectly attribute his sickness to the soda on the basis of certain logical syllogisms. Similarly, the learning process often leads animals astray. Such an instance of maladaptive learning is the sensory preconditioning of flavors discussed in Section 3.4. Another, more spectacular instance may be the capacity of certain experiences to result in behaviors which produce painful electric shock (Brown, 1969; Kelleher, Riddle, and Cook, 1963; McKearney, 1969). Of course, occasional maladaptiveness is characteristic of biological processes; for instance, immune reactions can produce allergies and perhaps also cancers. Given such limitations, learning may be considered a biological logic built into the animal which usually yields correct conclusions regardless of the particular situation in which it occurs.

## 4.1. Rationalization for a Lack of Precision

Associative learning will be treated here as the operation of a biological mechanism, essentially a logic machine, which is adapted for dealing with the causal relationships in biological environments. By the standards of traditional learning theories, the present treatment will seem very loose, almost chaotic. However, I think that it is usually best that a scientific analysis reflect the precision of the actual knowledge of the subject matter. Although precision not justified by knowledge has sometimes led to new scientific insights, its role in the study of learning has often been to create a muddle.

Traditionally, such important factors in learning as the number of learning trials, amount of reward, intensity of stimulation, and the like, were explained in terms of intervening variables or hypothetical constructs, if they were explained at all. Intervening variables are logical symbols anchored both to the experimental operations and the resulting changes in behavior. The shortcoming of this methodology is that intervening variables are simply summaries of facts about learning which are not related to any independent reality. For instance, the Hullian intervening variable of habit strength is a summary both of the operation of subjecting the animal to learning trials and of the effects of this operation. Thus, it is not related to independent information in the same way as an analysis of, say, respiration in terms of the interaction of the chemical and physical properties of oxygen and blood in the lungs. Intervening variables in learning theory are like the homunculi and behaviorunculi described in Section 1.1.

The main purpose of the intervening variable approach was to permit precise analysis of the interactions of different factors important in learning. For instance, Spence's (1956) equation, $E = (D + K)H$, means that reaction potential E can be quantified in terms of intervening variables; E is the sum of drive D and incentive K multiplied by habit strength H. Unfortunately, this quantitative analysis promises more precision than it can deliver. It is reminiscent of Boyle's law in physics, which describes the interaction of volume, pressure, and temperature in a fluid, but it does not yield comparable insights because measurements and definitions in psychology are not nearly as precise as those in physics. Admittedly, more recent mathematical learning theories have benefited from Spence's work, as well as the earlier work of Hull, by becoming narrower and hence more precise. But the present concern is with a general description of the learning process, not a description of a few narrow situations. It seems unlikely to me that the intervening variable approach can be useful for such a general description at the present time.

Although the present proposal to study learning as a reflection of causal relationships which exist in biological environments lacks precision, it is not circular in the way that the intervening variable methodology is circular. The causal relationships which actually exist in biological environments are not simply restatements of learning effects; causal relationships would exist even if animals could not learn them. Thus, the proposed analysis is like a biological analysis in that it depends on information about the environment which is independent of behavior, but it is unlike a biological analysis because it does not depend on facts of anatomy, chemistry, and physics. The latter is a serious defect, but we can only summarize knowledge which we actually have.

## 4.2. The Epistemic Process in Action

Below, an imaginary anecdote will be used to show how the learning mechanism acts like a biological logic machine. A sophisticated logician gets sick at 3:00 p.m. and wants to find out why. His reasoning process is divided into two major steps. First, he collects important information about the sickness and about all events which occurred prior to the sickness which will help him solve his problem. Then he combines all the information which he has collated and reaches a conclusion or set of tentative conclusions. I will show below that there are parallels between the way our imaginary logician uses sophisticated hypotheses and inferences to reach a logical conclusion and the way an animal learns about the causes of sickness or any other kind of event.

## 4.2.1. Information about Single Events

*a. History with Sickness.* If the sickness had repeatedly occurred in the past in the absence of any specific prior cues, the logician would be less likely to suppose that the present instance of sickness was caused by the cues which had preceded it. The net result is that he would assign to all prior cues a lower probability of responsibility for the sickness. This parallels animal learning. As Cappell and LeBlanc have shown in Chapter 4 of this volume, when animals are repeatedly subjected to toxicosis in the absence of a prior cue likely to become strongly associated with toxicosis, toxicosis loses some of its capacity to create food aversions. Similarly, the capacity of shock to produce fear reactions to prior cues is reduced after shock has repeatedly been presented in the absence of prior cues (Mis and Moore, 1973; Rescorla, 1973).

*b. Relevance of Cues.* Our man will pay special attention to what he ate during the hours preceding sickness because sickness is often caused by what has been eaten. He will tend to discount the remote possibility that the sickness was caused by ordinary external cues or by those of his own behaviors that do not involve ingestion. Of course, the stimulus relevance principle insures that animals will behave in the same way. There probably are relevance principles related to feeding that are even more specific than the stimulus relevance principle described in Section 3.5.1, such as a propensity to associate between particular tastes and particular physiological aftereffects (Frumkin, 1971, 1975; Weisinger, Parker, and Skorupski, 1974). Later, in Section 4.4, it will be explained how relevance principles also are applicable to traditional learning experiments.

*c. Psychophysical Intensity of Cues.* The logician will suppose that strong-tasting substances are more likely to cause sickness than weak-tasting substances because taste intensity is correlated with the concentration of important chemicals in a substance. Rats also behave in this manner, both in the feeding situation (Dragoin, 1971; Garcia, 1971) and in conventional learning situations. Presumably, in nature, more intense cues are usually more important (although certainly not always).

*d. Prior Experience with Cues.* If substances consumed prior to his present sickness had been repeatedly consumed in the past without the occurrence of sickness, our man would tend to suppose that these substances are unlikely to have produced the sickness. This is how animals behave, regardless of whether they are associating between foodstuffs and sickness or between external cues and external aftereffects (Lubow, 1973).

*e. Temporal Proximity.* Our man knows that sickness usually develops relatively soon after the consumption of a poisoned substance (although not always). So substances consumed during lunch at 1:00 p.m. would seem more likely to be responsible for a sickness that begins at 3:00 p.m. than substances consumed during breakfast at 8:00 a.m. Of course, animals behave in a similar way. The nearer in time that a cue is to an aftereffect, the more likely it is that it will become associated with the aftereffect.

### 4.2.2. Integration of Information

By now, our logician has collected a great deal of information about single events and their conceivable relationship to his sickness. That is, he has combined the use of each of the preceding criteria to assign to each of a number of prior events a probability that it is responsible for the sickness. But these probabilities are merely initial unadjusted probabilities. Our logician now changes each of these probabilities in light of the probabilities he has assigned to other events. An effect, such as sickness, is likely to have but one immediate cause; that is, it is relatively seldom that a person has consumed two poisoned substances or that two normally harmless substances have interacted to produce a poison. Thus, the actual likelihood that event $A$ is the cause of an aftereffect $X$ depends not only on the unadjusted probability based solely on information about $A$ and $X$, but also is inversely related to the probability that some event other than $A$ is the cause of $X$. Suppose the unadjusted probability that $A$ causes $X$ is high, but the unadjusted probability that $B$ causes $X$ is much higher; then, because an effect is likely to have but one cause, the actual probability that $A$ causes $X$ is lower than the unadjusted probability. Conversely, suppose the unadjusted probability that $A$ causes $X$ is low, but there is no $B$ which is more likely to have caused $X$; then, since an effect must have some cause, the actual probability that $A$ causes $X$ is higher than the unadjusted probability.

Having defined his task, our logician now gets to work. For each possible $A$, he considers the probability that other $B$ events have caused $X$. He then combines this probability for all possible $B$s and changes the unadjusted probability that $A$ caused $X$ accordingly. He does this for each $A$ which has preceded $X$; that is, he adjusts the unadjusted probability for each event which has preceded his sickness.

The logical system I am making our logician use is much more complex than any symbolic logic system I have been exposed to. The usual symbolic logic systems deal with information in an all-or-none fashion. A conclusion is shown to be true, false, or indeterminate; it is not assigned a probability which is then adjusted. However, a system for dealing with unknown causal relationships in a practical way must be able to operate in a probabilistic fashion rather than in an all-or-none fashion if it is to be maximally effective. This is not to claim that causality itself is probabilistic, but only that men and animals usually do not have enough information to be certain and hence must use the equivalent of a probabilistic logic system.

Consider a simpler logical system than the system our logician used. We take the unadjusted probabilities obtained by considering each event and the likelihood that it has caused the sickness. We do not adjust them in view of the probabilities that other events have caused the sickness. Instead, we simply choose the event with the highest unadjusted probability and say it is the true cause. Such a method would be effective only in a special case: the case in which one substance has a probability of responsibility for the sickness that is far higher than any other probability. However, such a method would not be able to cope with the frequent case in which a few of the substances have unadjusted probabilities far higher than the others; in such a case, a rational man or animal would have to avoid each of these substances in the future but sample them occasionally so as to determine which substance actually is harmful. Such a method would not be able to cope with the case in which none of the substances have high unadjusted probabilities; a rational man or animal would develop mild aversions to each substance which would strengthen or weaken with subsequent experience and also would have to consider the possibility that events not usually responsible for sickness might be responsible for this particular sickness. The point is that a really effective epistemic system must utilize all available information on a probabilistic basis and not assign causes to effects on an all-or-none basis.

Thus, if our imaginary logician is to be effective, he actually must do some equivalent of changing the unadjusted probability that $A$ causes $X$ as an inverse function of the probability that some other event causes $X$. I do not know if real logicians are this effective, but animals are. Changes in the strength of learned associations between a cue and an aftereffect as an inverse function of the total strength of competing associations between other cues and that aftereffect parallel closely the behavior of our idealized logician. Section 3.2 summarizes some of the evidence for this both in food aversion experiments and in conventional learning experiments; the evidence is even clearer when presented in detail in the original papers. Admittedly, there have been a variety of experimental reports which show animals acting as if they associate between only one cue and an aftereffect and lose information about the other cues. But in every instance like this, more subtle experimental procedures show that the animal has retained information about a number of cues.

Remarkably and mercifully, it is unnecessary to postulate an homunculus or cognitive structure inside the animal's head to describe the process by which it compares all the cues likely to be responsible for an aftereffect. A simple rule, *concurrent interference,* is an adequate description: *the strength of an association between any cue and an aftereffect changes as an inverse function of the number and strengths of competing associations of other cues with that same aftereffect.* In other words, first the strength of a reference association is determined by such factors as relevance, psychophysical intensity, prior experience, temporal proximity, and the like; this corresponds roughly to the assignment of an unadjusted probability by our logician. The concurrent interference rule then adjusts the strength of this reference association inversely in terms of the total strength of competing associations. This is done for each potential reference association. The net result is adjustment of the strength of each potential association in terms of the probability that some other cue is responsible for the aftereffect.

The concurrent interference rule described above only involves the case in which a number of cues precede a single aftereffect. Revusky (1971) suggested a parallel rule for the case in which a number of aftereffects follow a single cue: *the strength or likelihood of association between any reference cue and an aftereffect changes as an inverse function of the number and strengths of competing associations between the reference cue and other different aftereffects.* Just as the earlier concurrent interference rule reflected the presumed fact that an effect usually has only one immediate cause, the second rule reflects the presumed fact that a cause usually has only one immediate effect.

Regrettably, there is no direct experimental evidence for the second rule in the animal learning literature; Revusky (1971, p. 169) pointed out how a direct test of this second rule is extremely difficult due to the technical nature of animal learning experiments. Nevertheless, the second rule seems so intuitively compelling to me that I used it in Section 3.5 on delay learning. I hasten to add that the concurrent interference explanation of delay learning makes sense even in the absence of the second rule (Revusky, 1971, p. 169). The present use of the second rule without direct evidence is similar to the use of intervening variables in traditional learning theories without direct evidence for them. Regardless of whether use of the second rule is justified, it illustrates how considerations of epistemic learning lead to inference beyond the immediate data. It also illustrates the danger that the epistemic approach can easily degenerate into an armchair analysis of learning. There will be more about this danger in the next subsection, 4.3.

## 4.3. Speculations about Some Factors in Learning

The epistemic approach to learning is based on vague considerations: the causal relationships present in most environments and how animals cope with them adaptively. The approach lacks the discipline of approaches based on more specific and concrete facts. The very specific information involved in the biological analyses of other processes is lacking. The rigorous emphasis on procedural details and the development of specific responses involved in the traditional behavioristic approach is also lacking. Because the discipline imposed by consideration of very concrete facts is absent, an epistemic analysis is continually on the brink of becoming an armchair analysis similar to that of the British empiricists of two centuries ago. Nevertheless, I think the risks of the epistemic approach are necessary for reasons which have already been explained.

More discipline and structure will be imposed upon the epistemic approach as its vague implications are tested experimentally. This, after all, is how the more specific errors in more rigorous approaches have been corrected. Earlier parts of this chapter illustrate how corrections are made. Toward the end of Section 3.2, it was shown that a retrospective use of information, which would be highly adaptive and easily within the capability of a logician, is not possible for animals. In Section 3.4, it was shown that sensory preconditioning would develop in the feeding situation although it is illogical and maladaptive in that situation. In both of these cases, my *a priori* expectation based on the present viewpoint had been that the behavior of the animals would reflect causal relationships in almost a logical fashion. I was wrong. The epistemic mechanism is marvelously adaptive, but it is not perfect and its imperfections must be determined experimentally. Nevertheless, to supply some structure for the understanding of the actual epistemic mechanism, it is desirable to keep in mind the way a perfectly adaptive epistemic mechanism would function.

It is with awareness of my fallibility that I will speculate below on how two factors important in learning can be better understood through considerations of the causal nature of most biological environments.

### 4.3.1. Learning Trials

The mores of traditional students of learning seem to reflect their long exposures to the very artificial learning environments found in universities where the more thoroughly and quickly students learn, the better their learning is. Thus, there has been a tacit assumption that the faster an animal learns, the more intelligent it is and that the failure to learn perfectly in a single trial is to be considered a defect in the learning process.

In a classroom, it is worthwhile for the student to learn all that he is exposed to because the teacher will reward him for it; there is no great danger that the student will "lose" by learning academic material. Most environments differ from school environments in that the experiences upon which learning can be based often are deceptive. Two events may occur in sequence simply by accident, and if an animal or human learned perfectly on that basis, it would be likely to develop maladaptive behavior. Psychotherapists dealing with neurotics are likely to be as concerned with maladaptive learning as with learning which has not occurred. Indeed, Section 1 of this paper suggests that even in universities, overlearning of the accepted wisdom by students is likely to be counterproductive when they eventually become professors. A more mundane example of the danger of learning too fast is that of a man who has gotten sick as a result of a virus which had nothing to do with what he ate: development of a learned food aversion would be maladaptive.

The point is that learning is most effective when there is an appropriate trade-off between the necessity to learn about genuine causal relationships and the necessity not to learn erroneously on the basis of the accidental occurrence of two events in sequence. Thus, if the effects of number of learning trials reflect the causal nature of most biological environments, they will insure such a trade-off. After one occurrence of two events in sequence, a good learning mechanism ought to process the information and act tentatively on its basis, but only after repeated training trials ought it to treat the correlation between the two events as strong evidence for a causal relationship.

In these terms, consider the once-widespread belief that the underlying learning process is all-or-none; an increased number of learning trials increases the likelihood that learning will have occurred on one of these trials and apparent gradual learning over trials is an artifact of combining data from a number of animals. This type of learning mechanism seems unbiological to me, because biological processes are seldom quite this crude. Such a mechanism also does not seem compatible with the precise analysis of information of which animals are capable as demonstrated in Section 3.2. I think the theory of all-or-none learning reflects the cultural belief that learning ought to be fast as well as a behavioristic belief that its underlying mechanism ought to be simple. As for the data which seem to support all-or-none learning, Mackintosh (1974) has discussed how they are derived from experiments in which a graded measure of learning is not available; since the response either can occur or fail to occur, there is no measurement of an intermediate state.

## 4.3.2. Forgetting

From the present point of view, forgetting is an adaptation to a general rule in biological environments: the greater the elapse of time since learning, the more likely it is that the causal relationships responsible for the original learning have changed. It is, after all, the primary role of learning to allow adaptation to conditions which change throughout the lifetimes of individuals. The adaptive nature of forgetting is nicely implied in a rabbinical midrash I once read but cannot seem to find again: children must forget because an adult with a perfect memory of what he learned as a child would never be able to lose his childish outlook. Similarly, what is true in spring in an animal's environment may have become false by autumn. The dangers of not being able to forget are pointed up in Luria's (1968) description of the tragedy of a man with a perfect memory.

Forgetting is often considered a shortcoming, but this seems wrong. If it turns out that neural decay is involved in forgetting, then the decay is not a defect of the nervous system but an adaptation. If we turn a light switch on, it remembers indefinitely and it is unreasonable to suppose that a similar feat would be beyond the capacity of the nervous system if it were adaptive. Similarly, if it turns out that forgetting is due to proactive and/or retroactive interference, the interference ought not to be considered a defect in the animal, but an adaptive mechanism like concurrent interference.

## 4.3.3. Other Factors

In the parable of the logician trying to decide what had made him sick (Section 4.2.), there were allusions to the adaptive nature of other factors in learning. Since these are obvious and straightforward, further discussion of them and of other similar factors seems superfluous.

## 4.4. Relevance Principles

Relevance principles refer to innate tendencies to associate selectively between particular types of events. That is, the association of a cue with an aftereffect depends upon the particular type of cue and the particular type of aftereffect. It is only recently that there have been extensive investigations of relevance effects by learning psychologists, but it is already clear that relevance principles of various types are very widespread.

About a decade ago, James Miller of the Central Institute for the Deaf pointed out to me that electric shock was a more effective source of motivation than food reward in the study of audition in animals; food reward seemed more effective than electric shock in the study of vision.

Miller's impression was that the auditory modality tends to be involved in defense and the visual modality in feeding. Foree and LoLordo (1973) proved Miller was right by showing that the auditory cue tends to be dominant over the visual cue when a compound audiovisual stimulus is a signal for shock; vice versa, when the compound is a signal for food. There is also evidence that pigeons given a choice of pecking at eight differently colored but functionally equivalent keys, are more likely to peck at the blue key when the reward is water than when the reward is food (Delius, 1968). There have also been various reports that certain types of responses are selectively associated with particular types of rewards (Shettleworth, 1973; Thorndike, 1911) or with punishment (Bolles, 1970), although it is hard to determine the exact involvement of relevance principles.

Although serious study of the role of relevance in learning has only begun recently, the point to be made now is that it would be an overreaction to give relevance a unique theoretical status. In the parable of the logician who tried to decide what had made him sick in Section 4.2, relevance was treated as one among many other factors in learning, not as a different type of factor. To do otherwise is misleading because it reinforces a tendency to think of most aspects of learning as not innate; relevance becomes a special condition constraining a learning process which otherwise adheres to something like the *tabula rasa* model. From a naturalistic point of view, all aspects of the learning process are innate. For instance, the tendency of increased familiarity with a cue to reduce its associative strength relative to novel aftereffects (Lubow, 1973) is just as innate as a principle of relevance. Both effects are ways in which the epistemic process has evolved to process information about causal relationships in environments. In a world where external cues rather than feeding cues were related to sickness, we would have the opposite of the stimulus relevance principle which regulates feeding in our world. In a world where the probability that a cue would cause an aftereffect increased with its familiarity, we would have the opposite of the cue familiarity effect of our world.

There is only one, very special, sense in which an aspect of a biological process can be considered other than innate: it may have developed as a secondary result of other, more primary, aspects of the process. Mackintosh (1973) has tentatively suggested that this might be true of stimulus relevance: it might be a learned concept produced through the animal's experience that only feeding cues are related to sickness. I am sure this suggestion is wrong because investigators of food aversion learning have routinely used 30–40-day-old rats and because Grote and Brown (1971) have produced flavor aversions in weanling rats. It is unreasonable to suppose that young rats could have developed a broad concept of stimulus relevance on the basis of experience only with chow, water, and mother's milk, unless there was a powerful innate tendency to help that experience along. If the latter were true, stimulus relevance, like many other innate biological factors, simply requires some environmental input to become active. Conceivably, the same might be true of the effects of cue familiarity and other factors involved in learning.

It may seem like excessive pettifogging to make such a major issue of the verbal habit of treating some factors as "purely" experiential. However, I feel that invalid distinctions can distort the perspectives of investigators, particularly where there is a strong cultural force, the *tabula rasa* ideology, to create distortions. The thinking of students of learning must be addressed to scientific issues, not issues of concern to philosophers who lived centuries ago.

## 4.5. The Integrative Action of the Concurrent Interference Principle

We have seen in Section 4.2 how the concurrent interference principle acts to combine all the information which the animal has about the relationships of individual cues to an aftereffect. The net result is that men and animals act like idealized logicians who compare all potential causes to determine those most likely to be the true cause. That concurrent interference usually prevents long-delay learning is not a shortcoming, but an advantage; for in most natural situations in which long-delay learning is adaptive, the concurrent interference process allows it to occur.

Although a definitive description of concurrent interference awaits the future, it is obviously such a simple principle that there can be real hope that it depends on an understandable biological mechanism. Indeed, interfering (inhibitory) processes are ubiquitous in the nervous system. So there is real hope that the biological mechanism underlying concurrent interference can be discovered. Since this mechanism permits comparison of all potential causes and effects, it will be the integrative action of the nervous system with respect to learning. If and when this happens, learning will be studied in the same way as other biological processes.

After all the recent disillusionment, often shared by me, with the value of studying the learning process, I am simply astonished to find myself so optimistic about the scientific future of the study of learning. After all, learning is the source of all uniquely human knowledge and achievement. It is good to feel certain that it is a legitimate scientific subject matter.

ACKNOWLEDGMENTS

In many ways this chapter is simply a development of an approach to learning pioneered by Paul Rozin and James Kalat. I owe them a great intellectual debt, the magnitude of which is obscured in the chapter itself because of strong disagreements with part of their approach. I am also grateful to Bow Tong Lett and Linda A. Parker who carefully read the original manuscript and many revisions of it. They kept finding ways to make it more literate and clearer. Parker also got the list of references together. I also thank Beverley Hoyles for typing the manuscript and Margaret Crawford for proofreading it. Much of the experimental work mentioned in the chapter was supported by grants to me from the Canadian National Research Council and the United States National Institute of Mental Health.

## 5. References

Amsel, A. Partial reinforcement effects on vigor and persistence. In K. W. Spence and J. T. Spence (Eds.), *The psychology of learning and motivation. Vol. 1.* New York: Academic Press, 1967.

Best, M. Conditioned and latent inhibition in taste-aversion learning: Clarifying the role of learned safety. *Journal of Experimental Psychology: Animal Behavior Processes,* 1975, *1,* 97–113.

Best, P. J., Best, M., and Rudy, J. Blocking in conditioned toxiphobia. Paper presented at the 16th annual meeting of the Psychonomic Society, Denver, Colorado, 1975.

Bolles, R. C. Species-specific defense reactions and avoidance learning. *Psychological Review,* 1970, *77,* 32–38.

Bravemen, N. S. Poison-based avoidance learning with flavored or colored water in guinea pigs. *Learning and Motivation,* 1974, *5,* 182–194.

Bravemen, N. S. Relative salience of gustatory and visual cues in the formation of poison-based food aversions by guinea pigs *(Cavia porcellus). Behavioral Biology,* 1975, *14,* 189–199.

Breland, K., and Breland, M. The misbehavior of organisms. *American Psychologist,* 1961, *61,* 661–664.

Brown, J. S. Factors affecting self-punitive locomotor behavior. In B. A. Campbell and R. M. Church (Eds.), *Punishment and aversive behavior.* New York: Appleton-Century-Crofts, 1969.

Brown, P. L., and Jenkins, H. M. Auto-shaping of the pigeon's key-peck. *Journal of the Experimental Analysis of Behavior,* 1968, *11,* 1–8.

Capaldi, E. J. A sequential hypothesis of instrumental learning. In K. W. Spence and J. T. Spence (Eds.), *The psychology of learning and motivation: Advances in theory and research, Vol. 1.* New York: Academic Press, 1967.

Capaldi, E. J. Memory and learning: A sequential viewpoint. In W. K. Honig and P. H. R. James (Eds.), *Animal memory.* New York: Academic Press, 1971.

Capretta, P. J. An experimental modification of food preferences in chickens. *Journal of Comparative and Physiological Psychology,* 1961, *54,* 238–242.

Carr, A. F. Latent inhibition and overshadowing in conditioned emotional response conditioning in rats. *Journal of Comparative and Physiological Psychology,* 1974, *86,* 718–724.

Cousins, L. S., Zamble, E., Tait, R. W., and Suboski, M. D. Sensory preconditioning in curarized rats. *Journal of Comparative and Physiological Psychology,* 1971, *77,* 152–154.

Delius, J. D. Color preference shift in hungry and thirsty pigeons. *Psychonomic Science,* 1968, *13,* 273–274.

Denny, M. R. Recent explorations in a T-maze: Women's lib, long delays and all that. Paper delivered at the 46th annual meeting of the Midwestern Psychological Association, Chicago, 1974.

Dragoin, W. B. Conditioning and extinction of taste aversions with variations in intensity of the CS and UCS in two strains of rats. *Psychonomic Science,* 1971, *22,* 303–305.

Evans, R. I. Lorenz warns: "Man must know that the horse he is riding may be wild and should be bridled." *Psychology Today,* 1974, *8,* 83–93.

Foree, D. D., and LoLordo, V. M. Attention in the pigeon: The differential effects of food-getting vs. shock-avoidance procedures. *Journal of Comparative and Physiological Psychology,* 1973, *85,* 551–558.

Frumkin, K. Interaction of LiCl aversion and sodium-specific hunger in the adrenalectomized rat. *Journal of Comparative and Physiological Psychology,* 1971, *75,* 32–40.

Frumkin, K. Failure of sodium- and calcium-deficient rats to acquire conditioned taste aversions to the object of their specific hunger. *Journal of Comparative and Physiological Psychology,* 1975, *89,* 329–339.

Garcia, J. The faddy rat and us. *New Scientist and Science Journal,* 1971, *49,* 254–256.

Garcia, J., and Koelling, R. A. Relation of cue to consequences in avoidance learning. *Psychonomic Science,* 1966, *4,* 123–124.

Garcia, J., McGowan, B. K., and Green, K. F. Biological constraints on conditioning. In M. E. P. Seligman and J. L. Hager (Eds.), *Biological boundaries of learning.* New York: Appleton-Century-Crofts, 1972.

Grote, F. W., Jr., and Brown, R. T. Rapid learning of passive avoidance by weanling rats: Conditioned taste aversion. *Psychonomic Science,* 1971, *25,* 163–164.

Gustavson, C. R., and Garcia, J. Aversive conditioning: Pulling a gag on the wily coyote. *Psychology Today,* 1974, *8,* 68–72.

Hinde, R. A. Constraints on learning: An introduction to the problems. In R. A. Hinde and J. Stevenson-Hinde (Eds.), *Constraints on learning.* London: Academic Press, 1973.

Jenkins, H. M. Effects of the stimulus-reinforcer relation on selected and unselected responses. In R. A. Hinde and J. Stevenson-Hinde (Eds.), *Constraints on learning.* London: Academic Press, 1973.

Kalat, J. W., and Rozin, P. You can lead a rat to poison but you can't make him think. In M. E. P. Seligman and J. L. Hager (Eds.), *Biological boundaries of learning.* New York: Appleton-Century-Crofts, 1972.

Kalat, J. W., and Rozin, P. "Learned Safety" as a mechanism in long-delay taste-aversion learning in rats. *Journal of Comparative and Physiological Psychology,* 1973, *83,* 198–207.

Kamin, L. J. Predictability, surprise, attention, and conditioning. In B. A. Campbell and R. M. Church (Eds.), *Punishment and aversive behavior.* New York: Appleton-Century-Crofts, 1969.

Kelleher, R. T., Riddle, W. C., and Cook, L. Persistent behavior maintained by unavoidable shocks. *Journal of the Experimental Analysis of Behavior,* 1963, *6,* 507–517.

Lavin, M. J. The establishment of flavor-flavor associations using a sensory preconditioning training procedure. *Learning and Motivation,* 1976, *7,* 173–183.

Lett, B. T. Delayed reward learning: Disproof of the traditional theory. *Learning and Motivation,* 1973, *4,* 237–246.

Lett, B. T. Visual discrimination learning with a 1-min delay of reward. *Learning and Motivation,* 1974, *5,* 174–181.

Lett, B. T. Long delay learning in the T-maze. *Learning and Motivation,* 1975, *6,* 80–90.

Lett, B. T. Long delay learning: Implications for learning and memory theory. In N. S. Sutherland (Ed.), *Tutorial essays in experimental psychology. Vol. II,* in press.

Lockard, R. B. The albino rat: A defensible choice or a bad habit? *American Psychologist,* 1968, *23,* 734–742.

Lubow, R. E. Latent inhibition. *Psychological Bulletin*, 1973, *79*, 398–407.

Luongo, A. F. Stimulus selection in discriminative taste-aversion learning in the rat. *Animal Learning and Behavior*, 1976, *4*, 225–230.

Luria, A. R. *The mind of a mnemonist*. New York: Basic Books, 1968.

Mackay, B. Conditioned food aversion produced by toxicosis in Atlantic Cod. *Behavioral Biology*, 1974, *12*, 347–355.

Mackay, B. Visual and flavor cues in toxicosis conditioning in codfish. *Behavioral Biology*, 1977, *19*, 87–97.

Mackintosh, N. J. Stimulus selection: Learning to ignore stimuli that predict no change in reinforcement. In R. A. Hinde and J. Stevenson-Hinde (Eds.), *Constraints on learning*. London: Academic Press, 1973.

Mackintosh, N. J. *The Psychology of Animal Learning*. London: Academic Press, 1974.

McKearney, J. W. Fixed-interval schedules of electric shock presentation: Extinction and recovery of performance under different shock intensities and fixed-interval durations. *Journal of the Experimental Analysis of Behavior*, 1969, *12*, 301–313.

McLaurin, W. A. Postirradiation saccharin avoidance in rats as a function of the interval between ingestion and exposure. *Journal of Comparative and Physiological Psychology*, 1964, *57*, 316–317.

Mis, F. W., and Moore, J. W. Effect of preacquisitions UCS exposure on classical conditioning of the rabbit's nictitating membrane response. *Learning and Motivation*, 1973, *4*, 108–114.

Moore, B. R. The role of directed Pavlovian reactions in simple instrumental learning in the pigeon. In R. A. Hinde and J. Stevenson-Hinde (Eds.), *Constraints on learning*. New York: Academic Press, 1973.

Pavlov, I. P. *Conditioned Reflexes*. Oxford: Oxford University Press, 1927.

Pavlov, I. P. The reply of a physiologist to psychologists. *Psychological Review*, 1932, *39*, 91–127.

Petrinovich, L., and Bolles, R. C. Delayed alternation: Evidence for symbolic processes in the rat. *Journal of Comparative and Physiological Psychology*, 1957, *50*, 363–365.

Petrinovich, L., Bradford, D., and McGaugh, J. C. Drug facilitation of memory in rats. *Psychonomic Science*, 1965, *2*, 191–192.

Pschirrer, M. E. Goal events as discriminative stimuli over extended intertrial intervals. *Journal of Experimental Psychology*, 1972, *96*, 425–432.

Reiss, S., and Wagner, A. R. CS habituation produces a "latent inhibition effect" but no active "conditioned inhibition." *Learning and Motivation*, 1972, *3*, 237–245.

Rescorla, R. A. Variation in the effectiveness of reinforcement and nonreinforcement following prior inhibitory conditioning. *Learning and Motivation*, 1971, *2*, 113–123.

Rescorla, R. A. Effect of US habituation following conditioning. *Journal of Comparative and Physiological Psychology*, 1973, *82*, 137–143.

Rescorla, R. A., and Wagner, A. R. A theory of Pavlovian conditioning: Variations in the effectiveness of reinforcement and nonreinforcement. In A. H. Black and W. F. Prokasy (Eds.), *Classical conditioning II*. New York: Appleton-Century-Crofts, 1972.

Revusky, S. The role of interference in association over a delay. In W. K. Honig and P. H. R. James (Eds.), *Animal memory*. New York: Academic Press, 1971.

Revusky, S. Long-delay learning in rats: A black-white discrimination. *Bulletin of the Psychonomic Society*, 1974, *4*, 526–528.

Revusky, S. Animal learning: A review of N. J. Mackintosh's "The Psychology of Animal Learning." *Science*, 1975, *189*, 131.

Revusky, S., and Garcia, J. Learned associations over long delays. In G. H. Bower and J. T. Spence (Eds.), *The psychology of learning and motivation: Advances in research and theory, Vol. 4*. New York: Academic Press, 1970.

Revusky, S., Parker, L. A., and Coombes, S. Flavor aversion learning: Extinction of the aversion to an interfering flavor after conditioning does not affect the aversion to the reference flavor. *Behavioral Biology,* in press.

Rizley, R. C., and Rescorla, R. A. Associations in second-order conditioning and sensory preconditioning. *Journal of Comparative and Physiological Psychology,* 1972, *81,* 1–11.

Rozin, P., and Kalat, J. W. Learning as a situation-specific adaptation. In M. E. P. Seligman and J. L. Hager (Eds.), *Biological boundaries of learning.* New York: Appleton-Century-Crofts, 1972.

Sevenster, P. Incompatability of response and reward. In R. A. Hinde and J. Stevenson-Hinde (Eds.), *Constraints on learning.* London: Academic Press, 1973.

Shettleworth, S. J. Food reinforcement and the organization of behavior in golden hamsters. In R. A. Hinde and J. Stevenson-Hinde (Eds.), *Constraints on learning.* London: Academic Press, 1973.

Skinner, B. F. *Verbal behavior.* New York: Appleton-Century-Crofts, 1957.

Smith, J. C., and Roll, D. L. Trace conditioning with X-rays as an aversive stimulus. *Psychonomic Science,* 1967, *9,* 11–12.

Solomon, R. L., and Corbit, J. D. An opponent-process theory of motivation: I. Temporal dynamics of affect. *Psychological Review,* 1974, *81,* 119–145.

Spence, K. W. *Behavior theory and conditioning.* New Haven, Conn.: Yale University Press, 1956.

Taukulis, H. K., and Revusky, S. Odor as a conditioned inhibitor: Applicability of the Rescorla-Wagner model to feeding behavior. *Learning and Motivation,* 1975, *6,* 11–27.

Thorndike, E. L. *Animal Intelligence: Experimental Studies.* New York: Macmillan, 1911.

Tyler, D. W., Wortz, E. C., and Bitterman, M. E. The effect of random and alternating partial reinforcement of resistance to extinction in the rat. *American Journal of Psychology,* 1953, *66,* 57–65.

Wagner, A. R. Stimulus selection and a "modified continuity theory." In G. H. Bower and J. T. Spence (Eds.), *The psychology of learning and motivation: Advances in research and theory. Vol. 3.* New York: Academic Press, 1969.

Wagner, A. R., Logan, F. A., Haberlandt, K., and Price, T. Stimulus selection in animal discrimination learning. *Journal of Experimental Psychology,* 1968, *76,* 171–180.

Weisinger, R. S., Parker, L. F., and Skorupski, J. D. Conditioned taste aversions and specific need states in the rat. *Journal of Comparative and Physiological Psychology,* 1974, *87,* 655–660.

Wilcoxon, H. C., Dragoin, W. B., and Kral, P. A. Illness-induced aversions in rats and quail: Relative salience of visual and gustatory cues. *Science,* 1971, *171,* 826–828.

Williams, D. R., and Williams, H. Auto-maintainance in the pigeon: Sustained pecking despite contingent nonreinforcement. *Journal of the Experimental Analysis of Behavior,* 1969, *12,* 511–520.

# Appendix to Chapter 1

## Interference with Progress by the Scientific Establishment: Examples from Flavor Aversion Learning

This is a time of widespread concern with the reliability of psychological data. It now appears certain that classical studies relevant to the heritability of IQ were incompetent or fraudulent. The same appears to be true of some spectacular experimental results which implied that instrumental learning of autonomic functions can occur in curarized animals independently of the motor system. The doubt about the latter finding is of immediate relevance to flavor aversion learning. The "finding" about instrumental learning of autonomic responses became widely known at the same time as long-delay flavor aversions and was equally contrary to nearly axiomatic principles of traditional theories of animal learning. That it is now in doubt suggests the possibility that the findings of long-delay flavor aversions ought also to be in doubt.

In this historical context, Bitterman (1976) has come with allegations that the literature of flavor aversion learning is suspect because of the lack of elementary control procedures. He claims (a) a lack of controls for pseudoconditioning and (b) a failure to exclude indirect temporal contiguity between the taste and the onset of delayed sickness as the cause of conditioning. These allegations are very serious; for instance, an undergraduate who did not understand about pseudoconditioning controls could not obtain a high grade even in a first course in learning. In effect, Bitterman, a famous learning theorist, has claimed that students of flavor aversion learning are incompetent.

That Bitterman is one man arguing against the competence of many is no reason for an outsider to suppose that his claims are wrong. When scientists have staked their careers upon a fallacy, they are likely to defend that fallacy almost to the death. Certainly, scientists are capable of accepting gross errors once they have been seduced into allegiance to them; dozens of students of the heritability of IQ can be validly accused of incompetence because they uncritically accepted obviously incompetent data. It is perfectly plausible to an outsider that Bitterman is correct that students of flavor aversion learning are largely incompetent. It is naive to expect scientists not specialists in animal learning to evaluate Bitterman's evidence for themselves before reaching a conclusion; it is impractical to evaluate scientific evidence outside of one's immediate scientific area. Most of us accept the existence of viruses, hypothalamic hyperphagia, synaptic transmission, and the like on the basis of faith in the competence of the scientists who investigate them. Bitterman's suggestion that faith in those who investigate flavor aversions is not justified was published in *Science,* a journal for a general audience of scientists; its readers are more likely to accept his criticisms without reflection than would readers of a technical journal for specialists in learning.

Whatever damage was done to the flavor aversion field by Bitterman's criticisms will not readily be reversed. Together with Harry Taukulis, a student at Memorial University, I submitted a rebuttal to Bitterman's criticisms to *Science* but it was rejected for publication. A rebuttal presented here will reach few of the readers of *Science.* There is no need to convince readers of this volume that Bitterman is wrong because they have specialized knowledge of flavor aversion learning; Bitterman's arguments are so fallacious that they will sway very few who can evaluate the evidence for themselves.

Nevertheless, I will spend a number of pages demonstrating fallacies in Bitterman's criticisms, not to demonstrate that they are scientifically invalid, but to show that they contain such a large number of fallacies as to indicate that Bitterman desperately wants to disbelieve in long-delay flavor aversions; there is no other explanation of how a man with decades of experience in learning theory could make so many mistakes at once. If a need to disbelieve radically new findings which extends far beyond rational conservatism can be demonstrated in one leading scientist, it becomes tenable to suppose that similar needs are common among influential scientists and tend to interfere with scientific progress: this is my main thesis. In other words, Bitterman's criticisms are to be considered not for their scientific validity, but as suggestive evidence for a broad sociological hypothesis. Admittedly, this is not a nice way in which to use Bitterman's critique, but it is in the public interest; it is Bitterman himself who has chosen to place unreasonable criticisms in the public domain and thus I am free to demonstrate their full implications.

## 1. Specific Criticisms

### 1.1. Pseudoconditioning

In a flavor aversion experiment, pseudoconditioning may be defined as a flavor aversion produced by prior sickness independently of associative learning. Hence, the usual type of pseudoconditioning control group will be exposed to the sickness without prior exposure to the flavored test substance. Early investigators used such controls to rule out pseudoconditioning as an explanation of learned flavor aversions (Revusky and Garcia, 1970, p.16). In fact, a decade ago, Revusky and Bedarf (1967) did not bother to use pseudoconditioning controls in a flavor aversion experiment on the basis of failures to demonstrate pseudoconditioning by Scarborough, Whaley, and Rogers (1964) and by Smith, Taylor, Morris, and Hendricks (1965). Thus, pseudoconditioning controls are absent from most flavor aversion experiments simply because they are unnecessary. Requiring such controls would be like requiring Bitterman to control for the possibility that instrumental performance occurs only because the animal has experience with the reward rather than because the response precedes the reward. Bitterman has never to my knowledge used such controls (although, in fact, as students of autoshaping know, they sometimes are necessary).

Bitterman's failure to realize that pseudoconditioning had been excluded as the cause of flavor aversion learning over a decade ago might be considered excusable enough; certainly, we all have scholarly lapses. However, even a superficial acquaintance with the flavor aversion literature reveals a multitude of effects which are entirely incompatible with the hypothesis of pseudoconditioning. A person who knew of any of these effects and still thought flavor aversion learning could be due to pseudoconditioning would simply not be a competent student of animal learning. Some evidence is as follows:

1. There is a large literature (see Cappel and LeBlanc, Chapter 4, this volume) on the effects of prior sickness experience unpaired with ingestion on the subsequent capacity of sickness to produce flavor aversions. In these experiments the amount consumed during the first flavor–sickness pairing is a direct test of the pseudoconditioning hypothesis, since animals with histories of sickness are exposed to novel flavored substances. None of these experiments has yielded pseudoconditioning. More importantly,

prior exposure to sickness retards the development of a learned flavor aversion—the exact opposite of the effect to be expected on the basis of pseudoconditioning. In fairness, it must be pointed out that Bitterman might not have known of these relatively recent findings.

2. If flavor aversions were due to pseudoconditioning, the aversion to a novel flavor would be just as strong as the aversion to a flavor paired with sickness. In fact, both Rozin (1969) and Revusky (1971) have shown that an animal will avoid the solution previously paired with sickness when given a choice between it and a novel solution. Since both of these papers are widely cited and have been available for the better part of a decade, Bitterman ought to have been aware of them. However, in fairness to Bitterman, it should be noted that neither Rozin (1969) nor Revusky (1971) pointed out that these results excluded pseudoconditioning since they felt it was obvious and did not think pseudoconditioning was a problem anyway.

3. As the delay between exposure to a flavor and sickness increases, the learned aversion becomes less marked (Andrews and Bravemen, 1975; Domjan and Bowman, 1974; Dragoin, McCleary, and McCleary, 1971; Etscorn and Miller, 1975; Garcia, Ervin, and Koelling, 1966; Green and Rachlin, 1976; Nachman, 1970; Nachman and Jones, 1974; Revusky, 1968; Rozin, 1969; Rozin and Ree, 1972; Smith and Roll, 1967; Taukulis, 1974). It follows directly from the definition of pseudoconditioning that if flavor aversions were due to pseudoconditioning, the delay of sickness would have no effect since it would not matter if the flavor had been paired with the sickness. Bitterman's failure to notice this obvious point is evidence of his active desire not to believe in flavor aversion learning, for it is not reasonable to suppose that he could have been ignorant of the very existence of a delay gradient.

4. There is a generalization gradient to other substances after an aversion has been produced to one substance just as there is generalization to other CSs after conditioning has been produced to one CS (Czaplicki, Borrebach, and Wilcoxon, 1976; Domjan, 1975; Kalat, 1974; Klein, Mikulka, and Hamel, 1976; Nowlis, 1974; Revusky, Parker, Coombes, and Coombes, 1976; Rozin, 1969; J. C. Smith, personal communication cited by Revusky and Garcia, 1970). If the effect were due to pseudoconditioning, there would be no generalization gradient, but equal aversions to the "poisoned" flavor and other novel flavors. Here even the most charitable will find it difficult to attribute Bitterman's failure to realize this point to ordinary oversight, for Bitterman (1976) himself alluded to the specificity of an aversion to the *concentration* of the flavored solution in the case of sucrose but somehow managed to *repress* the realization that this alone excluded pseudoconditioning. I use the term "repress" quite deliberately because I do not see how such a realization could otherwise fail to develop in an intelligent person with decades of experience in animal learning.

## 1.2. Temporal Contiguity

In traditional animal learning theories, whenever animals seemed to associate between two events over delays greater than a few seconds, there was a tendency to attribute the learning to indirect temporal contiguity produced, for instance, by sensory aftereffects. Bitterman seems determined to continue this tradition in the realm of flavor aversion learning and demands the exclusion of such sources of indirect temporal contiguity as lingering aftertastes and the regurgitation of ingesta when sickness occurs. These sources of contiguity were definitively ruled out long ago (Revusky and Garcia, 1970, pp. 17–19). Bitterman's failure to realize this is profoundly irrational given his long experience with animal learning. Some of the evidence is as follows.

1. There have been many studies showing that a rat can consume a single flavored substance between the ingestion of a test substance and the onset of sickness and still develop an aversion to the flavor of the test substance. A more spectacular case is reported by Kalat and Rozin (1971), who showed that a rat can consume three flavored solutions between consumption of a test solution and toxicosis and still develop an aversion to the test substance. It is very hard to imagine how consumption of three different flavored solutions could fail to mask an aftertaste of the test solution and thus prevent temporal contiguity between this aftertaste and toxicosis; but undoubtedly Bitterman can imagine this. However, not even Bitterman should have failed to notice that one of the test substances used by Kalat and Rozin (1971) was sucrose solution. It will be recalled that Bitterman (1976) himself affirmed that aversions to sucrose solution tend to be concentration-specific. If so, how could a weak aftertaste of sucrose become associated with toxicosis and produce an aversion to the strong taste of the actual sucrose solution itself?

2. A hungry rat made sick more than seven hours after it has been fed sucrose solution still develops an aversion to the taste of the solution (Revusky, 1968). Sucrose is nearly completely digested at the end of seven hours and so cannot be retasted at the time of sickness. Nor can it reasonably be supposed to leave an aftertaste strong enough to generalize to the original taste of the solution because sucrose aversions tend to be specific to particular concentrations (Bitterman, 1976).

3. Bitterman (1976) claims that increases in flavor preferences produced by injection of thiamine into thiamine-deficient rats can be attributed to temporal contiguity because the injections produce rapid alleviation of thiamine deficiencies. In fact, the increase has been reported by Garcia, Ervin, Yorke, and Koelling (1967) to occur with a 30-min delay of injection. Since Bitterman (1975) actually cited this paper and the effect was depicted in the second of but two figures, his failure to notice it is a severe deficiency on his part. Furthermore, the increase in preference for a flavored solution

based on delayed thiamine injection occurs even if the rat is allowed to drink a masking solution during the interval (Campbell, 1969). Finally, even preference increases resulting from immediate injection of thiamine cannot be attributed to temporal contiguity since the injection requires a few minutes to take effect and, according to the traditional studies, this delay is too long to permit learning to occur.

4. Bitterman (1975) suggested that long-delay flavor aversions could be explained by the hypothesis that "taste receptors are stimulated again at the time of sickness by food returned to the mouth." The usual belief has been that rats cannot vomit, but Bitterman has cited work suggesting that rats have been known to vomit. However, these instances are so rare that explaining flavor aversions in terms of them is like explaining human population explosions in terms of increases in virgin births. Even if rats vomited as readily as monkeys, vomiting could not account for the results mentioned in the preceding two paragraphs.

## 2. Type-2 Incompetence

As any student of flavor aversions will realize, the above material is only a portion of the evidence that flavor aversion learning is not due to pseudoconditioning or to indirect temporal contiguity between the flavor and the sickness. A variety of different sets of findings could have been used to refute Bitterman's criticisms. But such scholarly gymnastics are not necessary because my main point, Bitterman's colossal disregard of evidence, has been made. Now I will explain why I think this is an important point.

During the last decade, I have gradually become convinced that the scientific establishment which reviews scientific papers for publication and grants proposals for funding is incompetent in dealing with certain types of new ideas and actively suppresses scientific progress based on such ideas. Since reviews of papers and grant proposals are usually considered privileged information, there is no collection of them and I can only support my opinion from my experiences and those of my friends. This makes it very difficult to discuss my opinion; one who claims that he has frequently been victimized by scientific incompetence on the part of very eminent scientists seems like a bad sport, megalomanic, and addicted to self-pity. One who brings his friends into the fray will soon have few friends. However, I hope readers of this volume agree with the present evidence that Bitterman's criticisms of flavor aversion learning, prepared by an eminent learning theorist for the very large readership of *Science* magazine, are incompetent. If so, they should be ready to consider my hypothesis that far less eminent scientists anonymously reviewing papers and grant proposals for audiences of less than half a dozen, might be even more incompetent. Bitterman differs from these anonymous reviewers by having the courage to state his convictions publicly so that he can be publicly refuted. I honestly respect him for this; others do not give their opponents a chance.

Bitterman (1975) has explained clearly and frankly why the possibility of long-delay flavor aversion learning is disturbing to him. He is an advocate of what he calls a Thorndikian approach to the comparative psychology of learning. He agrees with a variety of claims that the very occurrence of flavor aversion learning mandates a more ethological approach. Hence, flavor aversion learning is a threat to his scientific work. Before he perceived matters in this way, Bitterman apparently was not disturbed by the possibility that pseudoconditioning might be involved in flavor aversion learning. Some years ago, Bitterman told me that he had favorably reviewed a paper about flavor aversions by Revusky and Bedarf (1967) for *Science;* I have already mentioned that this paper did not include a pseudoconditioning control.

None of this proves anything, but it agrees with the hypothesis of many sociologists of science (Gordon, 1977) that the unwillingness to accept radical results stems primarily from jealousy and a reaction to threat. Another factor may be scientific training which emphasizes the dangers of acceptance of false findings more than the dangers of failure to accept true findings. However, the extreme reaction of concern here is more than mere conservatism.

The type of incompetence exhibited by Bitterman (1976) is different from the type of incompetence alluded to earlier involving the study of intelligence and the study of operant conditioning of autonomic responses. In the latter two cases, there were false statements that facts had been discovered; by analogy with inferential statistics, they may be called Type-1 incompetence (T1). Bitterman's incompetence involves the use of spurious criteria to deny that facts have been demonstrated and may be called Type-2 incompetence (T2). Use of the term "incompetence" here rather than "error" reflects the hypothesis that real deficiences on the part of individual scientists are involved. For instance, T1 incompetence may occur when a senior scientist places an excessive demand upon subordinates to produce radical and exciting results and has no checks that their work is competent; he is similar to an industrialist who does not tell his subordinates to violate the law, but puts pressure upon them which insures that many will do so. It is misleading to call such states of affairs "error" although admittedly the term "incompetence" may not be pejorative enough. Similarly, it is obviously inaccurate to call the T2 incompetence of Bitterman "error" when it has the systematic effect of downgrading scientific contributions made by students of flavor aversion learning. In other words, ordinary error should not have the systematic effect of being in the interest of those responsible for the error.

## 2.1. Sociology of T2

A *scientific enterprise* is defined here as the study of a limited set of techniques, phenomena, and/or ideas as a coherent subject matter. Such an enterprise may be said to begin when a number of individuals are actively working on it and dies when the study of its subject matter has essentially been completed. For instance, the basic Skinnerian enterprise is the study of free operant performance as a topic of basic research. By my definition, it does not include applications of the study of operant performance to psychotherapy, physiological psychology, the study of perception and attention, and so on. Such applications are not primarily operant conditioning but the use of operant conditioning techniques to study something else. In other words, I am defining the primary operant enterprise as the study of schedules of reinforcement even though plenty of Skinnerians are interested in other things. Given this crude and arbitrary definition, the operant enterprise began about 1950 (before that, its adherents were too few and uninfluential to form an enterprise). It died about 1970 when it was no longer meaningful for a new Ph.D. to state that his work was to be basic research in operant conditioning, since the broad implications of the operant conditioning techniques and philosophy were already known.* It is emphasized that, given our definitions, the death of a scientific enterprise is a natural and proper end which reflects its success.

In other words, the length of life of a scientific enterprise is how long it takes to get the job done. This, in turn, depends on the breadth and difficulty of problems involved and the number of scientists involved in the enterprise. In the course of this century, scientific enterprises have tended to become narrower in scope and the number of scientists involved per enterprise has increased. These factors have tended to reduce the life of a scientific enterprise. The Hullian and Skinnerian enterprises lasted 20–25 years.

We can briefly sketch the history of a scientific enterprise. It begins after the initially powerful T2 has been broken down a bit; it has relatively few scientists and poor funding but because the area is essentially virgin territory, the results are very promising. After perhaps five years, graduate students are beginning to be attracted in mass and the enterprise is flowering. At about the chronological midpoint of its life, the enterprise begins to obtain substantial power in the scientific establishment and has input into the process of reviewing papers submitted to journals and grant proposals. Graduate students are increasingly jumping on the bandwagon, but the more important scientific work in the area has already been done. As the enterprise heads toward its inevitable death, it keeps attracting

---

* This, of course, does not mean that all experiments about operant conditioning done after 1970 are meaningless.

graduate students and grant resources even though it is getting very difficult to do meaningful work in the area. This, however, is not obvious from objective measures; there are so many people in the area that many papers about residual trivia are being published and are widely cited in other similar papers. As the enterprise dies, Ph.D.s with about ten years experience avail themselves of the right to begin doctoral programs in the area at third-rate universities. The in-group continues to be influential after the enterprise is dead and will not admit to itself that the enterprise is dead. In other words, it is claimed here that the situation among scientists can parallel that among generals who prepare for a past war and educators who train students in skills for which there is no longer any market.

This model implies that the proportion of human and financial resources absorbed by an enterprise is in almost inverse relationship to its usefulness. It is almost certain that the resources spent on an enterprise during the last 20% of its life and during an equal period after its death are much greater than the total resources spent earlier. A dying enterprise will attract new grant funds largely because it has representatives on the granting agencies and will attract students largely because they will receive financial support for working in the enterprise. There is no real possibility of a rational termination of the enterprise by those involved in it, for this would leave many of the workers in the enterprise effectively without major research work to do and hence with reduced status; it would be particularly unfortunate for new Ph.D.s. Thus, anything that suggests that the enterprise is completed or ought to change its direction constitutes a threat. T2 is a reaction to this threat and frequently consists of unreasonable applications of standards of rigor to the evidence for any new discovery. Occasionally an incident occurs which lends extra legitimacy to T2. It is found that the work of an honored leader of the enterprise is faulty. The honored leader is not blamed because that would impugn the enterprise. Instead the incident is taken as evidence there must be still more vigilance to maintain scientific standards; this, of course, is a rationalization for still more T2.

Like all models, the above model is certainly oversimplified. I have emphasized the role of the coming completion of an enterprise in eliciting T2, but certainly ordinary professional territoriality can be a factor. The in-groups of recognized scientists in a particular area will resent anybody without training in the area who has the gall to think he has important contributions to make. Another oversimplification is the assumption that a scientific enterprise has a relatively fixed task and relatively constant scientific techniques; in many cases a scientific enterprise is more open-ended and then it need not die. However, even in such cases, it is likely that a modified form of this model applies to more limited tasks within the enterprise.

This model can help explain why flavor aversion learning was not widely accepted in the psychological literature until nearly 15 years after the first clear and rigorous demonstration of the effect by Garcia, Kimeldorf, and Koelling (1955). It is my hypothesis that without T2 the lag for acceptance of the effect would have been less than five years and that within another few years, a substantial number of investigators should have been concerned with the effect. Instead, the lag was 15 years, largely because the effect was kept out of the more prestigious psychological journals through T2 reviews of submitted papers.

To determine the cause in terms of our model, we must consider the state of animal learning in the 1960s. The tone of the study of animal learning was set by two major in-groups, the Hullian and the Skinnerian. By our model, the Hullian enterprise began about 1945 and died about 1965. The Skinnerian enterprise began and died about five years later. In the early 1960s, the Hullians began to see the handwriting on the wall and the Skinnerians began to see it five years later. Because reviews of journal submissions are anonymous, I do not have any details about who was responsible for keeping Garcia's effect from the attention of people who might have benefited from learning about it although I have read some silly reviews. But there certainly was an atmosphere of fear of obsolescence on the part of many concerned with animal learning, and I conjecture that it was a factor in suppressing a new discovery.

Although I think there were few, by the late 1960s, who expected any exciting new developments in animal learning as a result of applications of Hullian and Skinnerian theory and methodology, it did seem certain that past use of these techniques had left a large corpus of reliable scientific principles. Garcia's discovery of long-delay food aversions produced by selective association between feeding cues and sickness demonstrated that principles of learning which had seemed incontrovertible were entirely incorrect. But this alone was not enough to elicit maximal T2 since the Hullians and Skinnerians were, in fact, capable of dealing objectively with substantial attacks on established principles, as shown by their studies of vicious circle behavior and autoshaping. It was two additional elements which made Garcia's discoveries too threatening to bear. First, Garcia was undeserving. He made his basic discovery while an assistant at an applied naval research laboratory and did not even have his Ph.D.; in fact, he was not really trained in learning theory in any rigorous sense. Both vicious circle behavior and autoshaping had been delineated by people in the appropriate in-groups in a manner which initially did not pose a major threat. Second, Garcia's original techniques involved production of flavor aversions by means of x-irradiation and measurement of the aversion by a simple test of consumption: weighing bottles. This meant that elaborate learning methodologies were not necessary and hence reduced the value of the educational investments made by members of the in-groups.

As indicated earlier, T2 is usually hidden in anonymous reviews so that an historian can obtain the impression that the scientific enterprise involves a much freer interchange of ideas than actually is the case. For instance, an historian in 1990 might conclude from a library investigation of journals that the learned flavor aversion effect got into the mainstream psychological literature in the late 1960s and was widely accepted in only a few years. If he were puzzled as to why learned flavor aversion experiments were not reported in this literature (with rare exceptions) for such a long period since the paper of Garcia *et al.* (1955), he might conjecture that early investigators made a poor choice of journals to publish in. The historian would have no evidence either of early suppression of publication or of editorial deletion of more threatening implications when publication finally was permitted.

An historian looking at the objective record will see a rapid acceptance of Garcia's importance as a scientist after the Garcia effect became known. In 1969, just a few years after belated receipt of his Ph.D., Garcia obtained a prestigious academic post at the Stony Brook Campus of the State University of New York. One might infer that after 1969, Garcia was no longer penalized for his radical stance, but I do not believe that. Those who failed to recognize an important effect for over a decade were not about to admit to their own failure but were to blame Garcia for it. I believe this because I have heard the same story from a number of sources that Garcia indeed discovered the effect but did not know how to do a rigorous experiment to prove it. Paul Rozin and/or Sam Revusky allegedly did the definitive experiments. Of course, this is completely without foundation; both Rozin and Revusky presupposed the effect and neither have made claim to discovering or establishing it more definitively. Indeed, as I indicated earlier, Revusky and Bedarf (1967) were so sure of the basic effect that they did not even bother with a pseudoconditioning control group.

Another instance of the way truth is distorted involves the classic demonstration of constrained association in the feeding system by Garcia and Koelling (1966). This paper had been rejected by a number of prestigious psychology journals. It then was drastically condensed for submission to a nonrefereed journal with a then-strict limit on the length of articles. The condensation made the paper difficult to read. Garcia was then blamed for poor writing when, in fact, the choice was either to condense the material or not to get the information on the record. The point is that a T2 establishment, like any establishment, will protect itself from its mistakes as much as it can. I do not think Bitterman would have been so quick to infer the existence of widespread incompetence among students of flavor aversion learning if he did not periodically move in a social milieu in which such incompetence was implied.

Of course, this sounds like a classically paranoid analysis. But it is compatible with the following facts. (1) When the Garcia effect was finally recognized, Paul Rozin was invited to address the convention of the American Psychological Association about it instead of John Garcia. (2) In 1967 and in 1968, with only one or two published papers on food aversion learning, I was invited to contribute chapters to two prestigious volumes on learning instead of Garcia.* (3) *The Journal of Comparative and Physiological Psychology,* which regularly prints a list of its guest reviewers, has never, as far as I know, asked Garcia to review a paper for it in spite of publishing many papers in taste aversion learning. Indeed, as I remember, Garcia told me in 1974 that he had only been asked once to review a paper for a journal of the American Psychological Association. The point is not so much that Garcia was penalized, but that the single most qualified man in an area was kept out of the review process. It was not fair to people submitting flavor aversion papers to journals of the American Psychological Association or to readers of those journals.

I will now describe how I believe I have been subjected to T2. To increase my credibility, I emphasize that I initially benefited from T2 at the expense of Garcia in a manner which increased my prestige immensely; I am probably a net gainer from T2. Nevertheless, my scientific style elicits T2 because I use insights from my area of expertise to shed light upon areas in which I am not trained or expert and emphasize my belief that work within the invaded area should be strongly affected by what I have to say. Obviously, this is bound to elicit territorial reactions from those within the in-group which controls the area. It is my impression that this is the only time I have serious trouble with reviewers of papers for publication and with grant applications. If my work doesn't threaten anybody, I have no trouble publishing or getting funded even though I am convinced that my unthreatening work is not nearly as important as my threatening work. Similar beliefs have been expressed by others (Gordon, 1977).

It would require a great deal of space to prove that I have been subjected to severe T2, although I have no doubt I could do so to the satisfaction of most readers of this volume if I were to bother to write 100 pages on the topic and they were to bother to read it. Consider that the present incomplete analysis of Bitterman's T2 required a number of pages. To demonstrate that I have been subjected to T2, I would have to include

* Conceivably, the poor readability of the 1966 Garcia–Koelling paper might have been a factor in these editorial decisions. It is, of course, awkward for me almost to blame people for offering me tremendous opportunities and I would like to emphasize that I am personally grateful. Furthermore, there were certain advantages to having a person with a background in traditional learning theory like myself do the chapters. Nevertheless, I think it necessary to suggest these editorial decisions were indicative of a sociological process. Finally, it is to be noted that Garcia was invited to the 1969 McMaster Conference on Classical Conditioning.

my submissions, the reviews I received, and then explain the role of T2. But nobody should make the mistake of supposing that I am confusing T2 with genuine inability to understand the submission. In the case of inability to understand a submission, the reaction is befuddlement and a few irrelevant remarks. To define something as a T2 reaction, one needs some indication that more than befuddlement is involved. Here is an example from somebody in a runway and T-maze business which happens to be the most recent T2 reaction I have received:

> I cannot recommend publication of 062-6 because discrimination learning was not obtained. If it had occurred, I would have recommended against publication on two other grounds. First, the paper is poorly written. Consider an example. "The present experiment was an attempt . . . " (pg 3). More seriously, the authors lump together a variety of different procedures under delayed reward. It is this gross procedural confusion which allows then *(sic)*, in my view, to conclude essentially that excepting themselves, all of psychology has failed to understand delayed reward. What utter nonsense.

This was followed by another paragraph which, if it was not due to T2, proved statistical incompetence and/or illiteracy on the part of the reviewer.

As may be inferred from the above example, the hallmark of T2 is sputtering rage at the effrontery of the submission. This suppresses all normal intelligence. However, technical terms are remembered and uttered in a sort of jumbled incantation to drive the devil away. A typical T2 ploy is that the work is incomplete and detailed technical knowledge allegedly possessed only by members of the in-group is required to complete it. For instance, when my early long-delay flavor aversion studies threatened somebody in the neuroanatomical-regulation-of-food-intake business, he claimed that to explain a sugar aversion in terms of ingestion-contingent X-irradiation was not sufficient; I had to explain the neuroanatomy by which the association developed. When I infringed on psychopharmacology territory by demonstrating a learned association between pentobarbital sedation and lithium sickness, I was informed that I had to explain this learned association in terms of the interactions of the pharmacologies of the pentobarbital and lithium reactions. Since this pharmacology is known neither for pentobarbital nor lithium, such a demand can be used to stop any inconvenient investigation; it is never used to stop investigations by members of the in-group. Of course, I cannot delineate here every type of T2 I have encountered, but the examples given here are not extreme.

It is, I know, considered bad taste to describe a sociological process in terms of anecdotes, but there seems to be no other way because there are no available records of T2. However, the use of anecdotes does introduce a methodological bias: my friends and I come out as heroes and adherents of traditional learning theories come out as villains. But if my model is correct, this is bound to be true. My friends and I were involved in founding and developing a new scientific enterprise and adherents of traditional learning theories were involved with maturing and dying enterprises; thus, we were bound to be victims of T2 and they were bound to exert it. If the anecdotes were obtained at a different time, the roles of heroes and villains might be different. When the traditional learning theories were younger, their adherents were victims of T2; I distinctly remember the T2 inflicted on Skinnerians while I was a graduate student in the late 1950s. I expect that flavor aversion learning is at about the midpoint of its life and will soon begin to exert substantial T2. My aim in writing this note is not to serve the flavor aversion learning in-group, but to try to make it aware of the damage it is likely to do in the future. Nor is my aim self-serving in any narrow sense, since I do not expect T2 to be a major problem for me in the future. I would like scientific institutions somehow to protect people like the Sam Revusky of a decade ago from people like the Sam Revusky of a decade hence.

## 2.2. How T2 Is Hidden

It is remarkable that there are so few complaints about T2 if the present thesis about the extent of its interference with scientific progress is correct. If as much injury is being inflicted as I suggest, one would expect to hear more screams from the victims even if these are not in the usual scientific literature.

There are a number of reasons the victims are silent (except in occasional anecdotes in scientific biographies). The victim who never gains scientific recognition for potential contributions (and I suspect there are many such) cannot publicize the matter with any credibility because it is his word against the word of eminent scientists. A man with some limited scientific reputation who is still actively sciencing is likely to be afraid of being penalized by harsh reviews of his work or simply of being considered unbalanced. The man who has overcome T2 will not mention it because he is now a success, is not threatened, and has no desire to be considered a sorehead. Imagine a Nobel Laureate beginning his acceptance speech like this. "Thank you. But if my colleagues had not been so incompetent, my discovery would have been recognized four years earlier, the field would be two years further advanced, and my own work would be a year ahead of where it is now. I single out for special recognition Professors X, Y, and Z, who not only did stupid experiments themselves for five years because they would not recognize the truth and importance of my work, but penalized their students by preventing them from doing many clever experiments based on my theories."

There is a related factor which keeps T2 hidden. A scientific in-group is subjected to it early in its formation. As the group becomes more successful it encounters less T2 and the early T2 is forgotten by the group. For instance, in the 1950s, Skinnerians were very disturbed about the bias against them in journals and in grant review panels. By the 1960s they had their own journal and representation on the grant review committees. So they forgot their concern with T2 and probably many of these same people once concerned with T2 are now concerned with the maintenance of standards; the latter often boils down to inflicting T2 upon others. It is a sad thing that the concern with scientific freedom among scientists is much like the concern with religious freedom among adherents of many religions. Their concern is only that they have religious freedom, but they do not care about others.

## 2.3. Society and T2

It is conceivable that T2 incompetence is more harmful to the scientific enterprise than T1. T1 can disseminate falsehood which can mislead scientists for decades, but because it is public, it is eventually due to be refuted. T2 is far more insidious; it usually occurs in anonymous and privileged reviews of scientific papers for journals and research proposals for granting agencies. Thus, the very nature of T2 insures that there will be no record of it no matter how much it holds the field back. Doctors can bury their mistakes, but eventually it is noticed when a doctor buries too many patients. An incompetent in a high position (such as grant reviewer, journal editor, etc.) whose work is anonymous can continue his harmful work for many decades and gain acclaim for doing an important job; he can justify his lack of important published scientific work by claiming that he works so hard on his anonymous tasks that he really is a coauthor of much important work that appears under other people's names. In reality, he may only be interfering with scientific progress without any public record of the damage he does. Bitterman's placement of evidence for T2 on the public record is an exceptional event.

But although T2 is a real problem, it is not clear how to solve it. Scientific power structures are necessary. If the concept of T2 became popular and everybody who screamed that he was a victim got his way, many unreadable papers would be published, many wasteful research enterprises would be funded, and many students without the discipline or intelligence to do good scientific work would be given credentials as researchers. In the large majority of cases, the people in power in scientific communities make their decisions on valid technical grounds. It is only with regard to the novel and threatening that they frequently become incompetent. But, of course, these are the cases in which it is most important that they be competent because these are mainly responsible for major advances.

One conceivable solution is to imitate the method which has developed in the United States to control the military propensity to prepare for the last war instead of the next war. The U.S. Department of Defense uses a civilian bureaucracy and external semiacademic think-tanks to control the generals. A parallel to this would be to use nonscientists to control the scientists. Yet I do not think this would work because the problems involved require expert knowledge to be solved. I have experience of the involvement of nonscientists in scientific decisions and it can be even worse than the involvement of scientists. It might be possible to use scientists to control the T2 process, but these would have to be removed from much connection with other scientists so that they would not be preempted by the scientific establishment; I am not sure this is possible or practical.

## 3. A Modest Proposal

Although I have no immediate solution for T2, I am convinced that development of a solution depends upon learning more about it. One possibility is open reviews to eliminate the anonymity which conceals T2, but this would be a mistake. The main drawback is that open reviewing might lead to a sort of reciprocity; it is hard for a reviewer to harshly review a grant proposal from somebody who had reviewed his own recent proposal favorably, particularly when the roles of reviewer and reviewee are likely to switch again in the future. Thus, the net result of open grant reviewing would be an even greater concentration of research funds among the established enterprises represented by currently eminent scientists. There also would be social drawbacks of open reviewing. A reviewer who felt obliged to negatively review the work of a friend would be chagrined at having to see him later; thus with open reviewing, it would be desirable to have only relative strangers do reviewing. However, most of the workers in narrower scientific areas know each other fairly well if they have been around for a while. In practice, then, if scientific work were only reviewed by relative strangers, most reviews would have to be done by people with relatively little knowledge of the area.

However, there is no need that the anonymity of reviewers be perpetual. It is reasonable to require that all records of journals and funding agencies be strictly preserved and that everything be open to public view five or ten years later. The cost of this would be trivial relative to the cost of operating journals and reviewing grants. Both journals and grants are mainly paid for, directly or indirectly, by public monies and this would allow at least a small element of accountability in the use of public funds by scientists. It is true that some unpleasantness might occur when records are finally made public but it would nearly always be minor. Most reviewees would not even look up the records and the unhappiness of the remainder would be mitigated by the passage of five or ten years.

Any remaining disadvantages of opening the records five or ten years later would be countervailed by substantial benefits, in addition to those of major concern here, as follows. (1) It is my experience as a reviewer and as a member of a reviewing panel that about 25% of anonymous reviews are quite slovenly even if T2 is not considered. If reviewers knew their reviews would be preserved for posterity, I think they would be more careful. (2) There is some feeling among investigators that scientific material is stolen by anonymous reviewers; a record of access to material might serve to confirm or disconfirm such claims. (3) There is some feeling that failures to replicate the work of influential psychologists are not published for invalid reasons; later opening of the record ought to mitigate any such problem, if it exists.

With a historical record which would allow detection of when and how it occurs, a method of controlling T2 might eventually be devised. It might be possible to have nearly objective criteria by which to identify submissions which elicit T2 and the reviewers likely to exhibit T2. Journals and granting agencies might develop criteria by which to handle these cases. From my experience, I imagine that special attention would be necessary for less than 10% of submissions.

Even if T2 cannot be controlled, the availability of the historical raw data of the scientific process is necessary if there are to be detailed histories of relatively narrow areas; such histories would have a sharper intellectual quality than the fuzzy generalities contained in histories covering all of experimental psychology. It is accepted by students of diplomatic history that public statements by governments are often unreliable as guides to the truth of what really happened, and so they demand that the confidential records of foreign offices eventually be made public. The same applies to the history of a scientific area; published scientific papers in journals are the end products of a great deal of history but are selected in too biased a fashion to be real history.

With so much material available, some proportion of scientists might choose to become scholarly historians of narrow areas rather than active participants in some scientific enterprise. I have been told that such an outcome would be unfortunate since university psychology departments might become like those departments of English literature brimming with critics and historians of literature, but with few, if any, creators of literature. However, it is unlikely that more than 20–30% of scientists would choose to become critics or historians and this might be the right ratio.

Maybe the presence of so many relatively objective observers of the scientific process might, by itself, reduce abuses.

ACKNOWLEDGMENTS

The criticisms of Bitterman's comments about flavor aversion learning contained herein were written in collaboration with Harry Taukulis and I would like to thank him. However, because this note is based largely on my experiences, which Taukulis has not shared, he could not meaningfully coauthor it. Bow Tong Lett, Nicholas Mackintosh, Tony Dickinson, and John W. Moore discussed the subject matter of this note with me. Lett edited an earlier version of this note and Mackintosh criticized it more generally. I thank Steve Klein and Pete Mikulka for letting me test this material in a colloquium at Old Dominion University. Finally, I am grateful to the hospitality of the Laboratory of Experimental Psychology at the University of Sussex, where I have been visiting while writing this note.

## 4. References

Andrews, E. A., and Braveman, N. S. The combined effects of dosage level and inter-stimulus interval on the formation of one-trial poison based aversions in rats. *Animal Learning and Behavior*, 1975, *3*, 287–289.

Bitterman, M. E. The comparative analysis of learning. *Science*, 1975, *188*, 699–709.

Bitterman, M. E. Technical comment. Flavor aversion studies. *Science*, 1976, *192*, 266–267.

Campbell, C. S. The development of specific preferences in thiamine-deficient rats. Evidence against mediation by after-taste. Unpublished master's thesis, 1969, University of Illinois at Chicago Circle.

Czaplicki, J. A., Borreback, D. E., and Wilcoxon, H. C. Stimulus generalization of an illness-induced aversion to different intensities of colored water in Japanese quail. *Animal Learning and Behavior*, 1976, *4*, 45–48.

Domjan, M. Poison-induced neophobia in rats: Rule of stimulus generalization of conditioned taste aversions. *Animal Learning and Behavior*, 1975, *14*, 809–813.

Domjan, M., and Bowman, T. G. Learned safety and the CS–US delay gradient in taste aversion learning. *Learning and Motivation*, 1974, *5*, 409–423.

Dragoin, W. B., McCleary, G. E., and McCleary, P. A comparison of two methods of measuring conditioned taste aversion. *Behavior Research Methods and Instrumentation*, 1971, *3*, 309–310.

Etscorn, F., and Miller, R. L. Variation in the strength of conditioned taste aversion in rats as a function of the time of inducement. *Physiological Psychology*, 1975, *3*, 270–272.

Garcia, J., Ervin, F. R., and Koelling, R. A. Learning with prolonged delay of reinforcement. *Psychonomic Science*, 1966, *5*, 121–122.

Garcia, J., Ervin, F. R., Yorke, C. H., and Koelling, R. A. Conditioning with delayed vitamin injections. *Science*, 1967, *155*, 716–718.

Garcia, J., Kimeldorf, D. J., and Koelling, R. A. Conditioned aversion to saccharin resulting from exposure to gamma radiation, *Science*, 1955, *122*, 157–158.

Garcia, J., and Koelling, R. A. Relation of cue to consequence in avoidance learning. *Psychonomic Science*, 1966, *4*, 123–124.

Gordon, M. Evaluating the evaluators. *New Scientist*, 1977, *73*, 342–343.

Green, L., and Rachlin, H. Learned taste aversions in rats as a function of delay, speed, and duration of rotation. *Learning and Motivation* 1976, *7*, 283–289.

Kalat, J. W. Taste salience depends on novelty, not concentration in taste-aversion learning in the rat. *Journal of Comparative and Physiological Psychology*, 1974, *86*, 47–50.

Kalat, J. W., and Rozin, P. Role of interference in taste-aversion learning. *Journal of Comparative and Physiological Psychology*, 1971, *77*, 53–58.

Klein, S. B., Mikulka, P. J., and Hamel, K. Influence of sucrose pre-exposure on acquisition of a conditioned aversion. *Behavioral Biology*, 1976, *16*, 99–104.

Nachman, M. Learned taste and temperature aversions due to lithium chloride sickness after temporal delays. *Journal of Comparative and Physiological Psychology*, 1970, *73*, 22–36.

Nachman, M., and Jones, D. R. Learned taste aversions over long delays in rats: The role of learned safety. *Journal of Comparative and Physiological Psychology*, 1974, *86*, 949–956.

Nowlis, G. H. Conditioned stimulus intensity and acquired alimentary aversions in the rat. *Journal of Comparative and Physiological Psychology*, 1974, *86*, 1173–1184.

Revusky, S. H. Aversion to sucrose produced by contingent X-irradiation: Temporal and dosage parameters. *Journal of Comparative and Physiological Psychology*, 1968, *65*, 17–22.

Revusky, S. The role of interference in association over a delay. In W. K. Honig and P. H. R. James (Eds.), *Animal memory*, New York: Academic Press, 1971.

Revusky, S. H., and Bedarf, E. W. Association of illness with the prior ingestion of novel foods. *Science*, 1967, *155*, 219–220.

Revusky, S., and Garcia, J. Learned associations over long delays. In G. H. Bower (Ed.), *The psychology of learning and motivation: advances in research and theory*. Vol. 4. New York: Academic Press, 1970.

Revusky, S., Parker L., Coombes, J., and Coombes, S. Rat data which suggest that alcoholic beverages should be swallowed during chemical aversion therapy, not just tasted. *Behavior Research and Therapy*, 1976, *14*, 189–195.

Rozin, P. Central or peripheral mediation of learning with long CS–US intervals in the feeding system. *Journal of Comparative and Physiological Psychology*, 1969, *67*, 421–429.

Rozin, P., and Ree, P. Long extension of effective CS–US interval by anesthesia between CS and US. *Journal of Comparative and Physiological Psychology*, 1972, *80*, 43–48.

Scarborough, B. B., Whaley, D. L., and Rogers, J. G. Saccharin avoidance behavior instigated by X-irradiation in backward conditioning paradigms. *Psychological Reports*, 1964, *14*, 475–481.

Smith, J. C., and Roll, D. L. Trace conditioning with X-rays as an aversive stimulus. *Psychonomic Science*, 1967, *9*, 11–12.

Smith, J. C., Taylor, H. L. Morris, D. D., and Hendricks, J. Further studies of X-ray conditioned saccharin aversion during the postexposure period. *Radiation Research*, 1965, *24*, 423–431.

Taukulis, H. K. Odor aversions produced over long CS–US delays. *Behavioral Biology*, 1974, *10*, 505–510.

# Biological Significance of Food Aversion Learning

2

**James W. Kalat**

An appropriate subtitle for this chapter might be *"De gustibus* (sometimes) *est disputandum."* Several years ago, Rozin and Kalat (1971) and Shettleworth (1972) used food aversion learning as the primary example to support the contention that learning is a diverse category including several specialized machanisms, each adapted to particular ecological situations and evolutionary pressures. This position has been somewhat controversial; Revusky, for instance (see Chapter 1), has championed the contrary position, that learning is a single, general process which, like gravity, is more or less the same wherever it occurs, except for parametric perturbations. It is now time to re-examine the issue of whether and to what extent learning involves situation-specific evolutionary adaptations. Even if we cannot yet reach full agreement on an answer, we should be able at least to make a little more sense of the question.

## 1. The "Learning-as-a-General-Process" Assumption

The assumption that learning is a single, general process is an enormously pervasive one. It lies behind attempts to describe human-like intelligence in other animals, an attempt which has persisted, with un-

**James W. Kalat** • Department of Psychology, North Carolina State University, Raleigh, North Carolina.

deniable success, for the last century (Romanes, 1884; Köhler, 1921; Maier and Schneirla, 1935; Rensch, 1973). The assumption is also inherent in the intelligence-testing enterprise, since there would be little point in assigning each person a single intelligence quotient if one believed that there were several, independent intelligent abilities. Perhaps the best illustration of just how pervasive is the assumption of intelligence as a single, general process is the message which NASA included in the spacecraft Pioneer 10. At the risk of seeming to digress, let us consider that message and its underlying assumptions.

Pioneer 10, the first man-made craft to leave our solar system, contained an engraved message intended for any intelligent being that might eventually intercept it, many light-years away and countless centuries hence. The engraving (Figure 1) is intended to describe our location in both time and space. Sagan, Sagan, and Drake (1972) fully describe the nature of the message; I shall attempt to summarize the highlights. The barbell structure in the upper left corner represents the hyperfine transition of neutral atomic hydrogen, which, according to Sagan *et al.* "should be readily recognizable to the physicists of other civilizations." This defines the unit of either time or distance to be used in the rest of the figure.

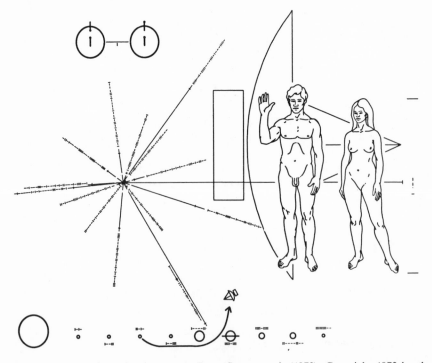

**Figure 1.** The message in Pioneer 10. From Sagan *et al.* (1972). Copyright 1972 by the American Association for the Advancement of Science.

This basic unit appears again in binary notation along the arms of the radial design in the center, which is to be interpreted as a representation of the location of 15 objects relative to some reference point. Given the number of significant figures provided, in the already-defined unit, the scientists from Somewhere Out There must say to themselves, "What useful information could this crude civilization possibly know to so many significant figures? Aha, obviously, the time periods of some pulsars. The length and positions of the lines must be estimates of the direction and distance of these pulsars relative to their home star. And the long line without a binary number must be the distance from their star to the center of the galaxy." Plugging this information into a computer (or working it in their heads, as the case may be), they compute our location in time and space. The diagram at the bottom represents our solar system, with the spacecraft originating at the third planet. Finally, the drawing at the right depicts two humans against a scale defined by a drawing of the spacecraft itself.

Presuming that some outer-space Smart Person catches Pioneer 10, notices the engraving, guesses that it is a message, and has some acquaintance with visual or tactile representations of information, then what is his/her/its likelihood of successfully decoding the message? It is probably safe to assume that the astronomy and physics of another civilization are in some sense isomorphic with our own, but it is hardly trivial to assume that our way of visually representing physical data will be comprehensible to beings elsewhere in the universe. It is easy (and entertaining) to try to imagine some ways in which the message might be misunderstood even by beings with patterns of intelligence essentially identical to our own. (Not long ago our own scientists would have failed to decipher the message, since our discovery of pulsars is relatively recent.) What about beings which share no evolutionary history with us, which are presumably adapted to a very different environment and way of life, and which may even be constructed of a very different set of chemicals?

Perhaps the message would be understandable to scientists of another planet. Perhaps reality is such that there can be only one form of intelligence effective enough to create a technology. Perhaps intelligence equals understanding of reality, in some absolute sense, such that it must be about the same wherever it occurs. We have little basis for speculation on this point, since extraterrestrial comparative psychology is a science which has not yet gotten off the ground, so to speak. Nevertheless, it is important to recognize all of one's assumptions, and it is certainly an assumption to regard intelligence as having any universal generality.

Back to earth now, restricting ourselves to species which share an evolutionary origin with us, are there demonstrable qualitative differences in the learning process? For the purposes of this chapter let us ignore invertebrates, though there is ample reason to believe that invertebrate learning processes may be quite different from those of vertebrates. We shall also ignore the substantial contributions of M. E. Bitterman. Bitterman claims to have found qualitative differences in learning among vertebrates; however, he describes these differences in terms of a linear hierarchy, as opposed to the possibility that species A might excel on one task and species B on another.

The primary question below shall be, are there differences in learning processes within the vertebrate subphylum—other than unidimensional, better-versus-worse comparisons—even though all vertebrates ultimately evolved from a common ancestor, which itself presumably had some learning abilities? This question refers not only to differences between one species and another, but also to differences within a species in how it learns in one situation versus another. That is, do learning abilities reflect specific evolutionary pressures?

## 1.1. Evolutionary Specializations in Learning

It is not difficult to find species differences in learning which show adaptations to a species' sensory abilities and experiences. For example, rats ordinarily fail miserably on simple oddity discriminations with which monkeys have little difficulty. However, if one sets up the same problem using olfactory instead of visual cues, the rat can solve the problem with ease. According to Langworthy and Jennings (1972), "When asked abstract questions in the proper idiom, these [rats] proceeded to make monkeys of themselves."

For another example, consider learning in earthworms (see review by Howell, 1974). Earthworms learn a simple T-maze so slowly that it has been suggested (Harlow, 1958) that the worm's learning ability would be of no value in nature. However, a left–right discrimination is probably particularly difficult for any animal with the body-plan of a worm; snakes seem to have the same difficulties with T-mazes as worms (Kellogg and Pomeroy, 1936; Wolfle and Brown, 1940; Crawford and Holmes, 1966). It may be that worms are well prepared for some types of learning, but very poorly prepared for left–right discriminations.

For a third example, a comparison of three ungulate species revealed that horses and donkeys learned better than zebras on visual discriminations among colors or between a white field and a checkerboard pattern. However, zebras were significantly better than the other two species on a discrimination between narrow and wide stripes (Giebel, 1958).

Additional examples of this type could readily be added. Animals show more effective learning in experiments similar to situations they typically face in nature. However, this point, while undeniably important, is not undeniably relevant to the issue at hand. To learn better is not necessarily to learn differently. Is the learning process itself different from one instance to another? We must look elsewhere for an answer to this question.

The first impressive apparent example of a specialized learning mechanism was imprinting, the process whereby a young bird follows a prominent moving object early in life and thereby learns (in nature) to recognize its own species. Unfortunately, our understanding of imprinting seems to have passed the point at which we thought we knew what was going on, but without yet reaching the point at which we are certain that we actually know what is going on. Thus, it is difficult to discuss imprinting both fruitfully and, at the same time, briefly.

On the other hand, the phenomenon of bird song learning seems to be closely related to imprinting, and illustrates some of the same points more conclusively. The white-crowned sparrow (Marler, 1970) learns its song only during a critical period (age 10–100 days) but does not begin to sing until sexual maturity, at age one year. Thus, learning takes place only during a limited time in life; it occurs without the animal making the to-be-learned response at all, and (as demonstrated by rearing birds in social isolation) the learning does not require "reinforcement" in any of the usual senses of that term. Furthermore, the bird forms a sensory template of its own song if heard during the critical period, but seems to ignore other species' songs altogether. In short, song learning, at least in white-crowned sparrows, depends on very different conditions from those characteristic of either classical or instrumental conditioning.

Besides imprinting and bird song learning, the other thoroughly investigated phenomenon which seems to show significant evolutionary specializations is food aversion learning. The prominent adaptations in this case are the specificity with which foods and illness are associated with each other rather than with other events, and the fact that taste and poison can be readily associated over several-hour delays. Rozin and Kalat (1971) argued that this type of learning represents an evolutionary specialization of the learning process, such as to make the laws of learning as adaptive as possible to the specific problems of food selection. For this argument to hold, it need not be the case that food aversion learning had a totally separate evolutionary origin from other types of learning, nor that its behavioral and physiological mechanisms have nothing in common with, say, shock avoidance learning. It would suffice to acknowledge a substantial parametric difference between food aversion learning and shock avoidance learning, provided that one regards that parametric difference as a difference *within the animal,* as opposed to being a by-product of the necessary differences in experimental procedure.

Let us now directly address the question, "Is food aversion learning fundamentally the same as, or fundamentally different from, other types of learning?" After surveying the reported similarities and differences, I shall conclude that yes, and also no, and besides that, the question does not make much sense.

## 1.2. Food Aversion Learning vs. Other Types of Learning

For the sake of brevity and simplicity, I shall present this section in tabular form. Table 1 presents some of the more striking similarities between food aversion learning and other forms of learning, which typically require short delays of reinforcement, such as shock avoidance learning. Table 2 presents some of the differences. Both tables are meant to be illustrative, not exhaustive. The generality of these comparisons varies, as some of the items in the right-hand column have been documented for a wider variety of situations than others.

## 1.3. So What?

The question under consideration is, "Is taste aversion learning fundamentally the same as, or different from, other types of learning?" Even with very incomplete lists, we can readily see that both the similarities and the differences are substantial. What is our net judgment on the original issue?

That depends. It depends on what we mean by "fundamentally the same" and "fundamentally different." Let us consider an analogy with human languages. Suppose we ask, "Are the English and Chinese languages fundamentally the same or different?" We could make lists analogous to Tables 1–2 of the similarities and differences between the two languages, including pronunciation, written symbols, grammatical rules, word order, manner of expressing certain relationships, and so forth. At the end, we would have lengthy lists of both similarities and differences, and we could then debate about which list was the more impressive. However, no matter how elaborate and detailed our lists, we would be unprepared to answer the question "Are English and Chinese fundamentally the same or different?" until we knew more precisely what the questioner had in mind. If he means by "fundamentally different" that the two languages are so different from one another that they ought not even to be classified under the single term "language," or if he means that the differences are so severe that the utterances of one language cannot be translated into the other, then we clearly could not regard the languages as different. On the other hand, if the questioner means by "fundamentally the same" that the two languages are demonstrably derived from a single ancestral language, or that these and other languages have so much in common that one can learn everything worth knowing about language by an intensive study of any one language, then clearly the languages are not the same.

**Table 1.** *Similarities between Food Aversion Learning and Other Types of Learning,*
*Such as Shock Avoidance Learning*

|  | Food aversion learning | Other associative learning |
|---|---|---|
| 1. Greater learning as CS intensity diverges from adaptation level | Kalat, 1974; Rozin, 1969a | Pavlov, 1927, Chapter 3 |
| 2. Greater learning with greater UCS intensity | Dragoin, 1971 | Passey, 1948; Church 1969 |
| 3. Less learning if CS is familiar | Revusky and Bedarf, 1967; Kalat and Rozin, 1973 | Lubow and Moore, 1959; Kremer, 1972; Siegel, 1970 |
| 4. Higher preference, less fear for familiar than novel stimulus | Siegel, 1974; Carroll, Dink, Levy, and Smith, 1975 | Welker, 1961 |
| 5. Weaker learning if previously exposed to unpaired UCS | Elkins, 1974; Gamzu, 1974; Vogel, 1974; Cannon, Bermon, Baker, and Atkinson, 1975; Cappell, LeBlanc and Herling, 1975; Revusky and Taukulis, 1975 | Ayres, Benedict, and Witcher, 1975; but this effect depends on parameters of experiment; see Church, 1969 |
| 6. Memory may improve, or "incubate" over time | Biederman, Milgram, Heighington, and Stockman, 1974 | Deutsch, 1973 |
| 7. Species vary in which modalities they can use for a single type of learning | Wilcoxon, Dragoin, and Kral, 1971; Braveman, 1974; Johnson, Beaton, and Hall, 1975 | Langworthy and Jennings, 1972 |
| 8. Learned helplessness | Cannon, Berman, Baker, and Atkinson, 1975 | Maier, Seligman, and Solomon, 1969 |

Similarly, if one asks whether taste aversion learning is so different from shock avoidance and other forms of learning that one should conclude that they originated totally independently of one another, and that one should find a new word rather than classify both as "learning" or "conditioning," then the answer should be no. If one asks whether they are so different that one should expect no more than coincidental similarities, then again the answer should be no. On the other hand, if one asks whether they are basically identical in the sense that one can discover all the principles of learning by an intensive examination of a single situation, then again the answer should be no, just as one should deny that chemists could learn the "laws of chemical bonding" by an intensive examination of a single bond.

**Table 2.** *Differences between Food Aversion Learning and Other Types of Learning,*
*Such as Shock Avoidance Learning*

|  | Food aversion learning | Other associative learning |
|---|---|---|
| 1. Time parameters | One-trial learning with CS–UCS delays as much as 24 h (Etscorn and Stephens, 1973) | Learning usually limited to CS–UCS delays of a few seconds; as high as 80 seconds in some experiments (Brush, Brush, and Solomon, 1955; Church, Brush, and Solomon, 1956) |
| 2. "Belongingness" | Poisons more readily associated with foods than with lights and sounds (Garcia and Koelling, 1966; Domjan and Wilson, 1972b; Green, Bouzas, and Rachlin, 1972) | Shock more readily with lights and sounds than with tastes (Garcia and Koelling, 1966; see also Wike, Wolfe, and Norsworthy, 1975) |
| 3. Specificity to training environment | Food aversion learning generalizes readily to a new environment (Garcia, Kovner, and Green, 1970) | Shock avoidance learning generalizes less readily to a new environment (Garcia, Kovner, and Green, 1970) |
| 4. UCS-specificity of CS salience | Some solutions more salient with particular poisons than with others (Weisinger, Parker, and Skorupski, 1974; Kalat (in prep.) | Salience of CSs has not been reported to vary as a function of UCS. |
| 5. Reinforcement value of amphetamine and morphine | Amphetamine produces food aversion even under conditions of voluntary self-administration (Cappell and LeBlanc, 1973) | Amphetamine positively reinforces bar-press even while producing learned food aversion (Cappell and LeBlanc, 1973) |
|  | Morphine is positive reinforcer for bar-press after dependence is established (Weeks, 1962) | Food aversions induced by morphine even in rats addicted to morphine (Jacquet, 1973) |
| 6. Maturation of learning abilities | Weanling rats equal to adults (Grote and Brown, 1971; Galef and Sherry, 1973) | Weanling rats worse than adults at passive avoidance of shock (Brunner, 1969; Riccio, Rohrbaugh, and Hodges, 1968) |

Table 2. *Continued*

|  | Food aversion learning | Other associative learning |
|---|---|---|
| 7. Synaptic pharmacology | Cholinergic and anticholinergic drugs have little or no effect on food aversion learning (Biederman, Milgram, Heighington, and Stockman, 1974; Smith and Morris, 1964; Gadusek and Kalat, 1975; Kral, 1971) | Cholinergic and anticholinergic drugs have large effect on shock avoidance learning (e.g., Deutsch, 1973; Margules and Stein, 1969; Feigley, 1974) |
|  | Little effect from loss of NE and DA synapses (Stricker and Zigmond, 1974) | Passive avoidance of shock is greatly impaired by loss of NE (Stein, Beluzzi, and Wise, 1975) or DA (Zis, Fibiger, and Phillips, 1974) |
|  | Food aversion learning may depend on histaminergic synapses (Levy, Carroll, Smith, and Hofer, 1974) | Role of histamine is unknown for other types of learning |
| 8. Effect of active vs. passive exposure to the CS | Less learning if taste is force-fed than if actively ingested (Domjan, 1973; Domjan and Wilson, 1972a; Smith and Balagura, 1969) | Active approach to CS is not regarded as important in other types of learning |
| 9. Learning under anesthesia? | Food aversion learning can occur with UCS presented under anesthesia (Roll and Smith, 1972) | No evidence for any other type of learning under anesthesia |
| 10. Effectiveness of electroconvulsive shock in inducing amnesia | More amnesia with ECS to posterior cerebrum (Kral, 1972) | More amnesia with ECS to anterior cerebrum (Kral, 1972) |
|  | ECS relatively ineffective in affecting food aversion learning (Nachman, 1970) |  |

Let us therefore rephrase the question in a more meaningful manner. To say that there are evolved situation-specific differences in learning is not necessarily to affirm that the learning process will depend on totally separate mechanisms in two situations. It is, however, to insist that the differences in learning between two situations are due to differences within the organism, not to differences in the experimental paradigms. Those internal differences might involve special situation-specific mechanisms, or quantitative variations in mechanisms employed in different situations. A further contention is that the differences in learning between one situation and another are, on the whole, adaptive. Thus, we substitute for the original "same-versus-different" question, two new questions: (1) Are the specialized features of food aversion learning—i.e., those features which distinguish it from other types of learning—particularly adaptive for the specific problems of food selection? That is, does the pattern of specializations characterizing food aversion learning suggest an influence of evolutionary pressures? (2) To what extent can we use our conclusions regarding one type of learning, such as food aversion learning, to infer mechanisms which apply generally to all forms of learning?

## 2. Are the Specialized Features of Food Aversion Learning Adaptive?

When considering the adaptive significance of food aversion learning, it is customary to think first of an animal avoiding poison. However, to appreciate fully the contribution of food aversion learning to the animal's adaptation, we must consider some other phenomena of food selection, perhaps no less important than poison avoidance.

To be healthy, an animal must avoid both deficits and excesses of each nutrient. Rozin and Kalat (1971) proposed that animals identify foods with needed vitamins largely by a process of elimination, acquiring incipient aversions to any diet which is deficient in some vitamin. Food aversion learning may also be involved in the avoidance of surfeits. Holman (1973) and Morrison (1974) found that rats temporarily shift their preference away from a solution they just drank. The basis for this may be that beyond a certain volume, additional consumption of a solution begins to produce aversive effects. For instance, Richter (1947, 1956b) reported that the amounts of various sugars that a rat will consume is directly proportional to the amount of each sugar that the rat can assimilate. That is, a rat ceases to consume a sugar at about the point at which additional sugar could not be assimilated, and would have to be excreted. Furthermore, according to Richter (1957a), "force feeding . . . amounts of hexoses larger than the rats eat voluntarily shorten rather than lengthen survival time." Presumably, rats learn this limit because consumption beyond this limit produces unpleasant effects.

The task of obtaining a balanced diet is further complicated by the fact that an animal's need for one nutrient may depend on how much it consumes of some other nutrient. For instance, since thiamine is necessary for the metabolism of glucose, a thiamine-deficient animal has no use for glucose; indeed, thiamine-deficient rats avoid glucose (Barelare, Holt, and Richter, 1938; Richter, Holt, Barelare, and Hawkes, 1938), presumably because its consumption produces aversive effects.

Finally, food aversion learning may be the key to the question of why some individuals consume more alcohol than others. Horowitz and Whitney (1975) found that the difference among strains of mice in how much alcohol they consume corresponds to a difference in their metabolism of ethyl alcohol. C57 mice, which readily convert alcohol to acetaldehyde, and acetaldehyde to acetic acid, drink large amounts of alcohol. DBA mice, however, which are relatively deficient in the enzyme which converts acetaldehyde to acetic acid, experience an accumulation of acetaldehyde (a poison) whenever they drink alcohol. These mice drink very little alcohol, almost certainly as a result of a learned aversion.

Similarly, in rats, it has been demonstrated that ethanol causes much less physiological damage to the internal organs in hypothyroid than in euthyroid or hyperthyroid rats. Not surprisingly, hypothyroid rats drink much more alcohol than others (Richter, 1956a, 1957a,b). Furthermore, artificially raising or lowering a rat's thyroid level lowers or raises its alcohol consumption, respectively. It is reported that human alcoholics tend to be hypothyroid and that thyroid administration can significantly reduce alcoholism (Richter, 1957a).

In short, food aversion learning plays a major role in the animal's selection of foods as well as its avoidance of poison. The biologically very important problems of food selection pose some special problems for learning. Rozin and Kalat (1971) argued that these special problems constituted a strong selective pressure to favor the evolution of a specialized learning ability. Garcia and his colleagues (Garcia and Koelling, 1966; Garcia, Ervin, and Koelling, 1966) initially discovered two major adaptations of food aversion learning: the animal's tendency to associate illness with foods rather than with lights and sounds, and the animal's ability to associate foods with poisons over several-hour delays. The adaptive significance of both points should be obvious.

To these two differences at least two more should be added: First, a taste which is artificially applied to the tongue but which is not swallowed is much less associable with poison than a similar taste which is swallowed (Domjan, 1973; Domjan and Wilson, 1972a; Smith and Balagura, 1969).

The adaptive significance is again obvious, since a solution which an animal tastes and spits out has much less chance to cause illness than one which the animal swallows. Second, rats seem to have some *a priori* "expectations" about the consequences of certain tastes. Kalat (in preparation) has found that intubations of large volumes of sucrose or NaCl can induce taste aversions, just like weak poisons. However, the taste of sucrose is more associable with an aversive sucrose intubation than with an NaCl intubation, while the reverse is true for the taste of NaCl.

The evolutionary approach to food aversion learning has, however, been subject to criticism on the grounds that food aversion learning shares many features with other types of learning, including some features which are not obviously adaptive, such as sensory preconditioning, conditioned inhibition, and intensity-specific discrimination learning. Since one would not expect evolution to provide these phenomena specifically for food aversion learning, it does seem likely either that food aversion learning has some mechanisms parallel to those of other learning, or that it taps into some of the exact same mechanisms of other learning. However, to concede some overlap of mechanisms for various kinds of learning does not vitiate the primary contention, that evolution has equipped animals with some special adaptations for food aversion learning as compared to other types of learning.

Evolution presumably equips animals with mechanisms that produce adaptive results as often as possible under natural conditions. But once those mechanisms are established, there will certainly be some circumstances in which they are nonadaptive or even maladaptive. For example, an animal's coloration may camouflage him in his natural environment, but leave him quite conspicuous if he is transported to a different place, or if his native environment changes. For another example, skunks' natural defense against approaching predators is to freeze in a conspicuous posture, and to spray a foul scent on those which continue to approach; this defense is highly effective against natural predators, but proves useless against the attack of one unnatural predator, the automobile. Similarly, the mechanisms of food aversion learning may be specifically evolved for normal food-selection problems, yet produce nonadaptive results under highly artificial laboratory conditions.

Perhaps the best way to study the evolution of learning is by examining some situations in which it appears that the results of food aversion learning would be maladaptive under natural conditions.

Even when a behavior appears maladaptive, the evolutionary point of view can sometimes be a helpful guide in interpretation and research. I refer to one example in particular, a phenomenon which would appear to be highly maladaptive under natural conditions: It has been demonstrated (Bond and DiGuisto, 1975; Bond and Harland, 1975; Barker, 1976) that the greater the volume of a solution drunk by an animal, the greater the aversion induced by subsequent poisoning. In other words, a rat which drinks 10 ml of a solution prior to poisoning will acquire a greater aversion to it than one that drank only 1 ml, all other factors being equal.

There is nothing unnatural or artificial about this paradigm; yet, on adaptive grounds one might expect the opposite result. If 1 ml of solution A causes the same amount of illness as 10 ml of solution B, then certainly solution A is the more toxic. But the results indicate that the rat learns a stronger aversion to B than to A.

How should one interpret the presence of such an evidently maladaptive law of behavior? We have no justification to assume that the brain, and the behavior it produces, are any less subject to evolutionary pressures than morphology and physiology are. Thus we must look for the kind of explanation that would be tenable for nonadaptive morphology.

Given this constraint, there are at least five possible types of explanations:

1. Most simply, when the data appear to be maladaptive, the data may be wrong. Three publications, cited above, reported that increased volume drunk causes increased associability. However, in all three experiments, increased volume drunk also meant increased time spent drinking. There is evidence that temporal duration of drinking is itself a factor in the associability of a solution (Domjan, 1972). It could be that it was the duration of presentation, not the amount drunk, that produced the reported effects. Smith and Morris (1963) held drinking duration constant and varied the amount drunk by altering thirst levels; they found no difference in learned aversion between groups that drank 4.6 or 9.2 grams of a saccharin solution prior to X-rays. Kalat (1976) controlled the duration of drinking and permitted volume drunk to vary spontaneously. In 29 groups varying in many aspects of procedure, the correlation between volume drunk and subsequent aversion was about normally distributed around a mean near zero. Evidently, with drinking duration held constant, the volume drunk does not seem to be a major factor in food aversion learning.

However, this conclusion changes our problem rather than solves it. Why should increased duration of drinking cause increased associability with poison? Practically the same problems and the same apparent maladaptiveness pertain as when we were talking about volume drunk.

2. What appears to be maladaptive may on closer scrutiny turn out to be adaptive. For instance, the striped coat of a zebra looks highly conspicuous to the human eye; however, in its natural habitat, surrounded by a broken shadow pattern, it turns out to be good camouflage. Similarly, it might be argued that it may be adaptive to form stronger aversions after drinking larger volumes of a solution than after drinking a small volume. This would be particularly plausible if an animal consumed several solu-

tions prior to poisoning; chances, are, the solution of which it drank the greatest amount is the most likely to have been poisonous. In support of this possibility, Der-Karabetian and Gorry (1974) found that the associability of a solution with poison decreases as a rat drinks increasing volumes of other, interfering solutions. On the other hand, rats tend to avoid consuming more than one novel substance in a brief period of time (Rozin, 1969b). In the common situation in which the rat consumes only one novel substance within several hours prior to poison, the direct relationship between consumption and associability remains apparently maladaptive.

3. The apparently maladaptive characteristic may be a necessary by-product of some other, highly adaptive feature. For instance, the human female pelvis is maladaptively narrow, considering the size of the infant's head at birth; however, if the pelvis were wide enough for easy childbirth, then upright locomotion would be more awkward. Conceivably, the effect of volume drunk on learned aversions may be a by-product of some other, more adaptive feature. If so, it is not obvious what the "more adaptive feature" is in this case, unless it be, as mentioned above, the desirability of associating poison with a solution of which one drank much, rather than a solution of which one drank less.

4. In some cases, a maladaptive feature is simply a physical necessity, given the chemical nature of the body and the principles of embryology. For instance, it may not be possible for a vertebrate to evolve wheels, or fireproof skin, or a resistance to high doses of radiation. However, it is not clear how this principle could help us explain the behavior in question.

5. Finally, some evolutionary developments may fail to occur simply because they would require a large number of genetic steps, and because the intermediate steps are not themselves adaptive. That is, the end result would be adaptive, but it would be too difficult for evolution to get from the start point to the end point. Presumably something of this sort is responsible for our failure to evolve eyes behind our heads.

An explanation of this type may well underly the rat's tendency to acquire stronger taste aversions after greater consumption of the solution. Let us presume, for instance, that we begin with a learning mechanism in which the better one remembers something, the better one associates it with something else. Furthermore, the longer one drinks a solution, the better one remembers it. The result, at least apparently, is maladaptive, and it would be desirable to superimpose an additional mechanism to monitor the amount drunk, then establish a poison-associability inversely proportional to that amount (if it is above some minimum threshold). But to establish such a mechanism, it must first be the case that the rat "knows" (in some sense) how much it has drunk. There is considerable evidence that a rat is ill-equipped to monitor how much it has consumed. Rats are evidently rather inept at calibrating their food intake to adjust for its caloric density or for their own state of deficiency. Rats and other animals do not eat larger meals after long intermeal intervals than after short intervals, within normal limits (Ardisson, Dolisi, Camous, and Gastaud, 1975; LeMagnen and Tallon, 1966; Snowdon, 1969). If given a high-caloric or low-caloric diet, they initially adjust their intake by decreasing or increasing the frequency of their meals, rather than the size (LeMagnen, 1971). Since evidently, rats are not well-equipped to monitor orally how much they have consumed (see also Young, Gibbs, Antin, Holt, and Smith, 1974), it might be asking too much to expect evolution to provide this ability simply for use in regulating taste aversions.

Where has all of this led us? We began with the question of whether the properties of food aversion learning are particularly adaptive, suggesting the effect of special evolutionary pressures. At this point it appears that several aspects are particularly adaptive, while some others—of less certain relevance in nature—are not apparently adaptive. The one aspect of food aversion learning which—at least to me—appears most likely to be maladaptive under natural conditions, can apparently be accounted for with the same types of explanations that one might apply to an apparently maladaptive morphological feature.

## 3. Does Our Understanding of Food Aversion Learning Have Implications Regarding the Mechanisms of Learning in Other Situations?

Several pages ago I posed two questions. So far, the discussion has considered only the first, i.e., whether food aversion learning appears to be an evolutionary specialization. However, to answer yes to this question does not necessarily affirm or deny that the mechanisms underlying food aversion learning have much in common with those of other types of learning. For an analogy, one might conclude that the properties of airplanes, automobiles, and motorboats are specifically adapted to particular situations, without knowing how much similarity there exists in the internal machinery of the three devices. We come, therefore, to our second question, somewhat independent of the first: To what extent can we use our conclusions regarding food aversion learning to infer mechanisms applying to other types of learning, and vice-versa.

There are at least a couple of potentially general principles which have been documented to some extent in food aversion learning and which had not previously been demonstrated in other situations. Perhaps these principles are unique to food aversion learning, or perhaps they apply generally but are simply easier to observe or demonstrate in food aversion learning.

Let us begin by examining what these principles are, concentrating on that aspect of food aversion learning which seems to have generated the greatest interest: learning with long delays between food and poison.

## 3.1. Possible Mechanisms of Long-Delay Learning

Long-delay food aversion learning has generated great interest, mainly because it seems to violate the principle of temporal contiguity which seemed so well-established in other situations. Perhaps it was natural that many observers sought at first to explain this property in terms of principles familiar in other types of learning. The proposals that some form of after-taste mediates the delay have been extensively contradicted (see Revusky and Garcia, 1970; Rozin and Kalat, 1971), and need not be discussed here.

Another possibility is that animals "learn to learn" over unusually long delays with regard to foods, based on their extensive experience with the consequences of foods. However, at least some species can associate foods with delayed poison as early as the day of birth (Kalat, 1975). Still another possibility is that slow-onset UCSs initiate longer backward scans for an appropriate CS than faster-onset UCSs do. (If so, this might help explain how humans learned the causes of certain diseases, where babies come from, and various other items involving long CS–UCS delays.) However, slow-onset shocks do not produce long-delay learning (Green, Bouzas, and Rachlin, 1972). Also, if one divides a dose of poison into several smaller doses, spread out over half an hour, so as to make the onset of illness even slower than usual, the resultant long-delay learned aversion is weaker, not stronger, than usual (Kalat, unpub.).

Given the apparent failure of previously familiar principles to account for long-delay food aversion learning, it makes sense to look for new principles. Revusky has proposed that the CS–UCS delay gradient is regulated primarily by interference from other CSs during the delay. If the UCS is associated mainly with the most recent potential CS, then any increase in the CS–UCS delay will introduce some additional CSs, and therefore decrease association with the CS in question. This process, according to Revusky, operates more slowly in food aversion learning, since a given delay will introduce far fewer stimuli associable with poisons (i.e., foods) than stimuli associable with other UCSs.

This mechanism is undoubtedly part of the story. However, Kalat and Rozin (1971) showed that the associability of sucrose with poison decreased less in 30 min with three novel, interfering tastes present, than in 3–6 h with no tastes present. Thus it appears that the associability of a taste with poison decreases with the passage of time, at least partly independently of the introduction of new tastes.

## 3.2. Learned Safety

Kalat and Rozin (1973) proposed a mechanism somewhat complementary to Revusky's. Revusky's hypothesis could be characterized as CS–CS$_i$ –UCS, in which uncontrolled CS$_i$s occurring during the CS–UCS delay interfere with that conditioning. Kalat and Rozin proposed another kind of interference which might be described as CS–UCS$_i$ –UCS, in which an additional UCS occurring during the CS–UCS delay interferes with conditioning. Specifically, they proposed that the passage of a period of time during which poisoning does *not* occur may constitute a UCS which can interfere with an association with poison. As time passes after the animal consumes a novel food, the animal associates that food with the *absence* of poisoning. The greater is the delay to poisoning, the greater is this association; and the greater this association, the less the taste is associable with poison. In effect, during the delay before poison, the animal reclassifies the solution as "safe," and the learned safety controls in part the decrease in associability during increased CS–UCS delays. This proposal contrasts with an explanation of the CS–UCS delay in terms of "trace decay," an explanation which has long remained popular despite the fact that there is no independent evidence for the existence of a decaying trace, and despite the fact that the concept of a decaying trace has not proven useful in studies of human memory (Tulving and Thomson, 1973).

There are several lines of evidence supporting the "learned safety" proposal. First, Rozin and Ree (1972) found that the effective CS–UCS delay could be greatly extended by anesthetizing the animal during the delay. While this result could be explained as easily in terms of Revusky's "concurrent interference" as in terms of learned safety, it clearly argues against an explanation in terms of the passive decay of a memory trace.

Second, it has been repeatedly established that a rat has a much greater preference for a taste when it is familiar than when it is novel (Barnett, 1958; Rzoska, 1953; Domjan, 1976), or even if it is similar to a familiar taste (Capretta, Petersik, and Stewart, 1975). Also, a familiar taste is much less associable with poison than a novel taste is (Revusky and Bedarf, 1967; Elkins, 1973; Fenwick, Mikulka, and Klein, 1975). Although many psychologists seem unacquainted with thinking of it this way, the process of reclassifying a taste from "novel" to "familiar" is itself obviously some kind of learning process—one which, in fact, evidently has the same properties posited for learned safety. As explicit evidence for this interpretation, it has been demonstrated that the transfer from "novel" to "familiar" is not instantaneous, but takes place gradually over several hours: The first time a rat tastes something, it shows "neophobia" for that food. As time passes following a rat's first experience with that taste, over a period of several hours, the rat's preference gradually increases (Nachman and Jones, 1974; Green and Parker, 1975). This is exactly what one would expect if the rat were gradually associating the taste with a period of safety during the delay. Furthermore, the increase of preference and decrease of associability with poison occur even if the taste (e.g., coffee or dilute vinegar) is force-fed to a nonthirsty rat, so as to minimize positive reinforcement (Domjan, 1972; Siegel, 1974). Thus the effect depends on the passage of time following the first presentation of the taste, but apparently does not depend on positive reinforcement, in any usual sense, from the metabolic consequences of the taste.

Third, there is decreased associability of a familiar taste with poison even if the familiarization consists of just a single exposure to the taste, three weeks prior to the pairing of that taste with poison (Kalat and Rozin, 1973, experiment 1). For this to be the case, obviously the rat must in some sense "remember" the taste over a 3-week period. Consequently, it is hardly plausible that it fails to associate the taste with poison over a 6-h delay because the memory trace has "decayed" during that time. Evidently what is lost during 6 h is not the trace itself but the associability of the trace; that is, the memory of the solution is in some way reclassified during that period.

Fourth and finally, if a rat drinks the same solution twice within the period normally defined by the CS–UCS delay gradient, and then is poisoned, the rat acquires less aversion than a rat which experienced only the second of the two exposures to the solution. Consider the following experiment: One group of rats drinks sucrose (briefly), and is poisoned 30 min later, thus acquiring a strong aversion. A second group drinks sucrose and is poisoned 4 h later, acquiring a demonstrable, but weaker aversion. The third group drinks sucrose, 3½ h later drinks sucrose again, and 30 min later is poisoned. This group acquires *less* aversion than the 30-min group (Kalat and Rozin, 1973; Bolles, Riley, and Laskowsky, 1973; Domjan and Bowman, 1974).

This result is exactly what one would predict on the basis of learned safety; the longer the delay since the first exposure to the taste, the greater the association with the absence of poisoning, and therefore the less the associability with poisoning. A trace-decay model would predict something quite different. There are, however, a variety of potential and real problems with the learned safety interpretation, to which we should now turn our attention.

### 3.2.1. Learned Safety or Positive Reinforcement?

One possible counter-interpretation of the results just described might be that the first presentation of the food decreases the later associability of that food not because the food is associated with the absence of negative consequences, but because it is associated with explicit pleasant feedback, i.e., positive reinforcement. This, I believe, is doubtful. First, the effect shows up with such solutions as isotonic saline (Kalat and Rozin, 1973) and sodium saccharin (Bolles *et al.*, 1973), which have no caloric or vitamin value. Second, if positive reinforcement from the solution itself interferes with association with poison, then learned aversions should decrease with increases in the amount drunk. The reader will recall from Section 2.1 that this prediction fails. Third, it has been demonstrated in slightly different paradigms that familiarization has equally potent effects on subsequent behavior even if the familiarization takes place while the animal is water-satiated (Domjan, 1972; Siegel, 1974).

Furthermore, consider the following: According to the learned safety hypothesis, the effects of familiarization with a solution on the subsequent poison-associability of that solution does not take place immediately during the rat's initial encounter with the solution, but depends on the uneventful, nonpoisoning period following the onset of drinking. Thus, the effect of familiarization should be minimal just after drinking and should increase gradually to asymptote over the next few hours. In the experiment in which rats drink a solution twice prior to poison, and thereby acquire less aversion than rats which drink it only the second time, the learned safety explanation insists that this effect is *not* due to the fact that there were two drinking periods instead of one, but rather depends on the uneventful delay between the two presentations of the solution. Let us describe the situation as follows:

solution A→ $x$ delay→solution A→30-min delay→poison

According to learned safety, if $x$ is a short delay, this group will react about the same as a group receiving only the second presentation. The longer $x$ is, up to a few hours, the less learned aversion should occur. On the other hand, if the effect depends on positive reinforcement, the delay between presentations should make no difference, provided that the minimum delay is sufficient for the solution to get through the digestive system.

To test these competing predictions, 58 experimentally naive rats were assigned to 5 groups. The control group drank 5% (weight/volume) casein hydrolysate twice, and was poisoned 24 h later with 1 ml/30 g 0.15 M LiCl. One experimental group drank casein hydrolysate for 2½ min and was poisoned 30 min later. Three other groups drank casein hydrolysate for 10 min, and after delays of 15 min, 1½ h, or 3½ h, respectively, drank casein hydrolysate again for 2½ min, 30 min later they were poisoned. On the next seven days all rats were given just water, 30 min daily. On the following day, all rats were offered casein hydrolysate and water simultaneously, for 30 min. Since all the experimental groups drank a median of 0 ml casein hydrolysate, an additional test was conducted the following day, on which the rats were offered just casein hydrolysate for 30 min. This test minimized the floor-effect problem.

The experiment was then repeated, using 30 new rats and substituting 10% sucrose for casein hydrolysate. The procedure was the same with the following exceptions: On the training day, all drinking periods lasted 5 min each. No fluid was available the day after the training day. Water was offered for 2 h on the third day, and the test took place on the fourth day. Since the groups were adequately differentiated on this day, an additional 1-bottle test was not necessary.

Figure 2 presents the results. According to a Mann–Whitney U-test, 2-tail, all the experimental groups differed significantly ( $p$ <.002) from the controls in both the casein hydrolysate and the sucrose experiments. In

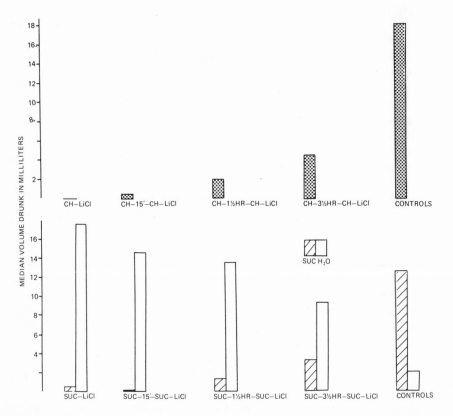

**Figure 2.** The effect of time since first exposure to a solution on the associability of a second presentation with poison. See text for explanation.

both experiments, two presentations of the solution did not differ significantly from one when the interval between them was only 15 min. However, as the delay between the two presentations increased (holding constant the delay between the second and poison), the learned aversion decreased. Thus the results are exactly what one would predict on the basis of learned safety, but not what one would expect on the basis of positive reinforcement.

### 3.2.2. "Learned Safety" or "Learned Irrelevance"?

Kalat and Rozin (1973) acknowledged that it was uncertain whether, during a delay after first exposure to a solution, a rat learns that the solution predicts no poison (i.e., it is "safe") or that it predicts nothing at all (i.e., it is "meaningless" or "irrelevant"). The basic question is whether a solution followed by an uneventful period is less associable with favorable consequences as well as with poison.

This question has been answered by Best's (1975) excellent experiments. Best found that if a rat drank solution A, which has previously been paired with poison, then drank solution B, and was *not* poisoned, this procedure enhanced the rat's preference for solution B. This preference was greater than that for a merely "safe" solution. Furthermore, this procedure was less effective in promoting the preference for B if the rat had previously been exposed to B than if B was novel. That is, to pair a solution with an uneventful period is to reduce its associability with both favorable and unfavorable events. Thus the process should be described not as "learned safety" but as "learned irrelevance," and I shall use the latter term henceforth.

A closely analogous process has been demonstrated in conditioned-suppression learning. Mackintosh (1973) has introduced the term "learned irrelevance" to refer to the fact that animals fail to associate a CS with subsequent shock if some other CS had already adequately predicted that shock. Actually, on the first trial they associate the new CS with shock just as much as if the additional, already-predictive CS were not present. They merely fail to increase this association on later trials, having learned to ignore the redundant CS (Mackintosh, 1973, 1975). As in the case of tastes, the decreased associability of a familiar stimulus is attributed to its previous association with no change in reinforcement.

### 3.2.3. Learned Irrelevance, Latent Inhibition, Habituation

Learned irrelevance refers to the decreased associability of a taste or other stimulus which has been paired with a period lacking any change in reinforcement. It is natural to investigate its relationship to latent inhibition and habituation.

Latent inhibition also refers to the decreased associability of a familiar stimulus. The only distinction from learned irrelevance is that the learned irrelevance position specifically affirms a learning process, in which the animal learns that the stimulus predicts nothing, while there is as yet no consensus on whether latent inhibition is a learning process. For contrasting views, see Weiss and Brown (1974) and Lubow (1973).

In most paradigms it is not easy to determine whether latent inhibition is or is not an associative learning process. The phenomenon is that the repeated, unpaired presentation of the stimulus decreases its later associability. To determine whether this involves a learning process, we need to know whether the decrease in associability simply depends on the repeated *presentation* of the stimulus, or depends on the *uneventful period* following the stimulus. In case of food aversion learning, this question can be tested, as above; the decrease in associability seems to depend on the uneventful period (Figure 2). But in other types of learning, the question is very difficult to test. Latent inhibition in other situations normally requires a large number of unpaired presentations of the stimulus. Since it is impossible to present the stimulus many times without consuming a fair amount of time, it is clearly difficult or impossible to test the independent contributions of the presentations and the uneventful time.

One might inquire, however, why there should be any doubt in the first place about whether latent inhibition is a learning process. After all, it is certainly a change in behavior as a result of experience, and thus fits most definitions of learning. The difficulty, presumably, is that there is no "reinforcer." For latent inhibition to be an example of associative learning, one must assume that the animal associates a stimulus with "nothing unexpected happening." At least to me, this is a perfectly reasonable assumption. Any animal *should* actively seek information; it *should* want to know what each stimulus predicts, even when the stimulus predicts nothing. The traditional—though usually unstated—assumption, however, has been that the animal learns only when "reinforcement" occurs.

This gratuitous assumption also underlies most theorizing on "habituation." Habituation refers to a decreased response to a stimulus, when that stimulus has been presented repeatedly and followed by nothing. In most cases it seems very natural to describe this as a learning process; for instance, the animal may learn that a particular stimulus, which originally alerted and perhaps frightened it, does not predict any danger. In the case of Tinbergen and Perdeck's (1950) gull chicks, the pecking response "habituates" to an artificial beak stimulus because the chicks learn that pecking it produces no food. In the case of male bettas attacking a mirror image, Rhoad, Kalat, and Klopfer (1975) suggest that the attack "habituates" because the fish learns that it cannot drive this "enemy" away. Indeed, after habituation of the betta's attack has taken place, the betta shows definite avoidance of the target (Rhoad *et al.*, 1975; Baenninger, 1970).

Despite the ease of explaining most habituation results as associative learning, most secondary sources refer to habituation as nonassociative learning, or as "the simplest type of learning," or as something other than learning. The only apparent reason for this attitude is the assumption that something-followed-by-nothing cannot produce learning, the assumption that learning can take place only if there is an explicit UCS present.

This assumption, I contend, should be abandoned. In the case of foods, a food followed by nothing produces some profound changes in the animal's subsequent behavior toward that food—changes which, in fact, take place gradually during the first few hours after the animal's first experience with the food. The evidence suggests that the animal associates the food with an uneventful period of time, and thus learns that it is irrelevant to both favorable and unfavorable visceral consequences. In short, the animal asks about any new stimulus, "What does it predict?" During the next few hours—or the next few seconds in the case of stimuli other than foods—it either associates the stimulus with some event, or associates it with the fact that nothing happened. The latter should be regarded as just as good an example of associative learning as the former.

### 3.2.4. The Primary Difficulty of the Learned Irrelevance Hypothesis

There is one problem with the learned irrelevance interpretation, which was acknowledged by Kalat and Rozin (1973), emphasized by Nachman and Jones (1974) and Domjan and Bowman (1974), and which must still be regarded as an unanswered question: Given that an animal fails to associate a food with poison over a few-hour delay because it has already associated the food with nonpoison, how is it that a rat ever learns an aversion to a familiar food? Familiar foods are much less associable with poison than novel foods are, but the associability is hardly negligible.

This is a problem for learned irrelevance in the sense that, evidently, learned irrelevance is not the whole story. If it were, then after the animal had associated a food with "no consequences," the animal could never learn an aversion to that food. However, in a sense this is not really a problem with the learned irrelevance interpretation itself; rather, the problem is that there is something else going on which is not yet adequately characterized.

To gain some perspective on this matter, Karen Rhoad and I have determined CS–UCS delay gradients for both familiar and unfamiliar tastes, using a single population of rats. Half the rats were familiarized with the test solution for two days, and half were not. Then all rats were given the solution for 2½ min, and poisoned with LiCl after 0 min, 30 min, or 24 h. Figure 3 presents the group medians and the statistical significance levels, using a Mann–Whitney U-test, 2-tail. Evidently the effect of familiarization is more apparent with a delayed poison than with an immediate poison. Certainly, it is not difficult to establish a strong aversion to a familiar solution via immediate poisoning.

The following is a tentative attempt to characterize the role of learned irrelevance in the CS–UCS delay gradient: After an animal drinks a novel solution, during the subsequent uneventful delay, the animal gradually associates the solution with uneventfulness, or "learns irrelevance." This process has two effects: First, it decreases the tendency for the solution to be associated with poison, should one be administered during the post-drinking interval. Second, it alters the animal's response toward the solution, the next time it tastes it. On that encounter it shows a stronger preference for it, and a more rapid tendency to again reclassify it as safe during a postdrinking delay.

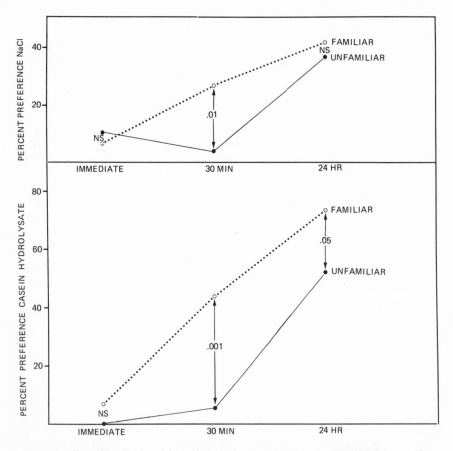

**Figure 3.** Effect of familiarity with casein hydrolysate or NaCl on the CS–UCS delay gradient.

## 3.3. Conclusions

We began this section with the question, "Can one draw conclusions about other types of learning from our studies of food aversion learning, and vice-versa?" I would hesitate to give an unqualified answer. I tend to suspect that both Revusky's concurrent interference process and the learned irrelevance process apply as much to other vertebrate associative learning as to food aversion learning. However, both are difficult to test in situations other than food aversion learning, since these other situations tend to require very short CS–UCS delays and very many trials before learning is clear. Thus it is difficult to make the desired experimental manipulations during the CS–UCS delay.

The above raises an interesting point: There are some principles which, even if they are true of, say, shock avoidance learning, would be very difficult to demonstrate in that situation, and probably even more difficult to notice in the first place. The same applies to food aversion learning: Because the learning takes place so rapidly, it would be difficult to test for such phenomena as the partial reinforcement effect. Perhaps for this reason as much as for any other, it pays to begin with the assumption that learning is a diverse category. Psychology for too long tested a few species in a few situations, confident of finding all the principles of all learning. The discovery of imprinting and of food aversion learning not only provided us with new, interesting phenomena, but also provided us with new, important, reinvigorating challenges for further investigation of previously familiar phenomena. Even if food aversion learning were to prove, in some final analysis, to have qualitatively the same laws as other types of learning, there are some principles we would have been unlikely to discover or demonstrate without the investigation of food aversion learning.

Therefore, it makes sense to adopt a working hypothesis that learning differs from one situation or species to another. Based on this assumption, we should test a wide variety of situations and species. If our working hypothesis is correct, then we shall profit from the labors. If in fact the laws of learning are the same for some groups of situations or species, we lose nothing by assuming the opposite, and we may gain something. There may be principles which apply generally, but which are much easier to observe and document in one context than in another.

## 4. References

Ardisson, J. -L., Dolisi, C., Camous, J. -P., and Gastaud, M. Rythmes spontanés des prises alimentaire et hydrique chez le chien: Etude préliminaire. *Physiology and Behavior*, 1975, *14*, 47–52.

Ayres, J. J. B., Benedict, J. O., and Witcher, E. S. Systematic manipulation of individual events in a truly random control in rats. *Journal of Comparative and Physiological Psychology*, 1973, *88*, 97–103.

Baenninger, R. Visual reinforcement, habituation, and prior social experience of Siamese fighting fish. *Journal of Comparative and Physiological Psychology*, 1970, *71*, 1–5.

Barelare, B., Jr., Holt, L. E., Jr., and Richter, C. P. Influence of vitamin deficiencies on appetite for particular foodstuffs. *American Journal of Physiology*, 1938, *123*, 7–8.

Barker, L. M. CS duration, amount, and concentration effects in conditioning taste aversions. *Learning and Motivation*, 1976, *7*, 265–273.

Barnett, S. A. Experiments on "neophobia" in wild and laboratory rats. *British Journal of Psychology*, 1958, *49*, 195–201.

Best, M. R. Conditioned and latent inhibition in taste-aversion learning: Clarifying the role of learned safety. *Journal of Experimental Psychology: Animal Behavior Processes*, 1975, *1*, 97–113.

Biederman, G. B., Milgram, N. W., Heighington, G. A., and Stockman, S. M. Memory of conditioned food aversion follows a U-shape function in rats. *Quarterly Journal of Experimental Psychology*, 1974, *26*, 610–615.

Bolles, R. .C., Riley, A. L., and Laskowski, B. A further demonstration of the learned safety effect in food-aversion learning. *Bulletin of the Psychonomic Society*, 1973, *1*, 190–192.

Bond, N., and DiGiusto, E. Amount of solution drunk is a factor in the establishment of taste aversion. *Animal Learning and Behavior*, 1975, *3*, 81–84.

Bond, N., and Harland, W. Effect of amount of solution drunk on taste-aversion learning. *Bulletin of the Psychonomic Society*, 1975, *5*, 219–220.

Braveman, N. S. Poison-based avoidance learning with flavored or colored water in guinea pigs. *Learning and Motivation*, 1974, *5*, 182–194.

Brunner, R. L. Age differences in one-trial passive avoidance learning. *Psychonomic Science*, 1969, *14*, 134.

Brush, F. R., Brush, E. S., and Solomon, R. L. Traumatic avoidance learning: The effects of CS–US intervals with delayed-conditioning procedure. *Journal of Comparative and Physiological Psychology*, 1955, *48*, 285–293.

Cannon, D. S., Berman, R. F., Baker, T. B., and Atkinson, C. A. Effect of preconditioning unconditioned stimulus experience on learned taste aversions. *Journal of Experimental Psychology: Animal Behavior Processes*, 1975, *1*, 270–284.

Cappell, H., and LeBlanc, A. E. Punishment of saccharin drinking by amphetamine in rats and its reversal by chlordiazepoxide. *Journal of Comparative and Physiological Psychology*, 1973, *85*, 97–104.

Cappell, H., LeBlanc, A. E., and Herling, S. Modification of the punishing effects of psychoactive drugs in rats by previous drug experience. *Journal of Comparative and Physiological Psychology*, 1975, *89*, 347–356.

Capretta, P. J., Petersik, J. T., and Stewart, D. J. Acceptance of novel flavours is increased after early experience of diverse tastes. *Nature*, 1975, *254*, 689–691.

Carroll, M. E., Dinc, H. I., Levy,C. J., and Smith, J. C. Demonstrations of neophobia and enhanced neophobia in the albino rat. *Journal of Comparative and Physiological Psychology*, 1975, *89*, 457–467.

Church, R. M. Response suppression. In B. A. Campbell and R. M. Church (Eds.), *Punishment and aversive behavior*. New York: Appleton-Century-Crofts, 1969.

Church, R. M., Brush, F. R., and Solomon, R. L. Traumatic avoidance learning: The effects of CS–US interval with a delayed-conditioning procedure in a free-responding situation. *Journal of Comparative and Physiological Psychology*, 1956, *49*, 301–308.

Crawford, F. T., and Holmes, C. E. Escape conditioning in snakes employing vibratory stimulation. *Psychonomic Science*, 1966, *4*, 125–126.

Der-Karabetian, A., and Gorry, T. Amount of different flavors consumed during the CS–US interval in taste-aversion learning and interference. *Physiological Psychology*, 1974, *2*, 457–460.

Deutsch, J. A. The cholinergic synapse and the site of memory. In J. A. Deutsch (Ed.), *The physiological basis of memory*. New York: Academic Press, 1973.

Domjan, M. CS preexposure in taste-aversion learning: Effects of deprivation and pre-exposure duration. *Learning and Motivation*, 1972, *3*, 389–402.

Domjan, M. Role of ingestion in odor-toxicosis learning in the rat. *Journal of Comparative and Physiological Psychology*, 1973, *84*, 507–521.

Domjan, M. Determinants of the enhancement of flavored-water intake by prior exposure. *Journal of Experimental Psychology: Animal Behavior Processes*, 1976, *2*, 17–27.

Domjan, M., and Bowman, T. G. Learned safety and the CS–US delay gradient in taste-aversion learning. *Learning and Motivation*, 1974, *5*, 409–423.

Domjan, M., and Wilson, N. E. Contribution of ingestive behaviors to taste-aversion learning in the rat. *Journal of Comparative and Physiological Psychology*, 1972a, *80*, 403–412.

Domjan, M., and Wilson, N. E. Specificity of cue to consequence in aversion learning in the rat. *Psychonomic Science*, 1972b, *26*, 143–145.

Dragoin, W. B. Conditioning and extinction of taste aversions with variations in intensity of the CS and UCS in two strains of rats. *Psychonomic Science*, 1971, *22*, 303–305.

Elkins, R. L. Attenuation of drug-induced bait shyness to a palatable solution as an increasing function of its availability prior to conditioning. *Behavioral Biology*, 1973, *9*, 221–226.

Elkins, R. L. Bait-shyness acquisition and resistance to extinction as functions of US exposure prior to conditioning. *Physiological Psychology*, 1974, *2*, 341–343.

Etscorn, F., and Stephens, R. Establishment of conditioned taste aversions with a 24-hour CS–US interval. *Physiological Psychology*, 1973, *1*, 252–253.

Feigley, D. A. Effects of scopolamine on activity and passive avoidance in rats of different ages. *Journal of Comparative and Physiological Psychology*, 1974, *87*, 26–36.

Fenwick, S., Mikulka, P. J., and Klein, S. B. The effect of different levels of pre-exposure to sucrose on the acquisition and extinction of a conditioned aversion. *Behavioral Biology*, 1975, *14*, 231–235.

Gadusek, F. J., and Kalat, J. W. Effects of scopolamine on retention of taste-aversion learning in rats. *Physiological Psychology*, 1975, *3*, 130–132.

Galef, B. G., Jr., and Sherry, D. F. Mother's milk: A medium for transmission of cues reflecting the flavor of mother's diet. *Journal of Comparative and Physiological Psychology*, 1973, *83*, 374–378.

Gamzu, E. Pre-exposure to unconditioned stimulus alone may eliminate taste aversions. Psychonomic Society, 1974.

Garcia, J., and Koelling, R. Relation of cue to consequence in avoidance learning. *Psychonomic Science*, 1966, *4*, 123–124.

Garcia, J., Ervin, R. R., and Koelling, R. A. Learning with prolonged delay of reinforcement. *Psychonomic Science*, 1966, *5*, 121–122.

Garcia, J., Kovner, R., and Green, K. Cue properties versus palatability of flavors in avoidance learning. *Psychonomic Science*, 1970, *20*, 313–314.

Giebel, H. D. Visuelles Lernvermögen bei Einhufern. *Zoologische Jahrbücher Abteilung für Allgemeine Zoologie*. 1958, *67*, 487–520.

Green, K. F., and Parker, L. A. Gustatory memory: Incubation and interference. *Behavioral Biology*, 1975, *13*, 359–367.

Green, L, Bouzas, A., and Rachlin, H. Test of an electric-shock analog to illness-induced aversion. *Behavioral Biology*, 1972, *7*, 513–518.

Grote, F. W., Jr., and Brown, R. T. Rapid learning of passive avoidance by weanling rats: Conditioned taste aversion. *Psychonomic Science*, 1971, *25*, 163–164.

Harlow, H. F. The evolution of learning. In A. Roe and G. G. Simpson (Eds.), *Behavior and evolution*. New Haven, Conn.: Yale Univ. Press, 1958.

Holman, E. W. Temporal properties of gustatory spontaneous alternation in rats. *Journal of Comparative and Physiological Psychology*, 1973, *85*, 536–539.

Horowitz, G. P., and Whitney, G. Alcohol-induced conditioned aversion: Genotypic specificity in mice (*Mus musculus*). *Journal of Comparative and Physiological Psychology*, 1975, *89*, 340–346.

Howell, D. N. The worm turns: An investigation of experimentation on the learning abilities of earthworms. *Megadrilogica*, 1974, *1*(10), 1–6.

Jacquet, Y. F. Conditioned aversion during morphine maintenance in mice and rats. *Physiology and Behavior*, 1973, *11*, 527–541.

Johnson, C., Beaton, R., and Hall, K. Poison-based avoidance learning in non-human primates: Use of visual cues. *Physiology and Behavior*, 1975, *14*, 403–407.

Kalat, J. W. Taste salience depends on novelty, not concentration, in taste-aversion learning in the rat. *Journal of Comparative and Physiological Psychology*, 1974, *86*, 47–50.

Kalat, J. W. Taste-aversion learning in infant guinea pigs. *Developmental Psychobiology*, 1975, *8*, 383–387.

Kalat, J. W. Should taste-aversion learning experiments control duration or volume of drinking on the training day? *Animal Learning and Behavior*, 1976, *4*, 96–98.

Kalat, J. W. Sucrose and isotonic saline intubations as USs for food-aversion learning. Manuscript in preparation.

Kalat, J. W., and Rozin, P. Role of interference in taste-aversion learning. *Journal of Comparative and Physiological Psychology*, 1971, *77*, 53–58.

Kalat, J. W., and Rozin, P. "Learned safety" as a mechanism in long-delay taste-aversion learning in rats. *Journal of Comparative and Physiological Psychology*, 1973, *83*, 198–207.

Kellogg, W. N., and Pomeroy, W. B. Maze learning in water snakes. *Journal of Comparative Psychology*, 1936, *21*, 275–295.

Köhler, W. *The mentality of apes*. 1921. (English translation, New York: Harcourt Brace Co., 1925.)

Kral, P. A. Effects of scopolamine injection during CS–US interval on conditioning. *Psychological Reports*, 1971, *28*, 690.

Kral, P. A. Localized ECS impedes taste-aversion learning. *Behavioral Biology*, 1972, *7*, 761–765.

Kremer, E. F. Properties of a pre-exposed stimulus. *Psychonomic Science*, 1972, *27*, 45–47.

Langworthy, R. A., and Jennings, J. W. Odd ball, abstract, olfactory learning in laboratory rats. *Psychological Record*, 1972, *22*, 487–490.

LeMagnen, J. Advances in studies on the physiological control and regulation of food intake. In E. Stellar and J. M. Sprague (Eds.), *Progress in physiological psychology*, Vol. 4. New York: Academic Press, 1971.

LeMagnen, J., and Tallon, S. La périodicité spontanée de la prise d'aliments ad libitum du rat blanc. *Journal de Physiologie (Paris)*, 1966, *58*, 323–349.

Levy, C. J., Carroll, M. E., Smith, J. C., and Hofer, K. G. Antihistamines block radiation-induced taste aversions. *Science*, 1974, *186*, 1044–1045.

Lubow, R. E. Latent inhibition. *Psychological Bulletin*, 1973, *79*, 398–407.

Lubow, R. E., and Moore, A. V. Latent inhibition: The effect of non-reinforced pre-exposure to the conditioned stimulus. *Journal of Comparative and Physiological Psychology*, 1959, *52*, 415–419.

Mackintosh, N. J. Stimulus selection: Learning to ignore stimuli that predict no change in reinforcement. In R. A. Hinde and J. Stevenson-Hinde (Eds.), *Constraints on learning*. London: Academic Press, 1973.

Mackintosh, N. J. Blocking of conditioned suppression: Role of the first compound trial. *Journal of Experimental Psychology: Animal Behavior Processes*, 1975, *1*, 335–345.

Maier, N. R. F., and Schneirla, T. C. *Principles of animal psychology*. New York: McGraw-Hill, 1935.

Maier, S. F., Seligman, M. E. P., and Solomon, R. L. Pavlovian fear conditioning and learned helplessness. In B. A. Campbell and R. M. Church (Eds.), *Punishment and aversive behavior*. New York: Appleton-Century-Crofts, 1969.

Margules, D. L., and Stein, L. Cholinergic synapses in the ventromedial hypothalamus for the suppression of operant behavior by punishment and satiety. *Journal of Comparative and Physiological Psychology*, 1969, *67*, 327–335.

Marler, P. A comparative approach to vocal learning: Song development in white-crowned sparrows. *Journal of Comparative and Physiological Psychology Monograph*, 1970, *71*, No. 2, part 2.

Morrison, G. R. Alternations in palatability of nutrients for the rat as a result of prior tasting. *Journal of Comparative and Physiological Psychology*, 1974, *86*, 56–61.

Nachman, M. Limited effects of electroconvulsive shock on memory of taste stimulation. *Journal of Comparative and Physiological Psychology*, 1970, *73*, 31–37.

Nachman, M., and Jones, D. Learned taste aversions over long delays in rats: The role of learned safety. *Journal of Comparative and Physiological Psychology*, 1974, *86*, 949–956.

Passey, G. E. The influence of intensity of unconditioned stimulus upon acquisition of a conditioned response. *Journal of Experimental Psychology*, 1948, *38*, 420–428.

Pavlov, I. P. *Conditioned reflexes*. Oxford Univ. Press, 1927.

Rensch, B. *Gedächtnis Begriffsbildung and Planhandlungen bei Tieren*. Berlin: Verlag Paul Parey. 1973.

Revusky, S. H., and Bedarf, E. W. Association of illness with prior ingestion of novel foods. *Science*, 1967, *155*, 219–220.

Revusky, S. H., and Garcia, J. Learned associations over long delays. In G. H. Bower and J. T. Spence (Eds.), *The psychology of learning and motivation*, IV. New York: Academic Press, 1970.

Revusky, S., and Taukulis, H. Effects of alcohol and lithium habituation on the development of alcohol aversions through contingent lithium injection. *Behavior Research and Therapy*, 1975, *13*, 163–166.

Rhoad, K. D., Kalat, J. W., and Klopfer, P. H. Aggression and avoidance by *Betta splendens* toward natural and artificial stimuli. *Animal Learning and Behavior*, 1975, *3*, 271–276.

Riccio, D. C., Rohrbaugh, M., and Hodges, L. A. Developmental aspects of passive and active avoidance learning in rats. *Developmental Psychobiology*, 1968, *1*, 108–111.

Richter, C. P. Carbohydrate appetite of normal and hyperthyroid rats as determined by the taste-threshold method. *Endocrinology*, 1947, *40*, 455.

Richter, C. P. Loss of appetite for alcohol and alcoholic beverages produced in rats by treatment with thyroid preparations. *Endocrinology*, 1956a, *59*, 472–478.

Richter, C. P. Self-regulatory functions during gestation and lactation. In C. A. Villee (Ed.), *Gestation: Transactions of second conference*. Madison, N.J.: Madison Printing Co., 1956b.

Richter, C. P. Production and control of alcoholic cravings in rats. In H. A. Abramson (Ed.), *Neuropharmacology*, III. Madison, N.J.: Madison Printing Co., 1957a.

Richter, C. P. Decreased appetite for alcohol and alcoholic beverages produced in rats by thyroid treatment. In H. Hoagland (Ed.), *Hormones, brain function, and behavior*. New York: Academic Press, 1957b.

Richter, C. P., Holt, L. E., Jr., Barelare, B., Jr., and Hawkes, C. D. Changes in fat, carbohydrate and protein appetite in vitamin B deficiency. *American Journal of Physiology*, 1938, *124*, 596–602.

Roll, D. L., and Smith, J. C. Conditioned taste aversion in anesthetized rats. In M. E. P. Seligman and J. L. Hager (Eds.), *The biological boundaries of learning*. New York: Appleton-Century-Crofts, 1972.

Romanes, G. J. *Animal intelligence*. New York: D. Appleton & Co. 1884.

Rozin, P. Central or peripheral mediation of learning with long CS–US intervals in the feeding system. *Journal of Comparative and Physiological Psychology*, 1969a, *67*, 421–429.

Rozin, P. Adaptive food sampling patterns in vitamin deficient rats. *Journal of Comparative and Physiological Psychology*, 1969b, *69*, 126–132.

Rozin, P., and Kalat, J. W. Specific hungers and poison avoidance as adaptive specializations of learning. *Psychological Review*, 1971, *78*, 459–486.

Rozin, P., and Ree, P. Long extension of effective CS–US interval by anesthesia between CS and US. *Journal of Comparative and Physiological Psychology*, 1972, *80*, 43–48.

Rzoska, J. Baitshyness, a study in rat behavior. *British Journal of Animal Behaviour*, 1953, *1*, 128–135.

Sagan, C., Sagan, L. S., and Drake, F. A message from earth. *Science*, 1972, *175*, 881–884.

Shettleworth, S. J. Constraints on learning. In D. S. Lehrman, R. A. Hinde, and E. Shaw (Eds.), *Advances in the study of behavior*, IV. New York: Academic Press, 1972.

Siegel, S. Retention of latent inhibition. *Psychonomic Science*, 1970, *20*, 161–162.

Siegel, S. Flavor pre-exposure and "learned safety." *Journal of Comparative and Physiological Psychology*, 1974, *87*, 1073–1082.

Smith, D. F., and Balagura, S. Role of oropharyngeal factors in LiCl aversion. *Journal of Comparative and Physiological Psychology*, 1969, *69*, 308–310.

Smith, J. C., and Morris, D. D. The use of X-rays as the unconditioned stimulus in 500-day old rats. *Journal of Comparative and Physiological Psychology*, 1963, *56*, 746–747.

Smith, J. C., and Morris, D. D. The effects of atropine sulfate and physostigmine on the conditioned aversion to saccharin solution with X-rays as the unconditioned stimulus. In T. J. Haley and R. S. Snider (Eds.), *Response of the nervous system to ionizing radiation*, II. Boston: Little, Brown. 1964.

Snowdon, C. T. Motivation, regulation, and the control of meal parameters with oral and intragastric feeding. *Journal of Comparative and Physiological Psychology*, 1969, *69*, 91–100.

Stein, L., Belluzzi, J. D., and Wise, C. D. Memory enhancement by central administration of norepinephrine. *Brain Research*, 1975, *84*, 329–335.

Stricker, E. M., and Zigmond, M. J. Effects on homeostasis of intraventricular injections of 6-hydroxydopamine in rats. *Journal of Comparative and Physiological Psychology*, 1974, *86*, 973–994.

Tinbergen, N., and Perdeck, A. C. On the stimulus situation releasing the begging response in the newly hatched herring gull chick. *Behaviour*, 1950, *3*, 1–38.

Tulving, E., and Thomson, D. M. Encoding specificity and retrieval processes in episodic memory. *Psychological Review*, 1973, *80*, 352–373.

Vogel, J. R. Prior exposure to a drug (US) attenuates learned taste aversions. Psychonomic Society, 1974.

Weeks, J. R. Experimental morphine addiction: Method for automatic intravenous injections in unrestrained rats. *Science*, 1962, *138*, 143–144.

Weisinger, R. S., Parker, L. F., and Skorupski, J. D. Conditioned taste aversions and specific need states in the rat. *Journal of Comparative and Physiological Psychology*, 1974, *87*, 655–660.

Weiss, K. R., and Brown, B. L. Latent inhibition: A review and a new hypothesis. *Acta Neurobiologiae Experimentalis*, 1974, *34*, 301–316.

Welker, W. I. An analysis of exploratory and play behavior in animals. In D. W. Fiske and S. R. Maddi (Eds.), *Functions of varied experience*. Homewood, Ill.: Dorsey Press, 1961.

Wike, E. L., Wolfe, V. L., and Norsworthy, K. A. The effects of low frequency, whole body vibration on rats: Prolonged training, predictability, incremental training, and taste conditioning. *Bulletin of the Psychonomic Society*, 1975, *5*, 333–335.

Wilcoxon, H., Dragoin, W., and Kral, P. Illness-induced aversions in rat and quail: Relative salience of visual and gustatory cues. *Science*, 1971, *171*, 826–828.

Wolfle, D. L., and Brown, C. S. A learning experiment with snakes. *Copeia*, 1940, *2*, 134.

Young, R. C., Gibbs, J., Antin, J., Holt, J., and Smith, G. P. Absence of satiety during sham feeding in the rat. *Journal of Comparative and Physiological Psychology*, 1974, *87*, 795–800.

Zis, A. P., Fibiger, H. C., and Phillips, A. G. Reversal by L-dopa of impaired learning due to destruction of the dopaminergic nigro–neostriatal projection. *Science*, 1974, *185*, 960–962.

# Stimulus Characteristics in   3
# Food Aversion Learning

**Marvin Nachman, Joan Rauschenberger,**
**and John H. Ashe**

One of the more intriguing issues in contemporary learning theory is the idea that stimuli are not equally associable. This idea, that some associations are more easily formed than others, has been formulated in various ways using such concepts as belongingness (Thorndike, 1932; Rozin and Kalat, 1971), stimulus relevance (Capretta, 1961), cue to consequence (Garcia and Koelling, 1966), and preparedness (Seligman, 1970). In food aversion learning, it is clear that animals readily learn to avoid ingesting material which was associated with sickness. (We use the words illness or sickness as arbitrary convenient terms in this chapter, realizing full well that they represent a gross oversimplification. The nature of the UCS is an important problem deserving of more consideration than can be given in this chapter.) The early field studies on bait shyness added poisons to bait and it became evident that animals learned to avoid the specific bait (Chitty, 1954). In subsequent laboratory experiments, the use of solutions permitted the control of other stimulus factors and it was possible to demonstrate that it was primarily the taste rather than any other sensory quality that was avoided (Garcia, Kimeldorf, and Koelling, 1955; Nach-

**Marvin Nachman and Joan Rauschenberger** • University of California, Riverside, California. **John H. Ashe** • University of California, Irvine, California.

man, 1963). Having established that animals readily learn taste–illness associations, many investigators sought to determine (1) the degree to which animals can form aversions to various sensory modalities, and (2) the parameters of the gustatory stimuli which are involved in the formation of these associations. These two issues and questions revolving around these issues are the subject of the present chapter.

## 1. Sensory Modalities

### 1.1. Taste

A typical experimental design in taste aversion research is to allow rats a limited drinking period each day in a standardized situation. On training days, they drink water; on acquisition or treatment days, they drink a distinctive-tasting solution and are made sick. For the next two or so days, they are again given trials with water and on the final test day, they are tested with the distinctive-tasting solution. On all days, stimuli and drinking conditions are identical except for the taste (and conceivably the odor) of the solution. Therefore, the fact that rats show a strong aversion to drinking the taste solution but not to water is clear evidence for the significant role played by the sense of taste. While odor may also be used as a cue (see below) it is clearly not a necessary one since anosmic rats show strong learned taste aversions.

#### 1.1.1. Taste Generalization

Further evidence of the role of taste is demonstrated by data which indicate that the learned aversion generalizes to other similar tastes but is strongest to the specific solution used in training. The learned taste aversion is so specific that this method of measuring generalization gradients provides a valuable tool for determining the similarity of various tastes to animals. For example, Nachman (1963) demonstrated the similarity of the taste of LiCl and NaCl to rats by showing that learned aversions to the taste of LiCl generalized to the taste of NaCl more than to the taste of $NH_4Cl$ or KCl. Similarly, Tapper and Halpern (1968) used the taste aversion learning technique to show that the taste of DL-alanine, glycine, and sodium saccharin are classed together by rats (all taste sweet to humans) while they are not classified as similar to D-glucose or KCl.

The stimulus generalization technique has been used more recently in our laboratory to further investigate the ability of rats to identify the taste of the sodium ion. It was previously established that sodium-deficient rats show an appetite which is highly specific to sodium salts in preference to nonsodium salts (Nachman, 1962). What is less clear and perhaps of greater theoretical significance for an understanding of neural coding of taste ions is whether, for rats, the presence of a sodium ion imparts a distinctive taste so that sodium salts all have a similar taste which is distinctive from the taste of nonsodium salts. For humans, this is apparently not the case. Humans cannot detect the presence or absence of sodium ions by taste and the specific taste class of "salty" contains both sodium and nonsodium salts.

To test rats for the similarity of tastes of various sodium and nonsodium salts to the taste of NaCl, nine groups of rats each were made sick with an intraperitoneal injection of LiCl after drinking .15 M NaCl for 10 min. The rats were then given five daily 10-min tests with water to extinguish any general aversion, and then each group was given a 10-min test with a different solution: one of the groups was tested with the original NaCl solution, four of the groups were tested with the same concentration of other sodium solutions, and four of the groups were tested with the same concentration of nonsodium solutions. The intake for each group on test day was compared with that of nine control groups which had each received the same testing as an experimental group except that they had not received an injection of LiCl. It should be noted that the various solutions were chosen because they are all relatively palatable to the rat, as evidenced by the fact that each control group drank somewhat more of each solution than they had of water on the previous day. As can be seen in Figure 1, the aversion to the original conditioning stimulus, NaCl, is greatest, and the aversion to every sodium-containing salt is greater than to any nonsodium salt, confirming that for the rat, sodium salts taste similar to each other as a class. In a variety of tests with college students, we were unable to find that the students could classify sodium-containing salts as a similar tasting group of compounds. It is logically possible, of course, that the discrimination was based on the intensity rather than the taste quality of the solutions and that, for rats, all sodium-containing salts are more similar in intensity than are nonsodium salts. Whether the discrimination is based on intensity or quality, however, it is clear that rats learn a taste aversion which only generalizes strongly to a relatively narrow class of similar tasting stimuli.

### 1.1.2. Role of Taste versus Ingestion

In most studies of taste aversion learning, the gustatory stimulus is provided by having the animals actively ingest a solution. A number of experiments have focused on the question of whether ingesting the solution is necessary or whether passively tasting the solution is sufficient as a

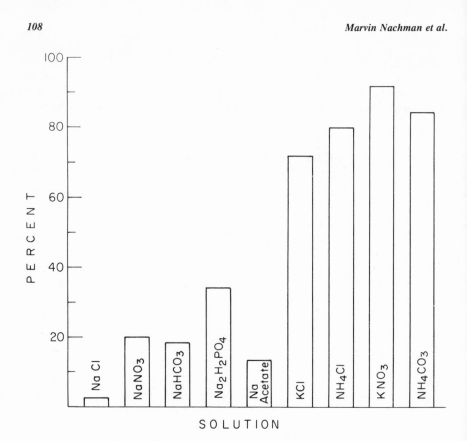

**Figure 1.** Relative intake of various sodium and nonsodium solutions by rats which had been made sick with LiCl after drinking NaCl. All solutions were .15 M.

conditioning stimulus. Clearly, the oral cavity must be stimulated for a learned aversion to occur. If the oral cavity is by-passed by stomach-tubing the solution, no conditioned aversion is obtained (Smith and Balagura, 1969). In a sense, this is obvious because, in the test for aversion, the animal would have no way of recognizing the taste of the solution to be avoided, unless it is assumed, contrary to all human experience, that one can taste a solution which is put into the stomach directly. On the other hand, there are data which show that some solutions, when given intravenously at a high enough concentration, can be tasted, apparently as a result of direct stimulation of taste buds via blood circulation (Geldard, 1972). Using this technique, Bradley and Mistretta (1971) demonstrated that rats learned a saccharin aversion when intravenous injections of saccharin were followed by illness produced by LiCl. Although the rats that received saccharin intravenously did not ingest the saccharin, they presumably did taste it, and may have mouthed it and perhaps even engaged in swallowing movements.

In the attempt to further delineate the role of taste, a number of studies compared the effects of active ingestion of solutions with various rinsing procedures (Burešová and Bureš, 1973; Domjan and Wilson, 1972b; Kalat, 1977). In the technique used by Burešová and Bureš (1973), the rat's mouth was held open and saccharin solution was dripped on the base of the tongue allowing the rat to swallow. When this procedure was followed by a LiCl injection, the rats learned a saccharin aversion but they did not learn as well as a comparable group of rats that had drunk an equal amount of the saccharin solution.

In the experiments of Domjan and Wilson (1972b) attempts were made to rinse the rat's mouth with the taste solution while minimizing the likelihood that the rat would swallow the solution. Swallowing was reduced by such procedures as having the solution flow very rapidly through the mouth, using nonthirsty rats, and using curarized rats. When swallowing was minimized, rats still learned the taste aversion but not as well as when some ingestion occurred. However, Kalat (1977) used a "learned safety" measure and found that rats only learned after ingesting the solution and did not learn "safety" when ingestion was minimized by rapidly infusing the solution through the mouth in nonthirsty rats.

The results of Domjan and Wilson certainly suggest that conditioning can occur with a rinse procedure, but the amount of learning they found was relatively small, and there are other considerations which make that conclusion somewhat uncertain. The main problem of course is the difficulty of knowing whether some tongue movements or ingestion may have occurred during the rinse procedure, despite all the precautions taken to prevent swallowing. It is also possible that following the rinse procedure, there was some solution left in the mouth which caused the rat to engage in active tasting, tongue movements, and swallowing.

One clear conclusion from this series of rinse studies is that greater learned aversion or learned safety occurs when a rat drinks the solution than when its mouth is rinsed with it. There are a number of reasons, apart from issues related to swallowing and motor movements, why this may be true. It is likely that the amount and kind of taste stimulation provided by a passive rinse simply does not compare with the amount and kind of taste stimulation when a rat drinks. From a generalization perspective, the stimuli are more similar when a rat actively drinks on both acquisition and test trials than when the mouth is rinsed during the acquisition trial and the test trial is a drinking test. Also, when the rinse procedures are used, there may be considerable overshadowing of gustatory stimuli by the unusual stimuli produced by the rinse.

### 1.1.3. Long-Delay Learning with Taste Stimuli

Undoubtedly, one of the most significant features of taste aversion learning is the fact that conditioning can occur even though long temporal delays intervene between the drinking of a flavored solution and subsequent illness. We shall discuss later some experiments by Revusky and Parker (1976) and Nachman, Rauschenberger, and Ashe (1977) which indicate that long-delay learning may also be possible when sensory cues other than taste are used. However, it is clear that the long-delay learning reported with other senses pales in comparison with the consistent findings of strong, single-trial long-delay learning when taste is used. Attempts made with other senses usually have been unsuccessful, or when successful, the results have been more variable, multiple trials have invariably been required, and the absolute amount of learned aversion has almost always been much less than when taste was used. With taste as a CS, strong learned aversions can occur with delays of several hours; the evidence suggests an asymptote at about 8–12 h (Nachman, 1970; Revusky, 1968; Smith and Roll, 1967), but there is even a report of taste aversion learning with a 24-h delay (Etscorn and Stephens, 1973). It is reasonable to ask whether there is anything special about the gustatory system which can account for long-delay learning. We shall discuss a few of the possible explanations.

*a. Aftertaste.* The possibility has often been considered that the taste of the solution persists in the mouth as an aftertaste so that the association between taste and illness is contiguous rather than after a long delay. This argument has been carefully reviewed and rejected by Revusky and Garcia (1970) and Rozin and Kalat (1971). Among the facts one can cite in rejecting the aftertaste argument is that rats can learn an aversion to water (Nachman, 1970), to the temperature of water (Nachman, 1970), to licking air (Nachman *et al.*, (1977), to a specific concentration of a solution (Rozin, 1969), and to a solution which has been followed by other tastes (Kalat and Rozin, 1970; Revusky and Bedarf, 1967). The fact that tactile stimulation to the tongue may also serve as a cue for rats (Nachman *et al.*, 1977) and visual stimuli as a cue for birds (Wilcoxon, Dragoin, and Kral, 1971) also argues against an explanation based on the continuous peripheral stimulation implied by the concept of aftertaste.

*b. Interference.* Revusky (1971) has proposed an interference hypothesis which he has combined with the concept of stimulus relevance to account for the fact that long-delay learning can occur more readily with taste–sickness associations than, for example, with auditory, visual, or proprioceptive-shock associations. During normal operant behavior of an organism, there is the likelihood of a continuous stream of visual, auditory, and proprioceptive stimuli, and any of these are presumably potential CSs for a shock UCS which may occur. On the other hand, taste stimuli are not continuously present, so that when a brief ingestion period is followed several hours later by sickness, there is less probability of interference of that association by the occurrence of other taste stimuli. It might be argued, of course, that during the taste–sickness delay period, various visual, auditory, and proprioceptive stimuli do occur and should become conditioned to the illness and thus interfere with the taste–sickness association. But here, Revusky hypothesizes that because of stimulus relevance, taste–sickness associations are favored, and visual, auditory, and proprioceptive stimuli do not readily become associated with illness. There have been relatively few experiments testing the interference hypothesis, although Kalat and Rozin (1971) have reported the results of one experiment which they interpreted as not fully supporting the interference hypothesis.

*c. Novelty.* The role of novelty in taste aversion learning will be discussed in some detail in a later section. Here we should first like to point out that in the usual taste aversion learning experiment, the taste stimulus as a CS is a far more novel stimulus than are the visual or auditory CSs used in other conditioning experiments. The laboratory rat normally lives a sheltered life as far as taste sensations are concerned. Thus, on the critical conditioning trial in which a saccharin solution may be presented for the first time, the potency of the taste cue from a novelty–distinctiveness–arousal perspective may be a contributing factor to the occurrence of long-delay learning. In this way, it might be argued that there is nothing unique about the sense of taste in producing long-delay learning and that the same effect might occur with any sensory input if we could make that input novel and sufficiently arousing. Of course, it can be countered that olfactory stimuli are also relatively novel but do not show the same potential for producing long-delay associations and that wild rats probably do have an abundance of taste experiences but nevertheless do learn taste aversions well (Chitty, 1954).

*d. Slow Decay of the Neural Trace.* Perhaps the simplest and most straightforward explanation which attempts to account for the role of taste in long-delay learning is to hypothesize that the neural representation of a taste input decays slowly, so that unlike other sensory inputs, it is still present several hours later when the UCS is presented. (This, of course, does not explain why visual and auditory stimuli which are present at the time of the UCS are not readily conditioned to the UCS.) The major difficulty with accepting the slow decay hypothesis, of course, is that it is pure conjecture. We know little about neural decay and certainly have no evidence regarding the parameters of the decay or any indication that taste systems differ in this regard from other sensory systems. A variation on the slow decay model is to suggest that the taste CS may alter for an extended period of time some of the neural parameters in the UCS pathway, thus facilitating conditioning when the UCS arrives (Thompson, 1976). It should also be pointed out that when we hypothesize a concept such as the slow decay of a neural trace, we are really referring to the decay of the associability of the taste CS with the UCS, not the memory of the CS (Nachman and Jones, 1974). While associability may decrease over a delay period of hours, it is clear that the memory of the CS experience may last for weeks or longer. For example, there may be an essentially permanent memory store of a single saccharin ingestion experience but that single ingestion experience is only associable with sickness if the sickness occurs within a matter of hours.

*e. Excitability of Specific Pathways.* Garcia and Ervin (1968) hypothesized that the direct projection of the gustatory and visceral inputs to the same anatomical locus in the medulla may be responsible for the facilitation of taste–sickness conditioning. This hypothesis could of course be extended to include the idea that the anatomical convergence also somehow plays a role in long-delay learning. Obviously, there is at present no evidence to support such an additional hypothesis; in fact, it is also the case that we do not have any insight into how anatomical convergence may be converted into a physiological facilitation of conditioning involving contiguous stimuli.

*f. Nothing Unique about Taste.* It is possible that taste–sickness long-delay learning occurs not because of any special characteristics of taste stimuli *vis à vis* other sensory modalities, but because of the nature of sickness as a UCS. Thus, it might be hypothesized that the state of sickness engages a type of scanning or neural retrieval mechanism which associates with prior events which have occurred over a more extended period of time. Here, of course, we would have to arbitrarily invoke a concept such as stimulus relevance to account for why the illness is associated with taste rather than other types of sensory input which have occurred during that time period. The important distinction between this type of explanation and one based on slow decay or on the excitability of specific pathways is that it ascribes specific long-delay conditioning properties to the nature of sickness as a UCS rather than to the nature of taste as a CS. Again, it should be pointed out that these are speculations without evidence.

## 1.2. Olfactory Stimuli

The role of odor in learned aversions has been of particular interest because of the interactions of gustatory and olfactory stimuli in feeding and drinking behavior. In fact, many investigations of the parameters of taste aversion learning have involved the use of flavor stimuli that are really composites of gustatory and olfactory cues (e.g., anise, chocolate, coffee, grape juice, . . . ). However, it is clear that olfactory cues are not necessary to form a taste aversion because peripherally anosmic rats do not show an impairment in the acquisition of an aversion to specific tastes (Barnett, Cowan, Radford, and Prakash, 1975; Domjan, 1973; Hankins, Garcia, and Rusiniak, 1973). It is then of interest to know whether odor, in the absence of gustatory cues, may itself serve as a discriminative stimulus in conditioning an aversion. A variety of techniques for presenting the olfactory stimulus have been used. In some experiments on learned odor aversions, the odorized agent was dissolved in a solution to be ingested (Larue, 1975; Lovett, Goodchild, and Booth, 1968; Pain and Booth, 1968). In other studies, the odor stimulus was presented near a drinking tube or in the region of the animal (Domjan, 1973; Garcia and Koelling, 1967; Lorden, Kenfield and Braun, 1970; Supak, Macrides, and Chorover, 1971; Taukulis, 1974). However, in any study using olfactory stimuli there are potential problems of confounding olfactory and gustatory stimuli. Because olfactory stimuli are airborne, water soluble substances (Somjen, 1972) they may be potential stimuli for both olfactory and gustatory receptors. This problem becomes more acute as the concentration of odorized molecules in air increases or if a stream of odorized air is directed at the head.

One way of showing that it is odor rather than taste that is involved in the learning of an aversion is to demonstrate that the learned aversion is dependent on an intact sense of smell. Larue (1975) found that unoperated rats could learn an aversion to odorized water in contrast to bulbectomized rats that were not able to learn the aversion. Similarly, Domjan (1973) found that rats which had acquired an odor aversion did not demonstrate it when they were made peripherally anosmic.

A common experimental design for demonstrating conditioned odor aversions is to make rats sick after they drink water in an odorized compartment. Learned odor aversions are then shown by the fact that the rats avoid drinking water when that odor is present. Another type of experimental design does not use ingestive behaviors, but simply makes rats sick in the presence of an odor. Domjan (1973) demonstrated that rats made sick in the presence of an odor show an aversion to a compartment containing that odor. However, the learned aversion was less strong than if the rat had been made sick after drinking water in the presence of the odor.

There seems little doubt that odor is a much less effective cue than is taste in learning aversions. Not only does relatively little learning occur when odor alone is used as the conditioning stimulus, but when compound stimuli of taste and odor have been presented, taste is clearly the cue to which the animal becomes conditioned and odor is largely ignored (Hargrave and Bolles, 1971; Supak *et al.*, 1971). Furthermore, taste aversions can be learned with long CS–UCS delays, but there is doubt as to whether odor aversions can be learned with temporal delays comparable to those seen for taste. There have been only two published studies investigating long-delay learning using odor stimuli and these two studies have reported somewhat conflicting results. Hankins *et al.* (1973), using peppermint odor on filter paper around the drinking tube, found that rats could learn an aversion with a 10-min but not a 30-min delay. Even with only a 10-min delay, relatively little aversion was learned in spite of repeated trials. In contrast, Taukulis (1974) used two concentric tubes arranged so that rats could drink water from the inner tube while a stream of amyl acetate vapor flowed from the outer tube. Under these conditions rats learned a strong aversion after one trial with delays of up to 4 h.

The most obvious factor which may account for the large difference in the results of these two studies is the method of presentation of the odorized stimulus. In the Taukulis study, a stream of amyl acetate was directed at the rat's mouth and it is therefore reasonable to infer that this method of presentation stimulated gustatory receptors. If this is true, the findings in the Taukulis study of a one-trial long-delay gradient of learned aversion cannot be assumed to be a gradient due to olfaction alone.

## 1.3. Visual–Auditory Stimuli

There is no doubt that taste cues can be readily associated with sickness. Considerable interest has focused on the question of whether learned aversions are limited to the use of taste cues or whether comparable aversions can occur when visual or auditory conditioned stimuli are used. In attempting to assess the effectiveness of these nongustatory stimuli, two general types of procedures have been used. Each of these has produced somewhat different results. In one procedure, the nongustatory cues are presented in conjunction with gustatory cues and the rat is made sick to this compound stimulus. In the other procedure, the nongustatory stimuli are presented by themselves while paired with sickness. Those studies, using the compound stimulus and then testing for the learning to each stimulus separately, consistently report that aversions are learned to the gustatory stimulus but not to the visual or auditory stimulus (Best, Best, and Mickley, 1973; Domjan and Wilson, 1972a; Garcia and Koelling, 1966; Garcia, McGown, Ervin, and Koelling, 1968; Green, Holmstrom, and Wollman, 1974; Hargrave and Bolles, 1971). On the other hand, in those studies which have used visual stimuli alone or have placed animals in a distinctive compartment, it has been possible to demonstrate that these nongustatory cues are somewhat effective in producing a learned aversion (Best *et al.*, 1973; Garcia, Kimeldorf, and Hunt, 1956; Martin and El-linwood, 1974; Mitchell, Kirschbaum, and Perry, 1975; Overall, Brown, and Logie, 1960; Rozin, 1969). Presumably, gustatory stimuli overshadow nongustatory stimuli, rendering them ineffective in a compound stimulus situation in learned aversion tasks.

When learned aversion does occur to a distinctive visual stimulus or place it appears to be particularly dependent upon the total environmental and training situation, including whether or not the animal drinks in the situation (Best *et al.*, 1973) and the amount of exposure to the training situation prior to conditioning (Mitchell *et al.*, 1975). Thus, while it is possible under special conditions for rats to learn an aversion to a place or to a distinctive visual stimulus, such learning does not always occur and is certainly not as strong as taste aversion learning.

Several studies have investigated whether rats can learn to avoid drinking from a specific container and whether such learning would occur with relatively long delays between drinking and illness (Rozin, 1969; Revusky and Parker, 1976; Nachman *et al.*, 1977). Rozin (1969) used a discriminative task in which rats drank saccharin from a Richter tube located in the left side of the cage versus from a cup located in the right side of the cage. He found that rats could learn an aversion to drinking saccharin from the particular container if they were made sick while they were drinking from the container but not when the sickness was delayed until 30 min after the drinking. Revusky and Parker (1976), and Nachman *et al.* (1977) each used a discriminative task in which rats drank water from a cup versus a spout and in both experiments it was found that in a few trials the rat could learn to avoid drinking from a particular container, even when sickness was delayed for at least 30 min after drinking. The relevant cues for the learning of this aversion are not at all obvious. The learning of the aversion may have been mediated by the differential appearance of the two solution containers, their different positions in the cage, or by the differential pattern of somatosensory stimulation that accompanied the drinking from each container. For example, in our study, the rats were acclimated to drinking from a glass jar, and conditioning trials were given when they were drinking from a glass drinking tube. In order to drink from the jar the rats had to place their heads down into the jar and lap at the fluid in a manner similar to a kitten lapping milk from a saucer. In contrast, drinking from the spout involves licking movements with the tongue touching the spout. These two patterns of drinking and their associated somatosensory stimulation are clearly different and may have become conditioned stimuli for the subsequent learned aversion.

## 1.4. Somatosensory Stimuli

Several studies have investigated whether somatosensory stimuli may be used as effective cues in learned aversions. We have found, for example, that rats can learn a LiCl induced aversion to the licking of air (Nachman *et al.*, 1977). Water-deprived rats were allowed to lick at a continuous stream of air for a 10-min period and were then made sick after various delays. When 1-min and 15-min sickness delays were used, the rats learned a strong aversion in a single trial, while no aversion was learned in a single trial when longer delays were used.

Similarly, it was found (Nachman, 1970) that rats could learn an aversion to the temperature of water. Rats learned to avoid either hot (43°C) or cold (0–1°C) water in a single trial and as in the air lick study, only the 1- and 15-min delay groups showed significant learned aversions after the one trial.

Additional evidence of the efficacy of somatosensory conditioned stimuli has recently been obtained (Nachman *et al.*, 1977). As a follow-up of the observation that rats can acquire an aversion to a specific solution container, several experiments were designed to factor out the relevant cues for this learning. To study the role of tongue tactile stimulation, rats were trained to drink a daily 10-min ration of water from glass drinking spouts. The spouts were made from 9-mm glass tubing which was fire polished so that the opening at the tip was either large (7 mm) or small (2.5 mm). On training days the rats drank water from a spout with a large opening. On conditioning days, the rats drank water from the spout with a small opening, and LiCl injections were given at various temporal delays. Strong learned aversions to drinking from the tube with the small opening were acquired after a few trials and clear aversions were seen with delays of at least 1 h. Because the tubes with the large and small openings had very similar appearances, it is quite unlikely that the rats could have utilized visual cues for the acquisition of this learning. In contrast, drinking from each of the tubes clearly provided for different patterns of tactile stimulation to the tongue.

While this evidence is not conclusive, these studies and additional follow-up experiments (Nachman *et al.*, 1977) certainly suggest that rats are capable of effectively utilizing information provided by somatosensory stimulation of the tongue in learning aversions.

It is of particular interest that somatosensory stimulation may be an adequate cue in long-delay learning, but it is also clear that these stimuli are not as effective as gustatory stimuli. With gustatory stimuli, one-trial learning and long-delay learning over several hours readily occurs, whereas with somatosensory stimuli, the learning appears to be considerably weaker on the first trial, more trials are needed, and the maximum delay is of the order of 1–2 h. Nevertheless, perhaps of greater significance is the finding that long-delay learning, in addition to occurring with gustatory stimuli, can occur with somatosensory stimuli.

It is interesting to note the anatomical similarity between the somatosensory projections from the tongue and the gustatory projections. *Nucleus solitarius,* in the medulla, receives direct projections from the trigeminal nerve in addition to projections from the chorda tympani and glossopharyngeal nerves (Torvik, 1956). The neuroanatomical hypothesis, outlined by Garcia and Ervin (1968), suggests that the direct convergence of gustatory and visceral afferents on the *nucleus solitarius* provides the anatomical substrate underlying taste aversion learning. Given this hypothesis, it is especially relevant that somatosensory stimulation of the tongue may be an effective cue for aversion learning and that the trigeminal nerve that conveys this information projects directly to the solitary nucleus. This issue has been further discussed in Nachman *et al.* (1977).

## 2. Parameters of Taste

Even though there is some suggestion that aversions may be formed to cues other than taste, we are confronted with the fact that the learning to nongustatory cues is not comparable to that seen with taste. The evidence is overwhelming that the taste of a substance is the most effective cue for rats learning to avoid that substance. In light of this evidence, there has been considerable emphasis on attempting to analyze the specific features of the taste cue which are significant for taste aversion learning. An important basic finding has been that not all tastes are equally associable. For example, Kalat and Rozin (1970) found that rats learn a better aversion to a sucrose solution than to a vanilla solution. They used the term "salience" to describe this phenomenon. Salience, of course, is not an explanatory concept, and Kalat and Rozin used it more as a way of describing the fact that aversions are reliably learned better to some solutions than to others. Perhaps a more fundamental question is what contributes to the salience of a solution or what factors are responsible for the fact that some solutions are more readily associated with illness than are other solutions. A variety of studies have focused on such variables as CS intensity, novelty, palatability, and specific taste qualities.

### 2.1. Quantitative Considerations

There are a number of quantitative aspects of the stimulus that have been reported to affect taste aversion learning. For example, increased volume of solution drunk, longer duration of drinking time, and more intense concentrations of solution have all been reported to enhance the degree of the learned aversion (Barker, 1976).

Findings that the strength of an aversion is directly influenced by the volume of solution consumed may be subject to qualification. In most of these studies rats were given different amounts of solution and left until the total volume had been drunk (Bond and DiGiusto, 1975; Bond and Harland, 1975). Thus, the duration of exposure was varied in addition to the volume of solution. On the other hand, studies in which duration has been held constant while allowing amounts to vary (Kalat, 1976; Smith and Morris, 1963) also require some clarification. These studies report that the amount consumed produced no effect on the strength of the aversion. However, in both studies, the fixed duration was relatively long, ranging from 20 to 60 min, and therefore all amounts drunk may have been at asymptote and not sufficiently varied to produce differences in taste aversion learning.

The effect of CS intensity has been examined by comparing various concentrations of particular solutions. In general, it has been found that the strength of a taste aversion varies as a function of CS intensity—that is, greater intensities provide greater aversions (Dragoin, 1971). Nowlis (1974) has found that increases in either training or testing intensities result in greater learned aversions, although the amount of aversion is also affected by whether the testing and training intensities are the same. The effect of intensity presumably is due to the fact that greater intensities produce increased neural afferent activity. Alternatively, the effect of intensity on learned aversion might also be explained in terms of the discriminative value of the taste. More intense (concentrated) solutions produce better taste aversions, perhaps, because they are more novel. Rats will show a greater aversion to a less concentrated solution when they have been reared on a more concentrated solution (Kalat, 1974). In this case, the less concentrated solution was the most novel. This suggests that the absolute value of concentration may not be as important as its relation to the normal or familiar taste experience. Intensity in this situation, then, might be considered as a measurement of novelty. It seems likely that both the quantitative value of neuronal activity and the relational value of the stimulus solution concentration play some role in the formulation of a learned taste aversion.

## 2.2. Novelty

The novelty of a solution is clearly one of the most significant factors in determining whether or not an aversion is learned to the taste of that solution. When novel and familiar solutions are presented to rats, a much stronger aversion is learned to the novel solution (Ahlers and Best, 1971; Revusky and Bedarf, 1967). Similarly, allowing rats to become familiar with a solution before pairing it with the UCS causes a marked diminution in learning to avoid that solution (Vogel and Clody, 1972; Nachman and Ashe, 1974).

The effects of novelty are dramatic and it is certainly appropriate to ask why novel solutions are so much more effective than familiar solutions in producing learned taste aversions. We shall consider two major theoretical explanations which may be used to account for the novelty effect. Although the two are related and clearly similar, one stresses attention and arousal mechanisms and focuses more on the effects of the novel stimulus, while the other explanation, employing the concept of learned safety, focuses more on the effects of the familiar stimulus.

### 2.2.1. Learned Safety

The concept of learned safety proposed by Kalat and Rozin (1973) has been used to account for both the long-delay gradient in taste aversion learning and for the fact that aversions are learned better to novel than to familiar solutions. Kalat and Rozin hypothesized that when a rat ingests a nontoxic, novel substance, it gradually learns in the ensuing hours that the substance is safe. The longer the time period after ingestion, and the greater the number of such experiences, the more safety is learned. Thus, potentially either of two incompatible habits may be learned. If ingesting a solution is followed by nontoxic consequences, the animal learns the solution is safe; if it is followed by toxic consequences, the animal learns an aversion. Thus, aversions are learned less well to familiar solutions because, as the taste becomes more familiar with increased experience, the learning that the solution is safe is incompatible with learning that the solution is toxic.

The concept of learned safety has received a good deal of attention and is clearly consistent with a number of experimental findings, such as: (1) aversions are learned less well to familiar than to novel solutions (Revusky and Bedarf, 1967), (2) aversions are learned less well the longer the toxic consequence is delayed after drinking (Revusky, 1968), (3) rats show a greater hesitancy to ingest a nontoxic substance on first exposure (neophobia) than on subsequent exposures (Barnett, 1963), (4) one toxic trial produces greater aversion than a safe trial followed shortly by a toxic trial (Kalat and Rozin, 1973), and (5) the amount of intake in a second trial, following a single nontoxic trial, is a function of the delay time (hours) between trials (Nachman and Jones, 1974).

By focusing on the changes produced by the process of familiarization to a stimulus, the concept of learned safety has been successfully used to account for and predict a number of experimental results. However, it should be noted that learned safety does not provide an explanation and in fact does not deal directly with questions surrounding the special characteristics of aversion learning. Thus, for example, while learned safety can be used to predict that a taste aversion is learned less well to a familiar solution than to a novel solution, it does not help us to understand or account for the great potency of learning to avoid the novel solution. Similarly, while it can be used successfully to predict that a 2-h toxic delay will be less effective than a 15-min delay, it does not explain the great strength of the learning after the 15-min delay. In other words, while varying amounts of learned safety may be used to account for variations in amount of taste aversion learned, the absence of learned safety is not sufficient to explain the robustness of taste aversion learning.

Similarly, the concept of learned safety, by itself, does not offer a solution to the perplexing problem of how associations are formed over long delays. The difficulty of explaining how toxic consequences can be effective after a long delay is not reduced by saying that a nontoxic consequence is also effective after a long delay. The problem still remains that the central effects of gustatory input appear to persist and can be associated with consequences, whether toxic or nontoxic, which occur after long delays.

Finally, learned safety does not easily account for the fact that, among a group of novel solutions, aversions will be learned more readily to some of the solutions than to others. A possible *post hoc* explanation is that some of the novel solutions are more similar to the tastes which have already acquired learned safety.

### 2.2.2. Arousal, Attention, and Neophobia

The fact that aversions can be readily learned to novel taste stimuli may be a direct result of the neural effects of a novel taste. In all sensory modalities, a novel stimulus elicits an orienting reflex (Sokolov, 1958). In the case of visual or auditory stimuli, arousal is clearly seen behaviorally in the form of various bodily and head adjustments, and neurophysiologically as a desynchronization of the cortical EEG. When novel taste stimuli are presented, there are presumably similar or analogous manifestations of orientation or arousal but these have not been well-studied. Instead, an indication of a type of orienting response which is usually measured with taste stimuli is the neophobic response or the tendency to ingest less of a novel substance.

Rats, for example, when presented with a novel food or solution show a great hesitancy to ingest the novel substance. This initial neophobic response is a relatively short-lived phenomenon. While the first exposure to a novel taste may produce strong neophobia, a few additional exposures to the same substance usually results in intakes which are normal or near normal for that substance even if there are fairly long intervals of time such as days or weeks between successive exposures. Not all novel solutions produce equally strong neophobic responses. As an illustration, we have presented in Figure 2 examples of solutions which produce three different levels of neophobia.

The data shown in Figure 2 were obtained from an experiment in which rats were adapted to receiving water for 10 min a day. After 6 days, they continued on this schedule but every third day, different groups received instead a 10-min trial with either a 0.2% saccharin solution, 0.5% banana flavored solution, or 0.5% cherry flavored solution. The fruit flavored solutions were made with artificial flavorings (Schillings). The ratio of intake of the flavored solution to the intake of water on the previous day was calculated for each of six trials. As can be seen in Figure 2, saccharin elicited a very strong neophobic response while there was much less neophobia to the banana flavor and there was no evident neophobia to the cherry flavor. The neophobic response was greatly reduced by the second exposure to the solutions and apparently absent by the third exposure.

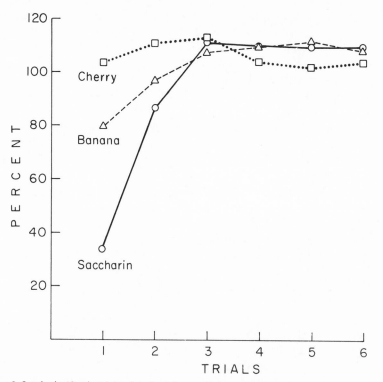

**Figure 2.** Intake in 10-min trials of each of three solutions, expressed as a percentage of water intake.

We have also found that different concentrations of solutions produce similar differences in levels of neophobia, and it is reasonable to consider that the differing neophobic responses to the saccharin, banana, and cherry flavored solutions may be more a reflection of the relative intensity of the taste of these solutions than to any qualitative dimension of these solutions. In any event, it appears that rats show differing levels of neophobia to different solutions and while we obviously have no direct measures of "attention" it seems logical to assume that a solution which evokes a strong neophobic response is a highly attention-getting solution and should therefore be a more effective solution in producing learned taste aversions.

To test this hypothesis, the degree of neophobic response produced by a solution was compared with the effectiveness of that solution in producing a learned taste aversion. Nine groups of rats were used. Each group was adapted to drinking water for 10 min a day for 6 days. On the next day each group received a different solution for 10 min and the intake was used to provide a measure of neophobia. A few minutes following the neophobia trial, half of each group was made mildly sick with 3.3 ml/kg of .15 M LiCl while the other half served as controls. (Mild sickness was used so that the degree of aversion would not be so strong as to mask any differences between groups.) All rats were tested the following day with the same solution they received in the neophobia trial. The nine fluids used were 0.2% saccharin, water, and the following seven solutions, each at a concentration of 0.5% artificial flavoring (Shillings): mint, lemon, anise, banana, vanilla, maple, and cherry.

Figure 3 shows the degree of neophobia found to each solution and the amount of taste aversion learned to that solution. The amount of neophobia was calculated as the ratio of flavored solution intake to the intake of water on the previous day and the learned aversion score was obtained by the ratio of intake of the experimental groups to control groups on the final test day.

As can be seen in Figure 3, the degree of neophobia shown to a solution is a good predictor of the relative amount of aversion learned to that solution. The rank-order correlation coefficient between the two rankings was .88. Let us consider two possible explanations of why there is a good relationship between neophobia and the amount of aversion learned to a solution. It may be that the neophobic response is a reflection of particular dimensions of a solution such as intensity, quality, or distinctiveness, and that these same dimensions are also involved in influencing the degree of learned taste aversion. Alternatively, if we conceptualize neophobia as the measure of the arousal or attention value of a solution, then the different levels of arousal or attention produced by solutions may account for differences in learning the taste aversion. To test these hypotheses, a second part of the experiment was continued with the

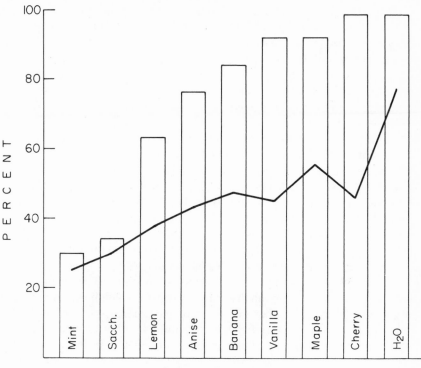

**Figure 3.** Neophobia measures (bar graph) and learned taste aversion measures (curve) for each of nine solutions.

control rats (which had not been given any previous aversion training). These rats were given repeated trials to familiarize them with their respective solutions. With increased familiarity, it was expected that there would be a decrease in any differences in arousal produced by the solutions. All rats were then given a single aversion training trial by injecting them with LiCl a few minutes after they drank their familiar solution. The test for aversion was conducted the following day. The results showed that the relative effectiveness of the nine familiar solutions in producing learned taste aversions was just about identical to their relative effectiveness when they were novel solutions. The rank-order correlation coefficient between the initial neophobia score and the relative effectiveness in producing learned taste aversion when the solutions were familiar was .91, thus indicating that the neophobia response was a good predictor of learned taste aversion to both novel and familiar solutions. Apparently, whatever qualities contribute to an initial neophobic response remain distinctive cues even after familiarization.

The implication of the term neophobia is clear, that there is an emotional or phobic reaction to a new taste. As Pfaffmann (1960) has pointed out in his discussion of the *Pleasures of Sensation*, tastes differ from visual or auditory stimuli in that they often have an hedonic or affective component in addition to their cue value. It may very well be that the affective states produced by taste stimuli involve specific neural structures such as components of the limbic system and that the special properties of taste aversion learning are a result of this neural involvement.

A number of studies have attempted to focus on limbic system involvement in neophobia and learned taste aversions (Kesner, Berman, Burton, and Hankins, 1975; Krane, Sinnamon, and Thomas, 1976; Nachman and Ashe, 1974; Rolls and Rolls, 1973a,b). In our laboratory, for example, we found that rats with amygdala lesions showed a decrease in neophobia to novel solutions as well as a deficit in ability to learn a taste aversion. Of additional interest was the fact that rats with amygdala lesions learned an aversion to novel solutions which was about the same as normal rats learning an aversion to familiar solutions. Also, amygdala-lesioned rats showed less discrimination of which solutions to avoid. Our conclusion was that it was not so much a memory function which was impaired by amygdala damage but rather that the rats had a perceptual deficit in their ability to recognize the significance of stimuli, whether rewarding or punishing and whether learned or unlearned. A similar conclusion was reached recently regarding the role of the hippocampus in neophobia and learned taste aversions (Krane *et al.*, 1976).

The data from lesion experiments contribute to the possibility that learned taste aversions may involve limbic system functioning and that the perceptual response to the taste input plays a major role in affecting the strength of learned taste aversions. While we have no evidence, it is certainly interesting to conjecture that the limbic system involvement in learned taste aversions may be responsible for the fact that taste aversions may be learned with long temporal delays between the CS and the UCS.

## 3. Species Differences

For any organism to survive, it must have adaptive mechanisms to avoid toxicosis. In the case of some species, the selection of foods is limited by various environmental constraints as well as by innate factors and the organism ingests only a very restricted number of different foods. Some examples of such food specialists include the koala bear, the monarch butterfly, and the giant panda. In contrast, generalists or omnivores such as the Norway rat select food from an enormous variety of acceptable foods and obviously run a greater risk of being poisoned. Recently, Rozin

(1976) has discussed at length the omnivorous character of the rat and has related this feeding behavior to the rat's ability to learn to avoid poisonous foods. For instance, being omnivorous entails a certain danger or increased risk of ingesting toxic substances. The rat handles this by exploring new items but also procedes cautiously (neophobia), eating only a small amount of food at a time. Additionally, even with safe foods, rats tend to eat only one food item at a time and generally wait a short period between successive eatings. Obviously, rats are very good at learning taste aversions. It would be of interest to know whether the omnivorous food selection of rats is related to their ability to learn food aversions and whether, in fact, there is an overall difference between specialists and generalists in their ability to learn food aversions.

Several mechanisms exist which allow generalists to avoid being poisoned. There are, of course, innate rejection mechanisms such as the rejection of toxic materials which taste bitter. In addition, there are other physiologically adaptive responses such as vomiting or alterations in the digestion and processing of toxic materials. And, finally, there are learned taste aversions so that a toxic experience which has occurred will be less likely to be repeated.

So far in our discussion of stimulus characteristics in food aversion learning, we have been dealing exclusively with studies using rats. However, learned aversion to food has been demonstrated in a wide variety of species both in naturalistic settings and in laboratory experiments.

In most of the studies of species other than rats, the specificity of the taste cue has not been the primary issue investigated. Rather, the studies have been demonstrations that food aversions can be established in those species using as many cues as possible. Therefore, in many of the studies, foods differed in taste, odor, texture, and visual characteristics, and it has not been possible to delineate which specific cues were involved in the food aversion learning.

For many species, it appears that aversions may be formed based on the association of the taste of a distinctive food with subsequent illness. However, other cues, such as olfactory or visual cues, may be secondarily associated with the taste and the animal may reject the substance without tasting it again on subsequent trials. For example, after a single pairing of ingestion of worms with LiCl injection, garter snakes continue to seize the worms but take longer to swallow them or often will drop the worms as soon as they strike. With additional trials, the snakes reject the prey without any attack and in some cases without even a tongue flick (Burghardt, Wilcoxon, and Czaplicki, 1973).

The use of aversion conditioning to control coyote predation also demonstrates that cues other than taste can be used to mediate the avoidance of food (Gustavson, Garcia, Hankins, and Rusiniak, 1974). After one or two trials in which a coyote is poisoned followed ingestion of a particular flesh (rabbit or sheep) the coyote will not only learn to avoid ingestion of that flesh, but the attack behavior will also be suppressed. Gustavson *et al.* (1974) suggest that this is due to the association of auditory, olfactory, and visual cues with the distinctive flavor.

Brower (1969) has described a similar pattern of avoidance in blue jays which have eaten a poisonous butterfly. He suggests that there are three physiological levels at which the bird can reject the poisonous butterfly. The first and most basic level is the automatic emetic effect brought about by ingestion of the poison. This is a relatively inefficient form of rejection since the bird is made sick and also loses food that was in its crop before eating the poison. Once this initial noxious rejection has been experienced the bird can learn to avoid the butterfly simply by tasting it. This second level of rejection is also somewhat inefficient since the bird must first catch the butterfly. The third level of rejection is the most efficient. This level is the association of the visual characteristics of the food with its unpalatable flavor. Now the bird need not get sick or catch the butterfly to avoid it.

In the species mentioned so far there is no clear evidence to determine whether or not taste must be the primary mediating stimulus. In some species, taste is a poorly developed sense and other senses are undoubtedly more relevant for food identification and selection. The particular sense that is used may also depend on the specific food being selected, as in the case of the terrestrial mollusks in which learned aversions are mediated by both gustatory and olfactory cues for one food (mushroom), while for another food (cucumber), the aversion is mediated only by olfactory input (Galperin, 1975).

A number of avians have been of particular interest for the study of food aversions formed to nongustatory cues, since many avians have a highly developed visual system relative to their gustatory system and appear to select food using visual cues. Quails (Czaplicki, Borreback, and Wilcoxon, 1976) and chickens (Capretta and Moore, 1970) are examples of birds showing very strong learned aversions solely on the basis of the color of the food. In the studies of learned aversions to visual cues, it has been found that quail are capable of long-delay learning with delays of up to 2 h (Wilcoxon, 1977). Also, the quail studies have demonstrated stimulus generalization and stimulus intensity effects in vision comparable to results seen in the taste aversion paradigm using rats (Czaplicki *et al.*, 1976).

The level of development of the visual system may influence the degree to which an animal uses that system in food selection, but the ability to form poison-based aversions to visual cues is not solely dependent upon a highly developed visual system. Braveman (1974) has shown that guinea pigs, which have relatively poor visual acuity, comparable to rats, can use both taste and visual cues in forming food aversions. Guinea pigs, unlike rats, and more like some of the avians, use visual cues as well as taste cues in their selection of food. Thus, it may be that the relevant or salient cues which become associated with illness are those cues which the animal uses in its normal feeding behavior.

Unfortunately, we do not yet have an abundance of comparative data on learned food aversions, particularly with regard to the stimulus characteristics of cues used by various species. However, the limited comparative data which does exist may have important implications for explanations which have been proposed to account for long delay taste aversion learning in rats. Of particular significance are the data that birds are capable of effective long-delay food aversion learning using visual cues.

In our discussion of long-delay learning in rats using taste cues, we examined the hypothesis that stimulus conditions such as aftertastes or lack of interference from other tastes may play a critical role in mediating the long-delay learning. However, it is clear that a comparable explanation is not appropriate to explain long-delay learning in birds using visual cues, since there is no likelihood of a visual after-sensation nor is there any absence of interfering visual stimuli between the CS and UCS.

Similarly, in attempting to account for taste-mediated long-delay learning in rats, it was proposed that there may be special neural properties of the gustatory system such as an hypothesized slow decay of the neural representation of gustatory input. Alternatively, it was proposed that involvement of specific pathways, such as the convergence of gustatory and visceral inputs to the solitary nucleus in the medulla, may somehow account for the robustness of taste aversion learning in rats. Such special hypotheses regarding neural mechanisms of the gustatory system would, of course, not explain how birds can use visual cues in mediating long-delay aversive conditioning. There is, of course, no evidence of any special anatomical convergence of visual and visceral input in the bird, nor is there any reason to believe that visual input "decays" more slowly in the bird.

Thus, the special taste mechanisms proposed to account for the success of long-delay learning in rats are unlikely to be applicable to the use of visual cues by birds. We are therefore left with postulating that multiple sets of specialized mechanisms exist, or stated another way, that differing neural mechanisms have evolved which allow organisms to adapt to their specific feeding requirements. It is clear that for rats, taste (and smell) play a major role in the selection and ingestion of foods, whereas for birds, visual cues play the predominant role. The rat recognizes its food by smelling and tasting it while the bird recognizes it by sight, and each may be specifically attuned to what is novel or different in its feeding environment. Each organism undoubtedly has developed specialized neural systems which correspond to these functional abilities and although the neural differences between species may, in part, be at the sensory level, they may also exist as the neural information is further processed and stored, and may be responsible for the ability to form specialized learned aversions.

## 4. References

Ahlers, R. H., and Best, P. J. Novelty vs. temporal contiguity in learned taste aversions. *Psychonomic Science*, 1971, *25*, 34–36.

Barker, L. M. CS duration, amount, and concentration effects in conditioning taste aversions. *Learning and Motivation*, 1976, *7*, 265–273.

Barnett, S. A. *The rat: A study in behavior*. Chicago: Aldine Press, 1963.

Barnett, S. A., Cowan, P. E., Radford, G. G., and Prakash, I. Peripheral anosmia and the discrimination of poisoned food by *Rattus rattus* L. *Behavioral Biology*, 1975, *13*, 183–190.

Best, P. J., Best, M. R., and Mickley, G. A. Conditioned aversion to distinct environmental stimuli resulting from gastrointestinal distress. *Journal of Comparative and Physiological Psychology*, 1973, *85*, 250–257.

Bond, N., and DiGiusto, E. Amount of solution drunk is a factor in the establishment of taste aversion. *Animal Learning and Behavior*, 1975, *3*, 81–84.

Bond, N., and Harland, W. Effect of amount of solution drunk on taste-aversion learning. *Bulletin of the Psychonomic Society*, 1975, *5*, 219–220.

Bradley, R. M., and Mistretta, C. M. Intravascular taste in rats as demonstrated by conditioned aversion to sodium saccharin. *Journal of Comparative and Physiological Psychology*, 1971, *75*, 186–189.

Braveman, N. S. Poison-based avoidance learning with flavored or colored water in guinea pigs. *Learning and Motivation*, 1974, *5*, 182–194.

Brower, T. P. Ecological chemistry. *Scientific American*, 1969, *220*, 22–29.

Burešová, O., and Bureš, J. Cortical and subcortical components of the conditioned saccharin aversion. *Physiology and Behavior*, 1973, *11*, 435–439.

Burghardt, G. M., Wilcoxon, H. C., and Czaplicki, J. A. Conditioning in garter snakes: Aversion to palatable prey induced by delayed illness. *Animal Learning and Behavior*, 1973, *1*, 317–320.

Capretta, P. J. An experimental modification of food preferences in chickens. *Journal of Comparative and Physiological Psychology*, 1961, *54*, 238–242.

Capretta, P. J., and Moore, M. J. Appropriateness of reinforcement to cue in the conditioning of food aversions in chickens *(Gallus gallus)*. *Journal of Comparative and Physiological Psychology*, 1970, *72*, 85–89.

Chitty, D. (Ed.). *Control of rats and mice* (Vols. 1 and 2). Oxford: Clarendon Press, 1954.

Czaplicki, J. A., Borreback, D. E., and Wilcoxon, H. C. Stimulus generalization of an illness-induced aversion to different intensities of colored water in Japanese quail. *Animal Learning and Behavior*, 1976, *4*, 45–48.

Domjan, M. Role of ingestion in odor-toxicosis learning in the rat. *Journal of Comparative and Physiological Psychology*, 1973, *84*, 507–521.

Domjan, M., and Wilson, N. E. Specificity of cue to consequence in aversion learning in the rat. *Psychonomic Science*, 1972a, *26*, 143–145.

Domjan, M., and Wilson, N. E. Contribution of ingestive behaviors to taste-aversion learning in the rat. *Journal of Comparative and Physiological Psychology*, 1972b, *80*, 403–412.

Dragoin, W. B. Conditioning and extinction of taste aversions with variations in intensity of the CS and US in two strains of rats. *Psychonomic Science*, 1971, *22*, 303–304.

Etscorn, F., and Stephens, R. Establishment of conditioned taste aversions with a 24-hour CS–US interval. *Physiological Psychology*, 1973, *1*, 251–253.

Galperin, A. Rapid food-aversion learning by a terrestrial mollusk. *Science*, 1975, *189*, 567–570.

Garcia, J., and Ervin, F. R. Gustatory–visceral and telereceptor–cutaneous conditioning: Adaptation in internal and external milieus. *Communications in Behavioral Biology*, 1968, *1*, 389–415.

Garcia, J., and Koelling, R. A. Relation of cue to consequence in avoidance learning. *Psychonomic Science*, 1966, 4, 123–124.

Garcia, J., and Koelling, R. A. A comparison of aversions induced by X-rays, toxins, and drugs in the rat. *Radiation Research Supplement*, 1967, 7, 439–450.

Garcia, J., Kimeldorf, D. J., and Hunt, E. L. Conditioned responses to manipulative procedures resulting from exposure to gamma radiation. *Radiation Research*, 1956, 5, 79–87.

Garcia, J., Kimeldorf, D. J., and Koelling, R. A. Conditioned aversion to saccharin resulting from exposure to gamma radiation. *Science*, 1955, 122, 157–158.

Garcia, J., McGowan, B. K., Ervin, F. R., and Koelling, R. A. Cues: Their relative effectiveness as a function of the reinforcer. *Science*, 1968, 160, 794–795.

Geldard, F. A. *The human senses*, 2nd Edition. New York: John Wiley and Sons, Inc., 1972.

Green, K. F., Holmstrom, L. S., and Wollman, M. A. Relation of cue to consequence in rats: Effect of recuperation from illness. *Behavioral Biology*, 1974, 10, 491–503.

Gustavson, C. R., Garcia, J., Hankins, W. G., and Rusiniak, K. W. Coyote predation: Control by aversive conditioning. *Science*, 1974, 184, 581–583.

Hankins, W. G., Garcia, J., and Rusiniak, K. W. Dissociation of odor and taste in bait shyness. *Behavioral Biology*, 1973, 8, 407–419.

Hargrave, G. E., and Bolles, R. C. Rat's aversion to flavors following induced illness. *Psychonomic Science*, 1971, 23, 91–92.

Kalat, J. W. Taste salience depends on novelty, not concentration, in taste-aversion learning in the rat. *Journal of Comparative and Physiological Psychology*, 1974, 86, 47–50.

Kalat, J. W. Should taste-aversion learning experiments control duration or volume of drinking on the training day? *Animal Learning and Behavior*, 1976, 4, 96–98.

Kalat, J. W. Status of "learned safety" or "learned noncorrelation" as a mechanism in taste aversion learning. In L. M. Barker, M. R. Best, and M. Domjan (Eds.), *Learning mechanisms in food selection*, Waco, Texas: Baylor University Press, 1977.

Kalat, J. W., and Rozin, P. "Salience": A factor which can override temporal contiguity in taste-aversion learning. *Journal of Comparative and Physiological Psychology*, 1970, 71, 192–197.

Kalat, J. W., and Rozin, P. Role of interference in taste-aversion learning. *Journal of Comparative and Physiological Psychology*, 1971, 77, 53–58.

Kalat, J. W., and Rozin, P. "Learned safety" as a mechanism in long-delay taste-aversion learning in rats. *Journal of Comparative and Physiological Psychology*, 1973, 83, 198–207.

Kesner, R. P., Berman, R. F., Burton, B., and Hankins, W. G. Effects of electrical stimulation of amygdala upon neophobia and taste aversion. *Behavioral Biology*, 1975, 13, 349–358.

Krane, R. V., Sinnamon, H. M., and Thomas, G. J. Conditioned taste aversions and neophobia in rats with hippocampal lesions. *Journal of Comparative and Physiological Psychology*, 1976, 90, 680–693.

Larue, C. Comparison des effets de l'anosmie périphérique et de la bulbectomie sur la séquence alimentaire du rat. *Journal de Physiologie (Paris)*, 1975, 70, 299–306.

Lorden, J. F., Kenfield, M., and Braun, J. J. Response suppression to odors paired with toxicosis. *Learning and Motivation*, 1970, 1, 391–400.

Lovett, D., Goodchild, P., and Booth, D. A. Depression of intake of nutrient by association of its odor with effects of insulin. *Psychonomic Science*, 1968, 11, 27–28.

Martin, J. C., and Ellinwood, E. H., Jr. Conditioned aversion in spatial paradigms following methamphetamine injections. *Psychopharmacologia*, 1974, 36, 323–335.

Mitchell, D., Kirschbaum, E. H., and Perry, R. L. Effects of neophobia and habituation on the poison-induced avoidance of exteroceptive stimuli in the rat. *Journal of Experimental Psychology: Animal Behavior Processes*, 1975, 1, 47–55.

Nachman, M. Taste Preferences for sodium salts by adrenalectomized rats. *Journal of Comparative and Physiological Psychology*, 1962, *55*, 1124–1129.

Nachman, M. Learned aversion to the taste of lithium chloride and generalization to other salts. *Journal of Comparative and Physiological Psychology*, 1963, *56*, 343–349.

Nachman, M. Learned taste and temperature aversions due to lithium chloride sickness after temporal delays. *Journal of Comparative and Physiological Psychology*, 1970, *73*. 22–30.

Nachman, M., and Ashe, J. H. Effects of basolateral amygdala lesions on neophobia, learned taste aversions, and sodium appetite in rats. *Journal of Comparative and Physiological Psychology*, 1974, *87*, 622–643.

Nachman, M., and Jones, D. R. Learned taste aversions over long delays in rats: The role of learned safety. *Journal of Comparative and Physiological Psychology*, 1974, *86*, 949–956.

Nachman, M., Rauschenberger, J., and Ashe, J. H. Studies of learned aversions using nongustatory stimuli. In L. M. Barker, M. R. Best, and M. Domjan (Eds.), *Learning mechanisms in food selection*, Waco, Texas: Baylor University Press, 1977.

Nowlis, G. H. Conditioned stimulus intensity and acquired alimentary aversions in the rat. *Journal of Comparative and Physiological Psychology*, 1974, *86*, 1173–1184.

Overall, J. E., Brown, W. L., and Logie, L. C. The shuttlebox behavior of albino rats during prolonged exposure to moderate level radiation. *Nature*, 1960, *185*, 665–666.

Pain, J. F., and Booth, D. A. Toxiphobia for odors. *Psychonomic Science*, 1968, *10*, 363–364.

Pfaffmann, C. The pleasures of sensation. *Psychological Review*, 1960, *67*, 253–268.

Revusky, S. H. Aversion to sucrose produced by contingent X-irradiation: Temporal and dosage parameters. *Journal of Comparative and Physiological Psychology*, 1968, *65*, 17–22.

Revusky, S. H. The role of interference in association over a delay. In W. K. Honig and H. James (Eds.), *Animal memory*. New York: Academic Press, 1971, pp. 155–213.

Revusky, S. H., and Bedarf, E. W. Association of illness with ingestion of novel foods. *Science*, 1967, *155*, 219–220.

Revusky, S., and Garcia, J. Learned associations over long delays. In G. H. Bower and J. T. Spence (Eds.), *Psychology of learning and motivation: Advances in research and theory*, Vol. IV, New York: Academic Press, 1970, pp. 1–84.

Revusky, S., and Parker, L. A. Aversions to unflavored water and cup drinking produced by delayed sickness. *Journal of Experimental Psychology: Animal Behavior Processes*, 1976, *2*, 342–353.

Rolls, B. J., and Rolls, E. T. Effects of lesions in the basolateral amygdala on fluid intake in the rat. *Journal of Comparative and Physiological Psychology*, 1973a, *83*, 240–247.

Rolls, E. T., and Rolls, B. J. Altered food preferences after lesions in the basolateral region of the amygdala in the rat. *Journal of Comparative and Physiological Psychology*, 1973b, *83*, 248–259.

Rozin, P. Central or peripheral mediation of learning with long CS–US intervals in the feeding system. *Journal of Comparative and Physiological Psychology*, 1969, *67*, 421–429.

Rozin, P. The selection of food by rats, humans, and other animals. In J. S. Rosenblatt, R. A. Hinde, E. Shaw, and C. Beer (Eds.), *Advances in the study of behavior*, Vol. 6, New York: Academic Press, 1976.

Rozin, P., and Kalat, J. W. Specific hungers and poison avoidance as adaptive specializations of learning. *Psychological Review*, 1971, *78*, 459–486.

Seligman, M. E. P. On the generality of the laws of learning. *Psychological Review*, 1970, *77*, 400–418.

Smith, D. F., and Balagura, S. Role of oropharyngeal factors in LiCl aversion. *Journal of Comparative and Physiological Psychology*, 1969, *69*, 308–310.

Smith, J. C., and Morris, D. D. The use of X rays as the unconditioned stimulus in five-hundred-day-old rats. *Journal of Comparative and Physiological Psychology*, 1963, *56*, 746–747.

Smith, J. C., and Roll, D. L. Trace conditioning with X-rays as an aversive stimulus. *Psychonomic Science*, 1967, *9*, 11–12.

Sokolov, E. N. *Perception and the conditioned reflex*. Moscow, USSR: Publishing House Moscow University, 1958.

Somjen, G. *Sensory coding in the mammalian nervous system*. New York: Appleton-Century-Crofts, 1972.

Supak, T. D., Macrides, F., and Chorover, S. L. The bait-shyness effect extended to olfactory discrimination. *Communications in Behavioral Biology*, 1971, *5*, 321–324.

Tapper, D. N., and Halpern, B. P. Taste stimuli: A behavioral categorization, *Science*, 1968, *161*, 708–710.

Taukulis, H. K. Odor aversions produced over long CS–US delays. *Behavioral Biology*, 1974, *10*, 505–510.

Thompson, R. F. The search for the engram. *American Psychologist*, 1976, *31*, 209–227.

Thorndike, E. L. *Fundamentals of learning*. New York Teachers College Bureau Publications, N. Y., 1932.

Torvik, A. Afferent connections to the sensory trigeminal nuclei, the nucleus of the solitary tract and adjacent structures: An experimental study in the rat. *Journal of Comparative Neurology*, 1956, *106*, 51–142.

Vogel, J. R., and Clody, D. E. Habituation and conditioned food aversion. *Psychonomic Science*, 1972, *28*, 275–276.

Wilcoxon, H. C. Long delay learning of ingestive aversions in quail. In L. M. Barker, M. R. Best, and M. Domjan (Eds.), *Learning mechanisms in food selection*, Waco, Texas: Baylor University Press, 1977.

Wilcoxon, H. C., Dragoin, W. B., and Kral, P. A. Illness-induced aversions in rats and quail: Relative salience of visual and gustatory cues. *Science*, 1971, *171*, 826–828.

# Gustatory Avoidance Conditioning by Drugs of Abuse

4

## Relationships to General Issues in Research on Drug Dependence

**Howard Cappell and A. E. LeBlanc**

The main reason that psychologists are interested in gustatory conditioning is because the phenomenon appears crucial to a comprehensive account of how organisms learn (Rozin and Kalat, 1971; Seligman, 1970). This interest, and examples of the contribution it has yielded, are amply evident elsewhere in this volume. One subarea in this general field has been circumscribed by a concern with psychoactive drugs and how they affect and control behavior. Although a grasp of conditioned gustatory aversion as an instance of complex adaptive behavior is necessary for this enterprise, what is paramount is a particular focus on a class of unconditioned stimuli, psychoactive drugs, and the properties that govern their pharmacological effectiveness as agents of conditioning. Consequently, we defer happily to our colleagues on the questions of learning as such in order to concentrate on more parochial matters.

**Howard Cappell and A. E. LeBlanc** • Addiction Research Foundation, Toronto, Ontario, Canada.

## 1. Some General Issues

### 1.1. Effective Drugs

Almost without exception, psychoactive drugs that man uses for both medical and nonmedical reasons have the interesting property that they also induce gustatory aversions in rats. The list is long and includes compounds representing the major drug classes: opiate analgesics, CNS stimulants, major and minor tranquilizers, barbiturates, nonbarbiturate hypnotics, and CNS depressants (Vogel, unpub.). Indeed, it is unusual to discover that a drug is ineffective in this conditioning paradigm; the one interesting partial exception is cocaine, of which more will be said later.

### 1.2. Toxicity and Effectiveness

In order to address many of the important behavioral issues related to gustatory conditioning, experimenters have chosen to use compounds selected intentionally for their presumed capacity to produce "illness" or "malaise" in rodents. Thus, massive doses of drugs that are emetics (in organisms capable of emesis), such as lithium chloride or apomorphine, have typically served as the UCS of choice. Where psychoactive drugs are concerned, the demonstration of conditioned aversion at toxic doses would be relatively uninteresting knowledge; high enough doses of any drug can cause what might be described as general malaise. Yet if general toxicity is to be eliminated as an explanation in particular cases, there is a catch—how is toxicity to be defined? In one sense, a dose of a drug that produces no more than a measurable effect might be described as toxic to the extent that any chemically induced disturbance of homeostasis represents a toxic state. There are a few tentative ways around this problem, but in the final analysis, it may be impossible to specify a criterion of nontoxicity that would be accorded universal assent.

One strategy (Cappell and LeBlanc, 1973) requires the demonstration that unit doses of a drug that are self-administered by rats are also capable of inducing conditioned avoidance of a flavor. Figure 1 illustrates the acquisition of avoidance when saccharin was paired with injections of isotonic saline or one of 3 doses of $d$-amphetamine. A conditioning trial* consisted of 10 min of exposure to a 0.1% solution of sodium saccharin followed in 5 min by the appropriate intraperitoneal (i.p.) injection. The

---

* With minor variations, all of the data collected in our laboratory involved the conditioning procedure described here.

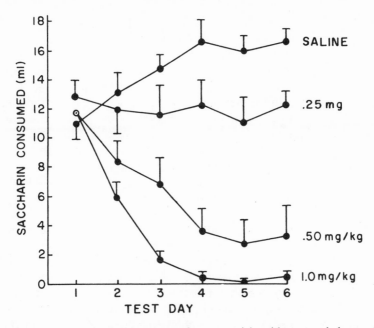

**Figure 1.** Acquisition of conditioned aversion over trials with repeated doses of amphetamine. From Cappell and LeBlanc (1973), by permission.

animals had been previously adapted to a schedule of restricted fluid access, and 2 days of comparably limited drinking intervened between conditioning trials. The results were straightforward. Avoidance of saccharin was evident with a dose as low as .25 mg/kg, and a reliable dose–response relationship was obtained. What is important is that each of the doses was well within the range of unit doses that rats will repeatedly self-administer (Pickens and Harris, 1968), albeit by the intravenous (i.v.) route. Of course, the mere fact of self-administration does not rule out the possibility that a dose of a drug produces toxicity; indeed, it is not uncommon for animals to self-administer drugs to the point of grave deleterious consequences (Deneau, Yanagita, and Seevers, 1969). Nonetheless, doses of *d*-amphetamine up to 1.0 mg/kg can certainly be described as low, and they clearly do not precipitate obvious acute toxicity during a single administration. Moreover, the lower doses used in this study are barely at the threshold required to produce detectable behavioral effects, even in sensitive tests (Maickel, Cox, Miller, Segal, and Russell, 1969).

A second approach to the issue of general toxicity was prompted by its suggestion as an alternative to a more specific pharmacological mechanism underlying some of the behavioral actions of drugs. For example, Nachman, Lester, and LeMagnen (1970) observed that two biochemical agents were capable of depressing alcohol intake in rats; because comparable doses of these agents induced conditioned avoidance of flavors, they proposed that the reduction in alcohol consumption reflected not a specific pharmacological action but general noxiousness that was conditioned to the taste of alcohol. In a somewhat different context, Elsmore and Fletcher (1972) attempted to account for a behaviorally disruptive effect of tetrahydrocannabinol in much the same way. Despite differences in procedural detail, what is common to both papers is the assertion that the sheer demonstration of conditioned gustatory aversion constitutes a *criterion* of nonspecific toxicity. We, with others (e.g., Berger, 1972), would prefer to argue that the phenomenon can occur *despite the absence* of the same order of toxicity.

Although the reasoning is not flawless, perhaps it is arguable that if a particular dose of a drug that is capable of conditioning a flavor aversion can also facilitate behavior, including appetitive behavior, the persuasiveness of the general toxicity claim is mitigated. Just such an argument, the support for which is illustrated in Figure 2, was advanced by Cappell, LeBlanc, and Endrenyi (1973). Dose–response functions were determined for doses of morphine, chlordiazepoxide, and ethanol that are frequently used in behavioral experiments. Significant conditioning was observed when the dose of morphine was 3.0 mg/kg or greater, when the dose of chlordiazepoxide was 6.0 mg/kg or greater, and only when the dose of ethanol was as high as 1200 mg/kg. The question is, do comparable doses inevitably have disruptive effects on behavior that might be caused by nonspecific toxicity? No. Alcohol at 1200 mg/kg has frequently been shown to facilitate food-directed behavior previously suppressed by punishment (Cappell and Herman, 1972). Similarly, the benzodiazepines, of which chlordiazepoxide is one, generally stimulate food intake (Bainbridge, 1970; Margules and Stein, 1967) and at a subcutaneous dose as high as 30 mg/kg, chlordiazepoxide greatly enhanced rats' intake of a saline solution (Falk and Burnidge, 1970). Finally, doses of morphine that produced conditioned aversion have been shown to facilitate, as well as disturb, food-reinforced behavior (Barry and Milier, 1965; Thompson, Trombley, Lake, and Lott, 1970).

To reiterate, neither counterargument can entirely demolish the assertion that conditioned aversion is in some or even all cases a reflection of toxicity, sickness, malaise, or whatever. Yet the available data are at least consistent with a rejection of the claim that these aversions, especially where low doses are involved, reflect *nothing but* toxicity. In short, it does not appear easy to trivialize the phenomenon as due to the application of poisonous dose levels.

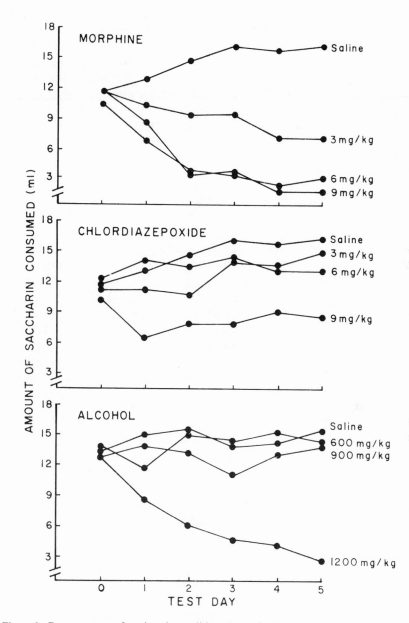

**Figure 2.** Dose–response functions in conditioned aversion by morphine, chlordiazepoxide, and alcohol. From Cappell, LeBlanc, and Endrenyi (1973), by permission.

## 1.3. Paradox or Not?

The occurrence of intravenous self-administration of drugs was well-established in animals before anyone thought to determine whether the same drugs were capable of inducing gustatory aversions. When the ease of establishing an aversion became clear, an apparent paradox was in the making (Cappell and LeBlanc, 1973). How could a drug like amphetamine, so powerful a positive reinforcer in the appropriate circumstances, also precipitate profound avoidance of a flavor after only two or three conditioning trials? Several attempts have been made to account for this seeming anomaly.

### 1.3.1. The Same Stimulus Events Need Not Have Invariable Behavioral Consequences

An event that can act as a positive reinforcer need not display that property in all possible circumstances; the same is true of events that are typically negative reinforcers. Reinforcement history, reinforcement schedule, stimulus intensity and quality, and a variety of current environmental and organismic variables may alter the status of an event as a reinforcer. For these reasons, Cappell and LeBlanc (1973) argued that the paradox may be little more than superficial. A compelling illustration in this context is McKearney's (1968) finding that an electric shock capable of eliciting avoidance behavior in monkeys would, with appropriate manipulation, *maintain* behavior that produced a contingent shock of identical intensity. Is it paradoxical that an electric shock reinforces both positively and negatively?

A somewhat different resolution of the apparent paradox derives from the proposition by Seligman (1970) that the associations that organisms make between responses and their consequences operate under biological constraints. Hence, rats may be "prepared" to develop particular forms of associations when a response involving the gustatory system is paired with an unconditioned drug effect but not when the same drug effect is paired with a response subserved by a quite different biological apparatus (lever-pressing, for example). A most pertinent illustration of this general proposition is readily available (Martin and Ellinwood, 1973). Methamphetamine in an amount of 3 mg/kg was sufficient to condition avoidance of a saccharin solution. The same dose, however, failed when an attempt was made to condition avoidance of a distinctive spatial location.

It should be emphasized here that the argument is not that responses governed by nongustatory mechanisms are not associable with drug-induced events at all, because if this were the case, the literature on the self-administration of drugs in animals could clearly not exist. Rather, the more modest assertion is that a particular form of association, namely one that favors avoidance of a UCS as opposed to approach, is enhanced to the extent that a novel gustatory CS is paired with a drug stimulus. Perhaps this reflects a "wired-in" predisposition of a species descended from scavengers. Of course there are exceptions to this generalization. For example, rats can be made to prefer distinctively flavored solutions that contain agents also capable of inducing gustatory avoidance (Stolerman and Kumar, 1970); but for the most part, in animals that have had no special pretreatment, in particular no prior experience with the UCS or the CS, the gustatory conditioning model seems much better suited to illustrating avoidance of, rather than approach to, drug-induced states. Similarly, and again there are exceptions, it appears that when a nongustatory system is involved as the controlling mechanism, the typically employed operant paradigms are more likely to yield evidence of approach or indifference rather than avoidance. The exceptions are that psychoactive drugs, including at least one that is a positive reinforcer, have been effective in generating conditioned suppression (Cameron and Appel, 1972; Whitney and Trost, 1970) and negative reinforcement (Hoffmeister and Wuttke, 1973).

In summary, there seems to be a case that there are constraints on the nature of the associability of certain conditioned stimuli with the unconditioned stimuli represented by drug effects. This is not an all-or-none argument about associability *per se*, but simply one that asserts that certain types of conditioned stimuli are *more likely* to provide evidence that drug effects are "aversive," whereas others are *more likely* to involve an association that favors approach. Obviously, this generalization is little more than a paraphrase of the available facts; why the facts should be so is a matter for speculation, of which some follows.

### 1.3.2. More of the Same with a Dash of Speculative Pharmacology

In the previous section the primary emphasis was on how the choice of the response system may bias a UCS toward acting like a positive reinforcer on the one hand or an aversive agent on the other. An elaborated approach to the same data adds another layer of speculation, this time involving an assumption about the affective consequences of the physical actions of some of the agents germane to this discussion. Consider a drug like amphetamine: As a UCS it represents a diverse constellation of physiological events. The question here is whether the same subset of these events is the UCS independent of the particular response system with which its presentation is experimentally correlated. Suppose, for the sake of argument, that amphetamine has effects $a$, $b$, $c$, and $x$, $y$, $z$; with some further indulgence, suppose that $a$, $b$, and $c$ are "intrinsically positive" events, and $x,y$, and $z$ are intrinsically "negative." Is it possible that even with the simultaneous occurrence of the entire set of events, rats are evolved to more probably associate $x$, $y$, and $z$ with a novel gustatory stimulus, and $a$, $b$, and $c$ with a response system not involving taste? While the suggestion is not outrageous, extracted as it is *ad hoc* to suit the preponderance of existing data, there is no direct empirical support for its credibility. However, there is some evidence that bears indirectly on such a line of reasoning. Pretreatment with alpha-methyltyrosine (AMT) has been shown to interfere with the self-administration of both morphine and amphetamine in rats (Davis and Smith, 1973a,b). At the same time, AMT failed to block the conditioning of gustatory aversion by amphetamine (Carey, 1973) or morphine (Coussens, Crowder, and Davis, 1973); indeed, in the latter study, AMT appeared if anything to enhance an aversion somewhat. On the basis of such findings (although, it should be admitted, Goudie, Thornton, and Wheatley [1975] have generated a positive result where Carey failed), Coussens *et al.* (1973) proposed that morphine and amphetamine share a "duality of opposing actions," namely, both positively reinforcing and punishing properties. The aversive properties of morphine, they reasoned, have been obscured in most studies by virtue of the particular circumstances that prevailed. Only when the reinforcing action is disabled (such as with AMT), or if an appropriate test is used, does the aversive component of morphine's action emerge. Presumably, an analogous argument could be made where amphetamine is concerned.

New even if this speculation is accepted, none of it tells us why there should be a selective association between a gustatory CS and the aversive dimension of a drug's total effect. What it does do, and tenuously at that, is to advance a case for the independent existence of positive and negative components in the action of the same psychoactive drug.

### 1.3.3. The Importance of Choice

Drug self-administration and gustatory conditioning differ entirely in the extent to which the presentation of the UCS is elective. This is a difference that has been emphasized by Vogel (unpub.) in attempting to resolve the "paradox" of conditioned aversion by drugs. The typical self-administration procedure permits an animal to exercise considerable control over the frequency and temporal distribution of drug injections. In contrast, the subject can do nothing to alter the inevitable administration of the drug when gustatory conditioning is attempted. Consequently, Vogel conjectured that a drug may have rewarding properties to the extent that its administration is under control, and aversive properties to the extent that control is precluded. Support for such an hypothesis derived from work on the phenomenon of electrical self-stimulation of the brain (Steiner, Beer, and Shaffer, 1969). Steiner *et al.* showed that rats would work to escape a pattern of brain stimulation that had previously been shown to be positively reinforcing; it was necessary only to impose the same pattern of stimulation independent of the animals' behavior to transform a reinforcer from positive to negative.

This speculation is certainly intriguing. Yet there is no overlooking that the discrepancy in electiveness is only one of many differences that distinguish typical studies of self-administration from those of gustatory aversion. Of course, this caveat applies to any single-factor resolution of the "paradox."

### 1.3.4. Route of Administration

One of the most salient differences in the usual procedures of experiments involving self-administration as opposed to gustatory aversion is in the customary route of administration—i.v. in the former case and i.p. in the latter. Coussens (1974) explored this difference as a possible basis for the paradox at issue here. Figure 3 compares the effectiveness of gustatory conditioning when saccharin was paired with 2.0 mg/kg of $d$-amphetamine by either the i.v. or the i.p. route. The figure depicts the volumes of saccharin consumed in each experimental condition when a test trial was conducted several days following a single conditioning trial. In the two control groups that received only saline injections (S-IV and S-IP), route of administration was inconsequential. However, when amphetamine was paired with saccharin, significant aversion was conditioned in either case, but more so when the route was i.p. (A-IV vs. A-IP, $p<.005$). This led Coussens to conclude that the ". . . difference in drug effects with different routes of administration might well acount for the paradoxical results obtained with self-infusion and taste-aversion procedures."

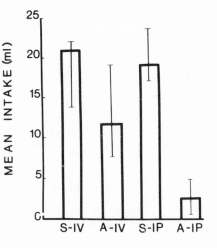

**Figure 3.** Intake of saccharin after a single conditioning trial with intravenous or intraperitoneal administration of amphetamine (2.0 mg/kg) or saline. (S-IV: intravenous saline; A-IV: intravenous amphetamine; S-IP: intraperitoneal saline; A-IP: intraperitoneal amphetamine.) From Coussens (1974), by permission.

These results are important for an issue to be considered later, but they do not really seem to address the paradox in a substantial way. The effect of route, although undeniable, was one of magnitude and not kind, since avoidance was seen in either case. Yet the paradox exists as a consequence of a *qualitative* difference, consisting of effects that appear opposite in direction. In short, an account based entirely on route of administration is inadequate. Moreover, even if the results were more persuasive, one would still be left to explain what it is about the different routes that might be responsible for their differential effectiveness.

### 1.3.5. Conclusions

It is evident that there is no difficulty in generating *ad hoc* resolutions for the apparent paradox posed by the fact that psychoactive drugs do not have reinforcing properties that are independent of situational constraints. Although it may be an interesting intellectual exercise to conjure these resolutions (and we must obviously plead guilty to this indulgence), clearly none of the proposals is more than speculative, and at least one is simply off the mark. Despite the considerable interest engendered by the "paradoxical" aspect of conditioned aversion by psychoactive drugs, one cannot help wondering whether too much importance has been accorded this feature of the phenomenon *per se*. Recently, Gamzu (1974) described the issue as a "pseudo-paradox"; but he did point out one beneficial consequence of paradoxicalness—it got him interested in doing some empirical work. Whether a paradox is specious or otherwise, it seems that non-obviousness endures as a pheromone for investigators.

## 2. Studies of Mechanism: How Does the UCS Work?

### 2.1. Central Versus Peripheral Locus of Effect

It seems safe to regard conditioned aversion by drugs as being something more interesting than a consequence of gross drug-induced illness. But even if it helps to know what something is not, it is always more satisfying to be able to make generalizations of a more positive kind. There have been several attempts to identify the features of a pharmacological UCS that might be responsible for aversive conditioning, with amphetamine the primary object of study.

#### 2.1.1. Surgical Manipulation

At a gross level, one fundamental question has been whether gustatory aversions are due primarily to central pharmacological action, peripheral action, or both. Where *d*-amphetamine is concerned, it appears likely that central effects of the drug are at least sufficient to induce an aversion. Berger, Wise, and Stein (1973) illustrated this point by examining the effect of lesions to the area postrema, a region of the brain believed to be an "emetic chemoreceptor trigger zone." They compared effects of thermal cauterization of the area postrema on aversions to milk induced by methylscopolamine and *d*-amphetamine. Interestingly, the lesion prevented the acquisition of an aversion only in the case of methylscopolamine. Like its design, the interpretation of the experiment was elegantly simple. First, it seemed reasonable to conclude that the two drugs induced flavor avoidance by different mechanisms. Because methylscopolamine penetrates the blood–brain barrier poorly, it is plausible to conclude that a peripheral action was responsible for its effectiveness in intact animals. In contrast, the lesion had no effect on the aversion created by amphetamine, a potent centrally acting drug. This might mean that amphetamine's effectiveness as a UCS is primarily due to its central action, and this was the conclusion that Berger *et al.* tentatively adopted. Clearly, such a conclusion is not inconsistent with the data; however, the same data do not rule out the possibility that amphetamine's ability to induce gustatory aversion is primarily due to peripheral pharmacological effects that have nothing to do with the particular function of the area postrema. Thus, any conclusion from these data is not without an element of uncertainty.

An important additional feature of the account by Berger *et al.* was the invocation of anorexia as a potential cause of amphetamine's aversive action. Before evaluating this further, it is worthwhile to consider the data behind a similar suggestion (Carey and Goodall, 1974), although one that has little to do with surgical intervention. Carey and Goodall compared the potencies of the *d*- and *l*-isomers of amphetamine and found the ratio for conditioned aversion to be on the order of 4 : 1 in favor of the *d*-isomer. This value suggested that conditioned aversion was mediated dopaminergically, although other biochemical explanations could not be excluded. Biochemical mechanisms aside, an important feature of the result was that a similar ratio obtained in the ability of the two isomers to suppress water intake when the drugs were administered prior to a drinking test. From this finding on adipsia, and by introducing evidence from other work, Carey and Goodall went on to propose that conditioned anorexia was responsible for amphetamine's effectiveness as a UCS in gustatory conditioning.

It is certainly within the realm of possibility that conditioned anorexia is the mechanism underlying the ability of amphetamine to cause conditioned avoidance of a flavor. But there is a serious oversight in any explanation that singles out a particular effect of a drug as *the* mechanism. Clearly, anorexia is not the only important action of amphetamine, central or otherwise, and it seems arbitrary to single it out as the culprit behind conditioned aversion. Moreover, since virtually every psychoactive drug is capable of producing conditioned aversion, including chlordiazepoxide, which stimulates food intake, it seems unlikely that a disturbance of ingestive behavior is necessary for conditioned aversion to occur.

## 2.1.2. Biochemical Manipulation

Another strategy for elucidating the properties of amphetamine that are aversive has involved the intriguing if dodgy techniques of direct biochemical intervention. Carey (1973) compared the effect of AMT on both conditioned and unconditioned suppression of saccharin intake in rats. AMT blocked the unconditioned effect of amphetamine administered prior to saccharin consumption, but the conditioned form of intake suppression was not affected. Carey took these results to rule out conditioned anorexia as a mechanism for conditioned aversion, favoring instead an unelaborated proposal postulating the involvement of conditioned central biochemical events. There is a bit of inconsistency here concerning the status of anorexia as a mechanism of aversion (cf. Carey and Goodall, 1974).

More recent evidence (Goudie *et al.*, 1975) indicates that the failure of AMT to affect conditioned aversion was due more to a procedural feature of Carey's (1973) study than a biochemical one. In Carey's study, treatment with AMT was not initiated until an aversion had been clearly established, in which case AMT would have required the ability to interfere with the retention of an existing aversion, rather than its acquisition; to expect a positive result is to postulate that AMT interferes with response retention rather than the pharmacological action of amphetamine. This problematic feature of Carey's study was detected by Goudie *et al.*, who undertook to examine the effect of AMT on the acquisition of conditioned aversion by amphetamine. The results were positive, but Goudie *et al.* were properly circumspect in drawing conclusions. They reasoned that the data were biochemically consistent with the suggestion that anorexia is involved in gustatory conditioning by amphetamine, but noted also that the same neurochemical systems mediate other central effects of the drug such as stereotypy and hyperactivity. Even more conservatively, they pointed out that a central mechanism was not necessarily involved, since AMT interferes with peripheral catecholaminergic mechanisms as well.

Given our present state of knowledge, it seems premature to identify particular physiological or behavioral consequences of drugs as those that are responsible for their effectiveness in gustatory conditioning. Indeed, the need for caution is underlined by the fact that there is only a single study (Berger *et al.*, 1973) that provided specific evidence on the gross question of whether the important drug effects were centrally or peripherally mediated.

## 2.2. A Nonspecific Mechanism: Novelty

In a context unrelated to gustatory conditioning, Amit and Baum (1970) hypothesized that in a pharmacologically naive rat, the sheer novelty of a drug is *per se* aversive. The primary evidence for this was that injections of alcohol retarded the extinction of an aversively controlled motor response in pharmacologically naive rats. The aversiveness of the novel drug state, Amit and Baum reasoned, combined with the aversive motivational state (i.e., fear), controlling avoidance to prolong extinction.

Intuitively, this hypothesis has a good deal of merit. Most of us can think of instances in which we have found a novel internal state to be less than pleasant. Nonetheless, intuition must bow to data when they are available, as they are in this case. If any novel drug state is aversive, and if such a state should be able to support avoidance behavior in extinction, then any novel drug state should prolong avoidance extinction. However, the results of a study reported by Cappell, LeBlanc, and Endrenyi (1972), illustrated in Figure 4, are inconsistent with this hypothetical requirement. Cappell *et al.* compared the effects of chlordiazepoxide and ethanol on the extinction of a lithium-induced gustatory aversion. Although the data lacked the elegance that would have been provided by neat dose–response functions, it was the case that alcohol significantly retarded extinction and chlordiazepoxide did the opposite. Thus, drug states that were equally novel had opposite effects on the extinction of an aversively based response.

To an extent then, the results were inconsistent with a mechanistic account based on drug novelty, but only to an extent. It would be possible to argue that the results of the study by Cappell *et al.* (1972) are not entirely damaging to a novelty hypothesis because the empirical test was not definitive. Moreover, the results with chlordiazepoxide may be complicated by the hyperdipsic action of chlordiazepoxide (Cappell and LeBlanc, 1973). Nonetheless, it is important that in its only direct test, one version of the novelty hypothesis fared poorly.

It is worth noting here that a novelty hypothesis has been stated and defended explicitly in the contest of gustatory aversion (Gamzu, 1974; Vogel and Nathan, 1975). Gamzu (1974) asserted that ". . . any sudden change from the normal state of eunoia that can be readily discriminated as a change should be categorized as potentially harmful in the absence of any information." As Gamzu pointed out, this hypothesis makes the prediction, confirmed by experience, that virtually all psychoactive drugs should produce gustatory aversions in pharmacologically naive animals. The hypothesis was distinguished from that of Amit and Baum, but not in detail, and the claim for its validity was modest. There will be reason to return to Gamzu's account later, but for now it should be said that the hypothesis is

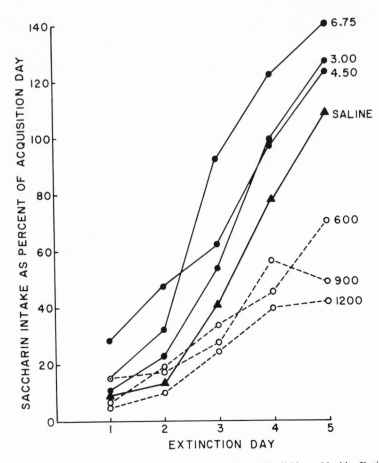

**Figure 4.** Extinction of an aversion to saccharin conditioned by lithium chloride. Extinction sessions began 72 h after a single conditioning trial in which a dose of lithium (2% of body weight of 0.15 M lithium) had been paired with saccharin. Chlordiazepoxide (closed circles), alcohol (open circles), or saline (triangles) was administered 30 min prior to each extinction trial. Numbers beside the Day 5 data points are doses in mg/kg. From Cappell, LeBlanc, and Endrenyi (1972), by permission.

still quite general and remains to be formulated in such a way that disconfirmation is possible.

## 2.3. The Importance of UCS Duration

Earlier, reference was made to Coussens's (1974) finding that conditioning by amphetamine was less effective when the route was i.v. than when it was i.p. Although Coussens suggested that this fact might have something to do with the "paradox" of conditioning by drugs, he did not go on to specify what it might be about differences in route that made the difference. Two possibilities immediately come to mind: the delay of onset of the drug effect, and its duration. Both would be affected by route of administration, but the first would seem to be ruled out in a study by Lester, Nachman, and LeMagnen (1970). They found that alcohol was equally effective in inducing avoidance of saccharin whether the route was i.p. or intracardiac (i.c.). Although the difference is slight in absolute terms, the i.c. route is even more efficient in producing a rapid onset of effect than either the i.v. or the i.p. methods. From this outcome, it is reasonable to conclude that delay of onset was not a crucial variable in the study by Coussens (1974).

Duration of effect, however, cannot be ruled out as readily, since the effect of an i.p. injection would be more protracted than an i.v. administration of the same compound. It is at this point that some intriguing data from an experiment using cocaine as the UCS become relevant (Cappell and LeBlanc, unpub.). Figure 5 provides a comparison of gustatory aversions induced by cocaine and caffeine. Because of discrepancies in the initial intake of saccharin the data are expressed as a proportion of intake on Trial 1, i.e., before any conditioning effects could be evident. Otherwise, our

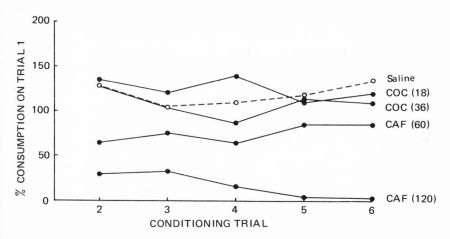

**Figure 5.** Acquisition of an aversion conditioned by various doses of caffeine (CAF) or cocaine (COC). Because of a sampling error, differences in baseline consumption were present on the first exposure to saccharin (i.e., before conditioning effects could be evident). These were adjusted for by calculating saccharin consumption on Trials 2–6 as a proportion of consumption on Trial 1. The first data point (Trial 2) thus reflects conditioning that occurred on Trial 1. No dose of cocaine, even one as high as 50% of the LD50 (36.0 mg/kg) was effective, but 50% of the LD50 of caffeine (120 mg/kg) induced profound avoidance of saccharin. Cocaine was tested at doses of 4.5, 9.0, 18.0, and 36.0 mg/kg and caffeine at 15, 30, 60, and 120 mg/kg. For the sake of clarity of the figure, only the results with the two highest doses of each drug are shown. The two lower doses of caffeine were entirely without aversive properties.

standard conditioning procedure was employed. Even the highest dose of cocaine, which at 36.0 mg/kg was roughly 50% of the LD50, was insufficient to produce avoidance of saccharin. The highest dose of caffeine, which was also roughly 50% of the LD50, induced profound avoidance of saccharin. Moreover, there can be no doubt that the doses of cocaine, especially at the higher levels, produced substantial central effects. Yet why was there no conditioning even at such potent doses? One property that sets cocaine apart from other CNS stimulants is its remarkably short duration of action, with a half-life perhaps as low as 20–30 min. Amphetamine, by contrast, has a half-life of 60 min, and caffeine a half-life of 120 min. Perhaps then, there is a minimal duration of action of the UCS that is required to engage the mechanisms of gustatory conditioning. Several threads of evidence indicate that this notion might have some merit. We first addressed the question in a way that, with hindsight, turned out to be simple-minded. It seemed logical that the best way to protract the effects of cocaine would be by giving multiple injections. Thus we spread 4 injections of cocaine, each of 9.0 mg/kg, at 15-min intervals after exposure to saccharin. The results are illustrated in Figure 6, in which our prediction was

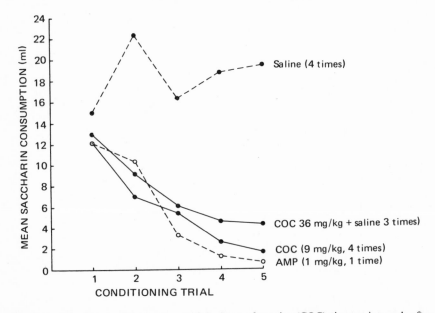

**Figure 6.** Aversive conditioning by multiple doses of cocaine (COC) given at intervals after saccharin. A group of animals conditioned with a dose of amphetamine (AMP) known to be effective (1.0 mg/kg) was included for comparison. Only a single injection was given in the amphetamine group instead of four as in the other conditions. The saline (SAL) data were collected at a later date using a group of animals that were older and heavier than those in the drugged groups. What is important, however, is that there was no evidence of aversion due to four saline injections *per se*.

amply confirmed. Unfortunately, there was a catch associated with the procedure. Since each animal had to be handled at every injection, rats that were already under the stress of a powerful CNS stimulant were futher stressed by being clutched, impaled, and otherwise disturbed. Perhaps it was the additional stress, rather than an extended drug effect *per se,* that was responsible for the effective conditioning. Indeed, when three additional saline injections were given after an initial cocaine dose of 36.0 mg/kg, conditioning was equally effective, even though the same dose given only once without further handling had failed earlier. Even though four injections of nothing but saline were insufficient to produce a learned aversion, the possibility of an interaction between the stress produced by the drug and that produced by the injection procedure cannot be eliminated. The confounding between duration and stressfulness of the drug experience is obvious; nonetheless, the result was positive if not unequivocal.

Another approach to the same issue was recently taken by Coussens (1975), who recast some old data and provided some new data. The old data were that pretreatment with AMT facilitated the production of gustatory avoidance by i.v. doses of morphine that were otherwise ineffective. The new data were that analogous results were obtained with cocaine. In each case, it was assumed that by depleting catecholamines, AMT effectively extended the action of morphine and cocaine, thereby making them effective as unconditioned stimuli. Coussens also reinterpreted his data on the differential effectiveness of the i.v. and i.p. routes of administration in terms of duration of action. Although it is comforting that someone else also attributes importance to duration of action, there is a loose end created by the data with AMT: Recall that Goudie *et al.* (1975) found that AMT *attenuated* the effect of amphetamine, presumably by the very same biochemical mechanism that Coussens referred to in explaining an effect in the opposite direction. Clearly then, some sorting out of these apparently discrepant findings remains to be done.

The final bit of evidence derives from a preliminary report by Braveman (1975a). Normally, electric shock is not effective in generating gustatory avoidance. However, Braveman found this not to be so when rats were subjected to 1 h of unavoidable shock on a VI-1 min schedule, 30 min after drinking saccharin. Although Braveman favored an interpretation in terms of the stressfulness of the UCS, its duration was also extraordinarily great.

In summary, there is no single bit of evidence that definitely supports duration of action as a key mechanism, and each bit is subject to alternative explanation or some other objection. But even though duration of action has not yet been manipulated clearly, it has been consistently correlated with increased effectiveness of the UCS. In the context of the teleological arguments that are often invoked in accounting for biological adaptations, it makes a certain amount of sense that effective gustatory conditioning would not occur unless the UCS were more than transient in its effects.

## 3. An Area of Conflict: Interpreting the Effects of Prior Exposure to the UCS on Subsequent Conditioning

The purpose of this chapter is to comment on general issues in research on drug dependence as they are related to gustatory aversion. Perhaps the most relevant facet of work in the area has been that which may relate to tolerance to and dependence upon drugs. The study of these phenomena inevitably involves the manipulation of an organism's history of exposure to drugs. If the earliest published paper on the topic (Elsmore, 1972) had been taken as definitive, there would be little else to say. Elsmore was interested in the effect of previous exposure to delta-9-tetrahydrocannabinol (THC) on the subsequent acquisition of an aversion to saccharin produced by that drug. Rats were given oral administration of 10 mg/kg of THC on 0, 1, 2, 4, or 8 occasions prior to conditioning trials with the same dose. Because no degree of prior treatment had any noticeable effect on conditioning, Elsmore concluded that no tolerance developed to the aversion-inducing property of THC.

Happily for the substance of this discussion, Elsmore did not have the last word. Indeed, we are far from hearing the last word on this subject.

### 3.1. Prior Exposure to Morphine: The "Artificial Need" Hypothesis

Among the first reports of an effect of prior drug history on later conditioning was one for which drug dependence as such constituted a secondary concern. Parker, Failor, and Weidman (1973) were actually more interested in assessing the ability of rats to associate flavors with the repletion of needed substances, and chose morphine because it generates a need for which repletion appears not to be governed by innate mechanisms. Essentially, they compared gustatory conditioning by morphine in dependent (addicted) and nondependent animals. It is safe to say that their schedule of exposure to morphine produced physical dependence, since there were 25 consecutive days of exposure to the drug to a level of 140 mg/kg; a control group received exposure to saline only. Conditioning involved the pairing of injections of morphine with the flavor of sucrose octaacetate (SOA) when the drug-treated animals had been deprived of morphine for 72 h. The results were clear: Without a history of exposure to morphine, the drug readily induced conditioned avoidance of SOA; however, this was not the case when the animals had been exposed to morphine and were in withdrawal (i.e., need) during conditioning trials. Parker *et al.*

reasonably interpreted the results "as a demonstration of the rat's ability to associate flavor cues with beneficial postingestional consequences." Withdrawal from morphine, they argued, constitutes an "unnatural need state" for which morphine is an effective medication. Hence the results turned out as they did.

This experiment constitutes an apt test of the hypothesis that inspired it, and the results provided solid support for the biological principle that was the focus of the work. However, there was nothing in the experiment that excluded potential alternative explanations, of which there are several.

## 3.2. The Tolerance Hypothesis

The manipulation of drug history chosen by Parker *et al.* (1973) certainly had the effect of creating what might be described as an artificial need; at the same time, however, it could have led to another, related consequence—the development of tolerance to many of the effects of morphine. Consequently, there is an alternative account for their data. Before elaborating the point, it is necessary to define tolerance operationally. Tolerance to a drug is evident when:

1. An increased dose is required to maintain an effect of constant magnitude.
2. A constant dose elicits an effect of diminishing magnitude.

These are operational requirements and, as such, do not address the important question of mechanism. It can be said, though, that there is no case for the existence of tolerance to a drug in the absence of achieving these criteria, regardless of the underlying mechanism.

This said, how can tolerance account for the data of Parker *et al.*? Their schedule of chronic exposure to morphine could easily have generated tolerance, since the duration and level of treatment were more than sufficient to have such an effect. Hence the efficacy of the dose they used in conditioning could have been reduced in comparing animals with and without prior exposure. What a tolerance argument asserts is that chronic exposure reduces the effectiveness of the UCS by making it less potent, the net effect of which is equivalent to lowering the dose of the UCS. Since it is well known that gustatory conditioning by drugs is dose-dependent, an impairment of acquisition would be predicted from a reduction in dose.

All of this is very well in theory. Empirically, the requirement of an ideal test would be to generate a drug history that produces tolerance without in turn creating an artificial need. LeBlanc and Cappell (1974) proposed that this might be achieved using amphetamine. Like morphine, amphetamine is a powerful positive reinforcer, and if i.v. self-administration is the criterion, both are potent drugs of dependence. However, if withdrawal-induced disturbance is the indicator, there is much less evidence of physical dependence (need) as a result of chronic exposure to amphetamine, although the possibility cannot be entirely discounted (Kalant, LeBlanc, and Gibbins, 1971).

Certainly, the sequelae of abrupt withdrawal from the two drugs are much less pronounced where amphetamine is concerned. Still another good comparison of amphetamine and morphine is provided by data on self-administration patterns in monkeys (Deneau, *et al.*, 1969). The self-administration of morphine was frequent and highly predictable; the diurnal pattern varied little over a period of weeks, and voluntary abstinence never occurred. By contrast, the self-administration of amphetamine involved "binges" of consumption interspersed with periods of voluntary abstinence lasting from a day to 2 weeks. Intake within days was also irregular. Obviously, these contrasts do not provide definitive evidence on the operation of a need-repletion mechanism. Nonetheless, it is not stretching a point to say that morphine appeared to be a drug that created a need for which satisfaction was sought consistently, whereas amphetamine, though clearly reinforcing, seemed governed in intake by a substantially different regulatory mechanism.

If there is a difference in the quality of need that can be generated by amphetamine and morphine, and if the position adopted by Parker *et al.* is basically correct, it might be expected that prior exposure would have different effects on aversive conditioning by the two drugs. A tolerance account, on the other hand, makes no differential prediction, since there is ample independent evidence that chronic exposure to either drug will result in tolerance. Our study (LeBlanc and Cappell, 1974) compared the effects of prior exposure to amphetamine and morphine on gustatory conditioning by these drugs. Since the morphine data essentially confirmed the results of Parker *et al.*, it is sufficient here to consider only the findings on amphetamine. Briefly, rats were assigned to one of three conditions of prior treatment. One group (ND) was a control treated with saline. A second group (LD) was pretreated with amphetamine to a level of 4.0 mg/kg, and a third (HD) to a level of 20.0 mg/kg. Within each prior treatment condition, equal numbers of rats were conditioned with saline (S) or 1.0 mg/kg of amphetamine (A) on trials that followed the chronic treatment regime. The outcome is illustrated in Figure 7, in which several points are worth noting. First, regardless of prior treatment, there was no difference in saccharin consumption among animals conditioned with saline (NDS, LDS, HDS), which means that chronic treatment *per se* did not affect the baseline of saccharin consumption. Parenthetically, amphetamine differs in this from morphine, a drug for which equal deprivation following prior treatment severely disturbed the baseline. Such differential disturbance gives additional evidence of the distinctiveness of the withdrawal effects of the

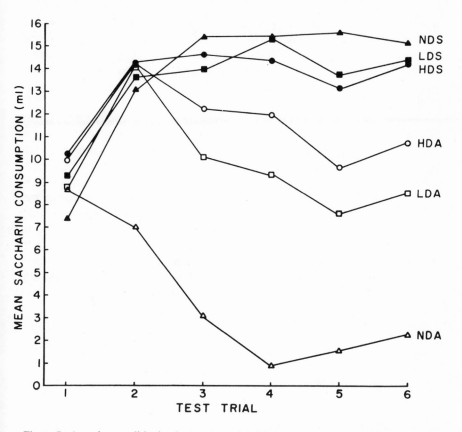

**Figure 7.** Aversive conditioning by amphetamine following pretreatment with saline (ND), 4.0 mg/kg of amphetamine (LD), or 20.0 mg/kg of amphetamine (HD). Conditioning was by saline (S) or 1.0 mg/kg of amphetamine (A). From LeBlanc and Cappell (1974), by permission.

different compounds. Amphetamine was an effective UCS in animals without prior experience, as is evident in the acquisition of pronounced saccharin avoidance in group NDA compared to all other conditions. Avoidance was not altogether mitigated by prior treatment, as groups HDA and LDA drank significantly less than their counterparts conditioned with saline (HDS and LDS). However, in both groups aversion was significantly less by far than it was in animals with no previous exposure to amphetamine.

To review the evidence, pretreatment with either morphine or amphetamine had comparable effects on conditioning by these drugs. Yet only in the case of morphine does chronic treatment establish a need state of the type required by the hypothesis of Parker *et al.* An account in terms of tolerance survives the same data, because there is independent evidence that tolerance develops to many of the effects of amphetamine and morphine. More recently (Cappell, LeBlanc, and Herling, 1975) we found that similar pretreatment effects were demonstrable with chlordiazepoxide. Applying the same argument as before, this was taken as further evidence in favor of a tolerance explanation but inconsistent with the artificial need hypothesis.

Another line of evidence that is consistent with an explanation in terms of tolerance derives from several parametric experiments. In the case of amphetamine (Cappell and LeBlanc, 1975a) we predicted that a particular time course of acquisition and loss of the effectiveness of prior treatment should occur if tolerance is involved. Specifically, the order of magnitude of the time courses in question should be measurable in a moderate number of days, rather than as a very short or very long time period. Figures 8 and 9 illustrate the parametric values that were determined. The first experiment (Figure 8) was concerned with the amount of pretreatment required to confer protection against aversive conditioning by amphetamine. The pretreatment dose was 7.5 mg/kg, administered on consecutive days, and the conditioning dose was 1.0 mg/kg. Although there was an apparent effect of

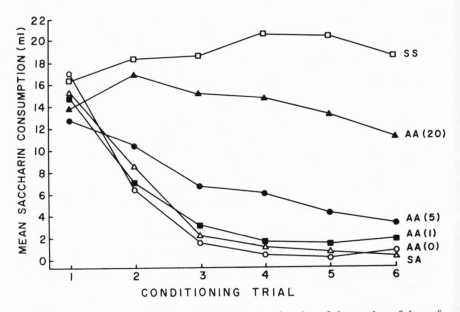

**Figure 8.** Conditioned aversion by amphetamine as a function of the number of days of pretreatment. The numbers in parentheses are the number of consecutive daily pretreatments with amphetamine that preceded conditioning trials. Group SS was pretreated with saline and conditioned with saline; Group SA was pretreated with saline and conditioned with amphetamine. All groups pretreated with amphetamine (AA groups) received maintenance injections of amphetamine during the period of conditioning trials. From Cappell and LeBlanc (1975a), by permission.

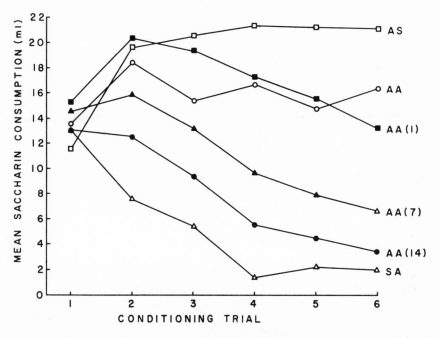

**Figure 9.** Effects of various durations of withdrawal from amphetamine on conditioned aversion by amphetamine. The numbers in parentheses indicate the number of days of withdrawal from pretreatment prior to the commencement of conditioning. Group AS was pretreated with amphetamine on a schedule that continued during conditioning trials, but conditioning was with saline. Group SA was pretreated with saline and conditioned with amphetamine. Pretreatment of Group AA with amphetamine continued throughout conditioning trials, which were with amphetamine as the UCS. Each of Groups AA(1), AA(7), and AA(14) were pretreated with amphetamine and conditioned with amphetamine following the indicated period of withdrawal. From Cappell and LeBlanc (1975a), by permission.

5 days of pretreatment (AA5), it did not attain significance. Only rats given 20 days of prior exposure (AA20) displayed significantly weaker conditioning than controls given pretreatment with saline (SA).

The decay of the effectiveness of pretreatment was studied following 26 consecutive days of exposure to amphetamine at a terminal dose level of 20 mg/kg (Figure 9). On acquisition trials 2–5, rats withdrawn from treatment for 7 days (AA7) still showed significantly weaker conditioning than controls given no pretreatment (SA). By the sixth trial, the steadily decreasing difference became nonsignificant. When withdrawal was for as long as 14 days (AA14), there was no significant residual effect of pretreatment, although there was some apparent effect.

Whether it was acquisition or loss of the effectiveness of pretreatment that was under scrutiny, the time courses of the effects were consistent with those to be expected if tolerance was involved (Kalant *et al.*, 1971).

Other possible explanations are not excluded, but tolerance remains as a viable candidate in yet another test.

Finally, there are some recent data on the persistence of pretreatment effects conferred by morphine (Cappell and LeBlanc, 1977). The procedure here was analogous to that with amphetamine except that the acquisition of aversion was examined following withdrawal for a period of 1, 7, 14, or 28 days. Pretreatment consisted of 26 consecutive daily injections of morphine terminating at a level of 120 mg/kg, and the conditioning dose was 15 mg/kg. As is apparent in Figure 10, there was a residual effect of pretreatment at all durations of withdrawal including the longest period (MM28), which was 28 days. Clearly, there should be reservations expressed about any comparison of these data with the results on duration of withdrawal from amphetamine; these were different experiments de-

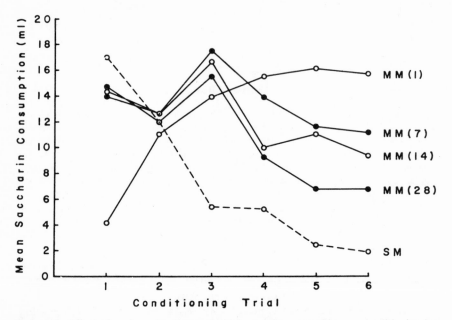

**Figure 10.** Effect of various durations of withdrawal from morphine on conditioning by morphine. The numbers in parentheses indicate the number of days of withdrawal from pretreatment prior to the commencement of conditioning. Group SM was pretreated with saline but conditioned with morphine. Each of Groups MM(1), MM(7), MM(14), and MM(28) was pretreated with morphine and conditioned with morphine following the indicated period of withdrawal. Some control groups that were included in the original experiment are not shown for the sake of pictorial clarity. Note, however, that after recovery from withdrawal-depressed saccharin consumption on Trial 1 in the case of Group MM(1), the groups began from almost identical levels of consumption on Trial 2. From Trial 3 onward, all groups pretreated with morphine showed reduced avoidance of saccharin ($p < .01$) compared to the control pretreated with saline (SM).

spite our attempt to equate the levels of pretreatment and the potency of the UCS across studies. Nonetheless, the durability of morphine's effect appears to be of a different order of magnitude from that of amphetamine. And, interestingly, morphine is a drug that stands out in conferring tolerance that may persist for a relatively long period after the cessation of treatment (Cochin and Kornetsky, 1964).

This discrepancy in the durability of pretreatment effects by morphine and amphetamine, if real, poses a problem for some accounts of the pretreatment phenomenon. The tolerance explanation, however, can contend with these data in view of the evidence that the retention of tolerance to morphine may be unusually long in comparison to other drugs.

In considering the case for tolerance, which is obviously favored here, it would be remiss not to mention that as a level of explanation, the account does not transcend descriptiveness (although this limitation is not unique to the tolerance explanation). Indeed, it would be premature to go beyond description at a stage in our knowledge of the phenomenon that precedes even a rudimentary understanding of why aversive conditioning by psychoactive drugs occurs in the first place. To ask what the underlying biological mechanism is when speaking of tolerance in this context is to ask the more general question of how tolerance to any drug effect is developed. This issue has been thoroughly addressed in other contexts (e.g., Kalant *et al.*, 1971), and there is no reason to believe that a new class of mechanistic explanation need be developed. For the time being the most useful approach appears to be to determine whether the descriptive account, based on the operational definitions specified earlier, is itself adequate. It does go a long way, but as will soon become evident, it is not without problems.

### 3.3. Habituation to Novelty

Inevitably, repeated exposure to any stimulus must reduce its novelty. If a drugged state is aversive to the extent that it is novel (cf. Section 2.2), an obvious explanation for pretreatment effects becomes available, and, in fact, has been proposed. It is difficult to pit this approach against a tolerance hypothesis because it is not entirely obvious where the two make clearly different predictions; moreover, operationally it is impossible to manipulate novelty without potentially affecting tolerance and vice versa. Nonetheless, some comparisons can be made.

Like the proponents of the tolerance hypothesis, those who favor novelty have relied upon the strategy of developing data that seem accountable only by their theoretical bias. Vogel and Nathan (1975) compared conditioning by amobarbital among animals that had been pretreated with amobarbital or saline, and found avoidance to be much less among pretreated animals. They also recorded sleeping time as a measure of tolerance. Although pretreatment clearly reduced sleeping time on the average, the rank correlation between sleeping time and saccharin consumption was marginal, and this was taken as evidence against the role of tolerance in explaining the effect of prior exposure on conditioning. Two observations are worth making here. First, the fact that there was significant tolerance at the group level should perhaps not be dismissed. Secondly, the correlation was certainly not trivial (0.41). Indeed, it could well be argued that a correlation of this size is somewhat remarkable given the small number of animals involved and the various other factors (i.e., potential "ceiling" or "floor" effects) that could have operated to restrain the size of a correlation. Thus, these data in themselves do no violence to a tolerance hypothesis.

Somewhat more problematic was the finding by Vogel and Nathan that prior exposure to amphetamine interfered with the acquisition of an aversion to amobarbital, but not to amphetamine itself. This outcome is clearly embarrassing to a tolerance notion, and was taken by Vogel and Nathan to indicate the generalization of habituation from one drug to another. There is no reason to suppose that there is cross-tolerance between amobarbital and amphetamine, hence the embarrassment for the tolerance explanation. At the same time it is difficult to conceive of a theory of habituation that predicts more habituation between different stimuli than within the same stimulus. Vogel and Nathan must also contend with the fact that their cross-drug "habituation" was not symmetrical; that is, although pretreatment with amphetamine reduced conditioning by amobarbital, the reverse was not true. Another proponent of an habituation hypothesis (Gamzu, 1975) has stated that asymmetry is an anomaly for the hypothesis.

Gamzu (1975) formulated an habituation hypothesis somewhat differently than Vogel and Nathan, implying a relatively specific mechanism whereby the process might work. Recall (see p. 145) that Gamzu proposed that any sudden change in an organism's affective homeostasis will be categorized as harmful (and thus avoided) unless shown not to be so. His argument is that prior exposure informs the animal that there is no harm and therefore obviates the need to avoid a substance that predicts a harmless, if aversive, state. The ability of prior information to minimize adverse reactions to drugs in man was cited in support of this view, but otherwise no crucial evidence was presented. This account provokes a few interesting observations. First, there is some question as to whether an habituation process is in fact being invoked; it seems somewhat like a learning process, hence as much akin to the associative mechanisms discussed in the next section of this chapter as to habituation. This observation obviously begs the question of defining habituation; does the process require that the unconditioned stimulus actually become less potent by some objective index, or is some other mechanism implied? The advocates of an habituation explanation have not spoken to this point. Gamzu appeared to argue that the animal *learns* to discount the danger of the stimulus, rather than to experience it in an objectively weaker form. A second point relates to the definition of "harmful," and requires peering into the rat mentality. It could well be questioned whether an animal should conclude that amphetamine is harmless after 26 exposures to a large dose (cf. Cappell and LeBlanc, 1975a) of a drug that interferes with sleep and feeding, causes hyperactivity and stereotypy, and so on. What a perspicacious rat should learn is not that the drug is not *harmful,* but if he is lucky, that it is not *lethal.* All this anthropomorphizing obviously does little more than beg the question of a rat's definition of harm. In any case, Gamzu did not present any specific evidence that would support this hypothesis over others, and it seems that it would be difficult to provide a direct empirical test of the mechanism as proposed.

A few other bits of data can be cited as inconsistent with the novelty hypothesis. One potential difficulty for the habituation notion is implied in the data illustrated in Figures 9 and 10. Both indicate that the effectiveness of pretreatment declines over time even with no special intervention. To account for these findings, an habituation hypothesis requires that habituation be lost over time. It is not difficult to fashion a version of an habituation hypothesis that would incorporate such a feature. However, Gamzu's (1975) version requires that the animals "forget" what they learned about the lack of harmful effects of the drugs in question even after prolonged, though somewhat remote in time, experience with them. This seems improbable. Nor can any habituation concept easily account for different rates of decay of the effectiveness of amphetamine and morphine. Yet both of these findings can be accommodated in the context of a tolerance explanation.

On the evidence presented thus far, the tolerance hypothesis appears to fare better than one based on habituation to novelty, though both, as will become evident in the next section, are not without problems. There is a sense, however, in which tolerance and habituation are not conflicting concepts. Tolerance, at least tolerance in the CNS, can be construed as a special case of adaptation or habituation to a stimulus. With protracted application, the stimulus becomes less effective. There may be special considerations that apply to habituation to the presence of a drug (e.g., the possibility of a "rebound" neural sensitivity on withdrawal), but habituation is nonetheless an appropriate generic category in which to place tolerance. The conflict lies mainly in the emphasis that what becomes habituated is the *novelty* of the drug stimulus *per se;* thus it should be clear that there are statements of an habituation hypothesis that could have much in common with one based on tolerance.

## 3.4. Associative Mechanisms

There are several ways in which an associative mechanism might account for pretreatment effects. One is that during prior exposure to the drug, unintended conditioned stimuli become associated with the to-be UCS and interfere with subsequent conditioning of an association with an intended CS. This notion has been rejected on the basis of data collected by independent investigators with entirely different explanations for the prior exposure phenomenon (Braveman, 1975a; LeBlanc and Cappell, 1974; Vogel and Nathan, 1975).

Other potential associative mechanisms have been postulated on the basis of the intriguing if perplexing data reported by Braveman (1975b). The impact of these data is not so much that they point to a particular explanation for pretreatment effects; rather they present a monumental task of explanation for other accounts, especially one based on tolerance. A brief exposition of Experiment 5 of Braveman's series illustrates the problem. In this experiment, rats were exposed to one of five pretreatments: injection with saline, rotation on a turntable at 60 rpm for a period of 5 min, injection with amphetamine, injection with lithium chloride, or injection with methylscopolamine. The pretreatments were given on 5 occasions at 5-day intervals. Ten days after the final pretreatment, conditioning trials were begun. These consisted of the pairing of the taste of saccharin with rotation, a treatment known to produce conditioned gustatory aversion. The results are illustrated in Figure 11. In animals previously exposed only to saline, rotation had the expected effect. But regardless of the specific nature of the other pretreatments, they were effective as long as they were not placebos. There is no way in which a reasonable construction of a tolerance hypothesis can account for these results, nor is the artificial need hypothesis very effective here either. An habituation notion could apply, but Braveman proposed two other potential mechanisms. One was derivative from Rescorla's (1973) observation that prior exposure to a UCS alone impaired its subsequent associative efficacy in conditioning when paired with a CS. Certainly this could apply in the case of gustatory conditioning, since the procedures are analogous although the nature of the stimuli is quite different. Another possibility was based on the notion of "learned helplessness." According to this argument, the animal learns during prior exposure that it can do nothing to prevent the aversive consequences of the treatment from occurring, and indeed that the experience is entirely capricious from its point of view. Such a learning history might have an effect on the associative value of a UCS when it becomes explicitly paired with a cue, as in conditioning; if the animal has learned that this type of stimulus occurs capriciously, it might be less likely to form an association based on its occurence, even if it is now more reliably informative.

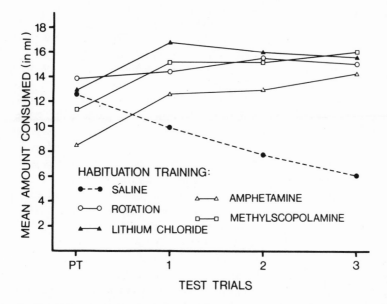

**Figure 11.** Conditioned aversion by rotation among animals previously exposed to a variety of treatments. Only when the pretreatment was with saline was it ineffective. From Braveman (1975b), by permission.

To reiterate, Braveman's data do not directly support these associative interpretations as much as they challenge others. And there is a major problem with an associative account in any case. What is interesting and challenging about the data is that the specific type of prior exposure is a virtual matter of indifference to its effectiveness in attenuating later conditioning; indeed, this is the basis for opting for some sort of associative mechanism. If this is the key feature, however, it would appear necessary that there *never be a negative result in a pretreatment experiment.* Yet Cappell *et al.* (1975) found that prior exposure to chlordiazepoxide had no effect on conditioning by amphetamine or morphine, even though it was effective against conditioning by itself. In unpublished work in our laboratory, prior exposure to amphetamine had no effect on conditioning by chlordiazepoxide or by caffeine, the latter of which, like amphetamine, is also a CNS stimulant. Vogel and Nathan (1975) also reported comparable findings in their work with amphetamine and amobarbital, as have Goudie and Thornton (1975) in experiments with amphetamine and fenfluramine.

## 3.5. Conclusions

Pretreatment effects are among the most interesting and important findings related to gustatory conditioning by psychoactive drugs. A comprehensive explanation for the existing data would be invaluable. Yet there is no account that is not subject to seriously damaging criticism stemming from data that are difficult if not impossible to incorporate. Each of the four alternatives that have been considered has some merit, just as each has deficiencies. It seems highly unlikely that a single-factor account will suffice, and with good reason. The good reason is that repeated exposure to a drug is not a simple manipulation. All of the consequences that have been suggested for this manipulation must be considered as real possibilities. The creation of an artificial need can occur, tolerance can develop, habituation can take place, and associative processes may be engaged. It is difficult to control a preexposure manipulation to the extent that only one of its properties is allowed to vary while the others are obviated or controlled in some way. Thus, "crucial" experiments are impossible to devise, except perhaps in the negative sense of failing to confirm, rather than unequivocally supporting, a particular viewpoint. Because a multiplicity of factors is involved, it seems likely that a multifactor account will be necessary to embrace all of the data. A strategic advantage of adopting a preference for a single explanatory system does exist, however, insofar as it provides an heuristic context in which to generate testable hypotheses. It is this advantage, rather than theoretical myopia, that seems to account for the pursuit of single-factor accounts by researchers in the area.

## 4. Summing Up

There can be no question that conditioned gustatory aversion *per se* constitutes a phenomenon that is both scientifically important and interesting. But it seems somewhat premature to ascribe a particular level of importance to the fact that the phenomenon occurs when a drug of abuse is the unconditioned stimulus. Before it will become possible to do so, it will be necessary to develop much more information on the properties of psychoactive drugs that are responsible for their effectiveness in gustatory conditioning. This does not promise to be a simple task, and our ability to recognize the need for such information may exceed somewhat the capacity of existing experimental techniques to provide answers. For example, although it has been proposed that drugs may possess properties that fall into the broad categories of "positive" and "negative" (Coussens *et al.*, 1973), clear-cut evidence is still lacking on this rudimentary point, plausible as the assertion may seem. In actuality, it is still not known whether the pharmacological events that are responsible for gustatory aversion are different from those that are responsible for positive reinforcement. The only generalization for which there would appear to be broad assent is that sickness, in the sense of gastrointestinal disturbance, cannot generally account for conditioned aversion by drugs of abuse. Such progress as has been made on this subject has come from such astute investigators as Berger *et al.* (1973), but even in this excellent work a serious problem was evident. This was the arbitrary selection of anorexia as a key mechanism despite the potential involvement of any number of effects of amphetamine. It may not in fact be the case that the important mechanisms need be related to feeding systems at all. The methods available to manipulate potential mechanisms remain relatively gross; even at a more refined level, it is not possible to affect any particular mechanisms without simultaneously incurring the possibility of affecting others. The level of analysis appears to be one of choosing between central or peripheral action, rather than, say, between conditioned anorexia and conditioned cardiovascular disturbance.

The original interest in gustatory conditioning by psychoactive drugs was initially stimulated by the assumption, perhaps somewhat naive, that it should not be possible to promote avoidance using unconditioned stimuli recognized as positive reinforcers. There is still no definitive resolution of this issue, but the surprise value of the phenomenon has worn off by now, and it will require more than simple demonstrations of conditioning by a psychoactive drug to warrant continued interest. One example of a worthwhile pursuit that has received its impetus in large part from a primary interest in psychoactive drugs is the general area of pretreatment effects. In this work there promises to be a dividend of knowledge concerning drug effects in particular and the conditioning process in general.

A contribution of considerable potential importance stems from an acceptance of gustatory conditioning by psychoactive drugs as a model of the *control of behavior* by the stimulus complex produced by drugs (Cappell and LeBlanc, 1975b). That is, gustatory conditioning provides an index of *disposition* toward drugs as stimuli, even if the dispositional response is avoidance rather than approach. This property of the conditioning model gives it promise as a supplement to techniques of self-administration in the general effort at understanding drug dependence. Moreover, some advantages over self-administration methods can be identified. For example, one feature of the traditional operant methods of self-administration is that an animal must usually undergo some degree of exposure to a drug before it acquires a stable baseline of behavior against which to assess the effects of independent variables that might be of interest. Indeed, it is sometimes the case that an animal must be trained to self-administer one drug before it can be reliably induced to work for another (Woods, Ikomi, and Winger, 1971). Such requirement may be problematic if one wishes to examine the control of behavior by drugs in a pharmacologically naive animal. The gustatory conditioning method, in contrast, demands a minimum of exposure to drugs before effective control of behavior by a pharmacological stimulus is established. A second feature of self-administration techniques that is occasionally problematic is that the sheer delivery of the reinforcer can have an effect on the behavior that is necessary to acquire the reinforcer. Thus, for example, if response rate on some reinforcement schedule is to be used as an index of disposition toward a particular dose of some drug, a potential confounding exists between the effects of a drug as a reinforcer and its direct effects on operant behavior. The problem is soluble by the use of appropriate controls, but it exists nonetheless. However, the drug that controls behavior need not be present when the dependent variable is measured using an index of gustatory aversion, and a relatively pure measure of dispositional tendency, unconfounded by effects of the unconditioned stimulus on the behavioral baseline, is available.

Despite the fact that some advantages can be claimed for the gustatory conditioning technique, it must be emphasized that it is not being proposed as a substitute for operant models based on well-documented principles of reinforcement. As a *behavioral* model, gustatory conditioning does not, in the final analysis, provide an experimental analogue of drug-seeking behavior. But it does provide a method in which behavior can be brought under the control of pharmacological events, and as such is of considerable interest to students of drug dependence. For example, it opens the possibility for research into interventions that can attenuate or break the control of the UCS. It is clear from such an analysis that the most promising avenue for exploiting the model lies in developing manipulations that might directly affect the action of the UCS. Pharmacological blockers or antagonists, for example, can be usefully assessed (e.g., LeBlanc and Cappell, 1975). In doing such research, it is important to be able to separate the effects of manipulations on the action of the UCS from effects on the learning process *per se*.

Finally, it is worth reiterating that what is being proposed is a line of research that is both a supplement and complement to self-administration methods. There are some issues (e.g., long-term studies of the maintenance of behavior by drugs) that can only be addressed using established operant techniques. And importantly, it remains to be determined whether the pharmacological events that govern behavior in the two behavioral paradigms are sufficiently similar for effective cross-fertilization to occur.

## 5. References

Amit, Z., and Baum, M. Comment on the increased resistance-to-extinction of an avoidance response induced by certain drugs. *Psychological Reports*, 1970, *27*, 310.
Bainbridge, J. G. The effect of psychotropic drugs on food reinforced behavior and food consumption. *Psychopharmacologia*, 1970, *17*, 204–213.

Barry, H. III, and Miller, N. E. Comparison of drug effects on approach, avoidance, and escape motivation. *Journal of Comparative and Physiological Psychology*, 1965, *59*, 18–24.

Berger, B. D. Conditioning of food aversions by injections of psychoactive drugs. *Journal of Comparative and Physiological Psychology*, 1972, *81*, 21–26.

Berger, B. D., Wise, C. D., and Stein, L. Area postrema damage and bait shyness. *Journal of Comparative and Physiological Psychology*, 1973, *82*, 475–479.

Braveman, N. S. Absence of taste aversion following prior exposure to sickness. Paper presented at a symposium entitled "Psychopharmacology and learned taste aversions," American Psychological Association, Chicago, September 2, 1975a.

Braveman, N. S. Formation of taste aversions in rats following prior exposure to sickness. *Learning and Motivation*, 1975b, *6*, 512–534.

Cameron, O. G., and Appel, J. B. Conditioned suppression of bar-pressing behavior by stimuli associated with drugs. *Journal of the Experimental Analysis of Behavior*, 1972, *17*, 127–137.

Cappell, H., and Herman, C. P. Alcohol and tension reduction: A Review. *Quarterly Journal of Studies on Alcohol*, 1972, *33*, 33–64.

Cappell, H., and LeBlanc, A. E. Punishment of saccharin drinking by amphetamine in rats and its reversal by chlordiazepoxide. *Journal of Comparative and Physiological Psychology*, 1973, *85*, 97–104.

Cappell, H., and LeBlanc, A. E. Conditioned aversion by amphetamine: Rates of acquisition and loss of the attenuating effects of prior exposure. *Psychopharmacologia*, 1975a, *43*, 157–162.

Cappell, H., and LeBlanc, A. E. Conditioned aversion by psychoactive drugs: Does it have significance for an understanding of drug dependence? *Addictive Behaviors*, 1975b, *1*, 55–64.

Cappell, H., and LeBlanc, A. E. Parametric investigations of the effects of prior exposure to amphetamine and morphine on conditioned gustatory aversion. *Psychopharmacology*, 1977, *51*, 265–271.

Cappell, H., LeBlanc, A. E., and Endrenyi, L. Effects of chlordiazepoxide and ethanol on the extinction of a conditioned taste aversion. *Physiology and Behavior*, 1972, *9*, 167–169.

Cappell, H., LeBlanc, A. E., and Endrenyi, L. Aversive conditioning by psychoactive drugs: Effects of morphine, alcohol, and chlordiazepoxide. *Psychopharmacologia*, 1973, *29*, 239–246.

Cappell, H., LeBlanc, A. E., and Herling, S. Modification of the punishing effects of psychoactive drugs in rats by previous drug experience. *Journal of Comparative and Physiological Psychology*, 1975, *89*, 347–356.

Carey, R. J. Long-term aversion to a saccharin solution induced by repeated amphetamine injections. *Pharmacology, Biochemistry and Behavior*, 1973, *1*, 265–269.

Carey, R. J., and Goodall, E. B. Amphetamine-induced taste aversion: A comparison of *d*-versus *l*-amphetamine. *Pharmacology, Biochemistry and Behavior*, 1974, *2*, 325–330.

Cochin, J., and Kornetsky, C. Development and loss of tolerance to morphine in the rat after single and multiple injections. *Journal of Pharmacology and Experimental Therapeutics*, 1964, *145*, 1–10.

Coussens, W. R. Conditioned taste aversion: Route of drug administration. In J. M. Singh and H. Lal (Eds.), *Drug addiction: Neurobiology and influences on behavior*, Vol. 3. Miami: Symposium Specialists, 1974.

Coussens, W. R. Route of administration and conditioned taste aversion. Paper presented at a symposium entitled "Psychopharmacology and learned taste aversions," American Psychological Association, Chicago, September 2, 1975.

Coussens, W. R., Crowder, W. F., and Davis, W. M. Morphine induced saccharin aversion in α-methyltyrosine pretreated rats. *Psychopharmacologia*, 1973, *29*, 151–157.

Davis, W. M., and Smith, S. G. Blocking of morphine based reinforcement by alphamethyltyrosine. *Life Sciences*, 1973a, *12* 185–191.

Davis, W. M., and Smith, S. G. Blocking effect of α-methyltyrosine on amphetamine based reinforcement. *Journal of Pharmacy and Pharmacology*, 1973b, *25*, 174–177.

Deneau, G., Yanagita, T., and Seevers, M. H. Self-administration of psychoactive substances by the monkey. *Psychopharmacologia*, 1969, *16*, 30–48.

Elsmore, T. F. Saccharin aversion induced by delta-9-tetrahydrocannabinol: Effects of repeated doses prior to pairing with saccharin. *Proceedings of the 80th Annual Convention of the American Psychological Association*, 1972, *7*, 817–818.

Elsmore, T. F., and Fletcher, G. V. △⁹-Tetrahydrocannabinol: Aversive effects in rats at high doses. *Science*, 1972, *175*, 911–912.

Falk, J. L., and Burnidge, G. K. Fluid intake and punishment-attenuating drugs. *Physiology and Behavior*, 1970, *5*, 199–202.

Gamzu, E. Pre-exposure to unconditioned stimulus alone may eliminate taste-aversions. Paper presented at the 15th Annual Meeting of the Psychonomic Society, Boston, November 22, 1974.

Gamzu, E. Elimination of taste aversions by pretreatment: Cross-drug comparisons. Paper presented at a symposium entitled "Psychopharmacology and learned taste aversions," American Psychological Association, Chicago, September 2, 1975.

Goudie, A. J., and Thornton, E. W. Effects of drug experience on drug induced conditioned taste aversions: Studies with amphetamine and fenfluramine. *Psychopharmacologia*, 1975, *44*, 77–82.

Goudie, A. J., Thornton, E. W., and Wheatley, J. Attenuation by alpha-methyltyrosine of amphetamine induced conditioned taste aversion. *Psychopharmacologia*, 1975, *45*, 119–123.

Hoffmeister, F., and Wuttke, W. Negative reinforcing properties of morphine-antagonists in naive rhesus monkeys. *Psychopharmacologia*, 1973, *33*, 247–258.

Kalant, H., LeBlanc, A. E., and Gibbins, R. J. Tolerance to, and dependence on, some non-opiate psychotropic drugs. *Pharmacological Reviews*, 1971, *23*, 135–191.

LeBlanc, A. E., and Cappell, H. Attenuation of punishing effects of morphine and amphetamine by chronic prior treatment. *Journal of Comparative and Physiological Psychology*, 1974, *87*, 691–698.

LeBlanc, A. E., and Cappell, H. Antagonism of morphine-induced aversive conditioning by naloxone. *Pharmacology, Biochemistry and Behavior*, 1975, *3*, 185–188.

Lester, D., Nachman, M., and LeMagnen, J. Aversive conditioning by ethanol in the rat. *Quarterly Journal of Studies on Alcohol*, 1970, *31*, 578–586.

Maickel, R. P., Cox, R. H., Jr., Miller, F. P., Segal, D. S., and Russell, R. W. Correlation of brain levels of drugs with behavioral effects. *Journal of Pharmacology and Experimental Therapeutics*, 1969, *165*, 216–224.

Margules, D., and Stein, L. Neuroleptics vs. tranquilizers: Evidence from animal behavior studies of mode and site of action. In H. Brill, J. O. Cole, P. Deniker, H. Hippius, and P. B. Bradley (Eds.), *Neuropsychopharmacology*. Amsterdam: Excepta Medical Foundation, 1967.

Martin, J. C., and Ellinwood, E. H., Jr. Conditioned aversion to a preferred solution following methamphetamine injections. *Psychopharmacologia*, 1973, *29*, 253–261.

McKearney, J. W. Maintenance of responding under a fixed interval of electric shock. *Science*, 1968, *160*, 1249–1251.

Nachman, M., Lester, D., and LeMagnen, J. Alcohol aversion in the rat: Behavioral assessment of noxious drug effects. *Science*, 1970, *168*, 1244–1246.

Parker, L., Failor, A., and Weidman, K. Conditioned preferences in the rat with an unnatural need state: Morphine withdrawal. *Journal of Comparative and Physiological Psychology*, 1973, *82*, 294–300.

Pickens, R., and Harris, W. C. Self-administration of *d*-amphetamine by rats. *Psychopharmacologia*, 1968, *12*, 158–163.

Rescorla, R. A. Effect of US habituation following conditioning. *Journal of Comparative and Physiological Psychology*, 1973, *82*, 137–143.

Rozin, P., and Kalat, J. W. Specific hungers and poison avoidance as adaptive specializations of learning. *Psychological Review*, 1971, *78*, 459–486.

Seligman, M. E. P. On the generality of the laws of learning. *Psychological Review*, 1970, *77*, 406–418.

Steiner, S., Beer, B., and Shaffer, M. M. Escape from self-produced rates of brain stimulation. *Science*, 1969, *163*, 90–91.

Stolerman, I. P., and Kumar, R. Preferences for morphine in rats: Validation of an experimental model of dependence. *Psychopharmacologia*, 1970, *17*, 137–150.

Thompson, T., Trombley, J., Lake, D., and Lott, D. Effects of morphine on behavior maintained by four simple reinforcement schedules. *Psychopharmacologia*, 1970, *17*, 182–192.

Vogel, J. R. Conditioning of taste aversion by drugs of abuse. Unpublished manuscript.

Vogel, J. R., and Nathan, P. E. Paper presented at a symposium entitled "Psychopharmacology and learned taste aversions," American Psychological Association, Chicago, September 2, 1975.

Whitney, G. D., and Trost, J. G. Response disruption following amphetamine self- and programmed administration. In R. T. Harris, W. McIsacc, and C. R. Schuster (Eds.), *Drug dependence*. Austin: University of Texas Press, 1970.

Woods, J. H., Ikomi, F., and Winger, G. The reinforcing property of ethanol. In N. K. Roach, W. M. McIsaac, and P. J. Creaven (Eds.), *Biological aspects of alcohol*. Austin: University of Texas Press, 1971.

# Suppression of Interspecific Aggression Using Toxic Reinforcers

5

## N. W. Milgram, Mauro Caudarella, and Lester Krames

## 1. Introduction

The present chapter will focus on studies dealing with the control of interspecific aggression, the attacking and killing of members of one species by members of another, using interoceptive reinforcers. This body of literature arose partly out of an interest in the associative specificity of toxicosis to ingestive behavior. Earlier research had indicated that toxic reinforcers were far more effective in establishing aversions to eating or drinking than in suppressing other behavioral sequences. For example, Garcia, Kimeldorf, and Hunt (1961) found that about ten times as much X-irradiation was required to produce an aversion to entering a colored compartment than was necessary to establish an aversion to a flavor. Such evidence was of considerable theoretical significance in that it suggested a far greater specificity of the reinforcing properties of stimuli than had traditionally been assumed. Additional research was clearly required in order to establish the limits on the reinforcing properties of toxicosis; to this end, interspecific killing proved a convenient response to study.

N. W. Milgram, Mauro Caudarella, and Lester Krames • Department of Psychology, University of Toronto, Toronto, Ontario, Canada. The authors' research described in this chapter was supported by grants from the National Research Council of Canada to N. W. Milgram (Grant # NRC 7659) and to Lester Krames (NRC 7455).

There is a second reason that some investigators have been studying the effects of toxicosis on interspecific aggression. Many animal species satisfy their nutritive and caloric needs by the capture, killing, and subsequent ingestion of prey. Killing by these predatory animals can be considered an appetitive component of feeding and there is other evidence which indicates that appetitive behavior which leads to the presentation of specific foods can be disrupted by the establishment of aversions to those foods (Best, Best, and Ahlers, 1971). It consequently was of theoretical interest to determine whether predation could be controlled by the establishment of aversions to ingestion of prey.

The following section compares the effects of pairing toxicosis with two types of behaviors—killing and eating—by reviewing the literature on the suppression of mouse killing by laboratory rats. There appear to be differences between the rat and other species and these differences are considered in Section 3.

## 2. Muricide, the Mouse-Killing Response of Rats

Muricide is probably the most thoroughly studied example of interspecific aggression. Interest in this phenomenon is attributable in part to the convenience of using the laboratory rat and in part to the reliability of the occurrence of muricide in "killer rats." Only a small proportion of laboratory rats generally kill mice, but those that do, do so immediately and in a stereotyped manner whenever given the opportunity.

The biological function of muricide remains open to speculation. O'Boyle (1974) has argued that muricide is a predatory response related to food getting, a view supported by evidence of a close relationship between mouse killing and feeding. Deprivation of food increases the probability that naive rats will kill mice, and, moreover, rats will typically ingest mice prey. Additional support for the predatory nature of muricide is suggested by the manner in which rats kill mice: in contrast to other forms of aggressive encounters, muricide lacks display components, a clear similarity to the interspecific killing of other predators (O'Boyle, 1975).

Such evidence is not unequivocal in establishing muricide as predatory. Rats are thought to be scavengers in nature (Barnett, 1963) and it seems unlikely that prey are an important dietary constituent. In addition, the nature of the relationship between muricide and ingestive activity is far from clear. Rats which kill mice continue to do so regardless of either their deprivation state (Paul, Miley, and Baenninger, 1971) or whether they are permitted to eat mice prey (Myer and White, 1965). On the other hand, mouse killing cannot be induced by food deprivation in rats which do not kill (e.g., Karli, 1956). Finally, there are other possible explanations for muricide which seem at least as plausible as a predation interpretation, but have received little consideration. For example, muricide may represent an adaptation which serves to reduce interspecific competition, a possibility consistent with the fact that rats and mice can inhabit similar environments and consequently compete with each other for food.

The question of biological function clearly requires further consideration. It would be particularly desirable to be able to clarify the nature of the relationship between muricide and eating. Evidence of an apparently unique relationship between ingestive behavior and toxicosis suggests one way of infering the functional significance of muricide. As has been described previously in this volume, a single injection of a toxic chemical can produce an aversion to a food. If muricide is a component of ingestive behavior, it should also be possible to suppress mouse killing using toxic reinforcers. The first part of this section compares attempts to suppress muricide using post kill injections with food aversion learning. The second part considers the relationship between muricide and feeding from another perspective, that of the specificity of the effect of post kill injections on muricide. If muricide is a component of ingestive behavior, then mouse eating should be suppressed in animals which have been punished for just killing; conversely, mouse killing would be inhibited by establishing an aversion to mouse eating. The final topic considered in this section is a comparison of the effects of toxicosis and foot shock on muricide. This question is of importance in view of evidence that foot shock and toxicosis have differential effects on feeding.

## 2.1. Effects of Postkill Injections of Toxic Chemicals

The question of whether muricide could be inhibited by injections of toxic chemicals was initially raised in three separate studies (Clody and Vogel, 1973; Krames, Milgram, and Christie, 1973; O'Boyle, Looney, and Cohen, 1973), each of which used a similar procedure. Rats which reliably killed mice were selected from a larger population. During the subsequent conditioning trials, the rats were permitted to kill mice placed into their home cages; immediately following the kill, the mouse carcass was removed and the rat received an intraperitoneal injection of either lithium chloride (LiCl) (Krames *et al.*, 1973; O'Boyle *et al.*, 1973) or atropine methylnitrate (Clody and Vogel, 1973). Conditioning trials were repeated daily until the rats no longer killed during the alotted testing interval.

All three studies reported that rats stop killing mice following repeated postkill injections (e.g., Figure 1). Although a single treatment does not totally suppress killing, measurements of latencies to kill reveal increments over successive trials (O'Boyle *et al.*, 1973) which reflect both an increase in latency to attack and a decrease in the effectiveness of the attack response. Eventually, the attack response becomes totally suppressed and the rats are likely to avoid all contact with mice.

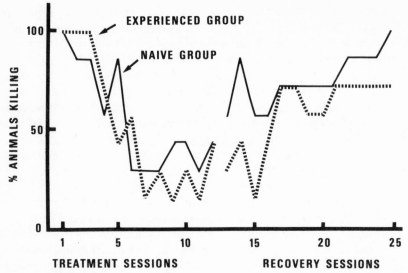

**Figure 1.** Suppression of mouse killing by lithium chloride treatments (.15 M, 2% of body weight). Intraperitoneal injections followed every successful kill during treatment sessions, but not during recovery sessions. Each session lasted 45 min. The "naive group" ($n = 7$) received their first LiCl treatment following their initial kill. The "experienced group" ($n = 7$) was first poisoned following their third kill.

### 2.1.1. Pretreatment Effects

*a. Prior Killing Experience.* Killer rats are typically selected from a larger population of animals after one or more screening trials. As a consequence, the subjects have experience with muricide prior to the first aversive conditioning session; however, such practice effects cannot account for the slowness of acquisition. When Krames *et al.* (1973) eliminated any possibility of practice effects by administering LiCl immediately following the first screening test in one group of rats, an average of 4.4 conditioning trials were required to suppress killing in these animals. Compared to food aversion learning, which typically occurs after a single trial, this acquisition rate is very slow. Surprisingly, a second group of animals, which were allowed two unpunished kills before conditioning sessions were started, stopped killing just as rapidly as the animals which were injected with LiCl following their initial kill (Figure 1). These findings were unexpected, since it is known that the acquisition of conditioned food aversions is inversely related to familiarity with the food. It consequently was important to determine whether this finding was attributable simply to insufficient experience. Possibly more than two prior kills are necessary before experience with killing has an effect on suppression.

Caudarella, Milgram, O'Dwyer, and Krames (in prep.) examined suppression in three groups of rats: a low-, medium-, and high-experience group. The low-experience group was injected with LiCl following the first screening session. These animals were then tested for mouse killing once a day for 24 consecutive days. Each daily test was terminated either immediately following a kill, or after 45 min without a kill. Lithium chloride was injected within 5 min after each of the first 12 tests but was not injected after the last 12 tests. The other two groups were treated identically except that, before the conditioning procedure was instituted, the medium-experience animals were permitted five unpunished kills and the high-experience animals were allowed ten unpunished kills. As can be seen in Figure 2, the results of this experiment were clear: it was more difficult to suppress killing in the high-experience group than in the low- or medium-experience groups. The medium-experience group animals were intermediate between the other two in terms of the number of treatment sessions required to produce suppression. In a separate experiment, Krames and Milgram (in prep.) attempted to establish an aversion to killing in 16 animals which had had 20 prior kills. Six of these animals continued to kill even after 20 consecutive conditioning sessions; the other ten animals required a mean of 7.9 injections of LiCl before they stopped killing during the 45-min session. These results indicate that prior experience with killing can have marked effects on the inhibition of killing by postkill injections. Indeed, it may not be possible to inhibit killing in some highly experienced animals.

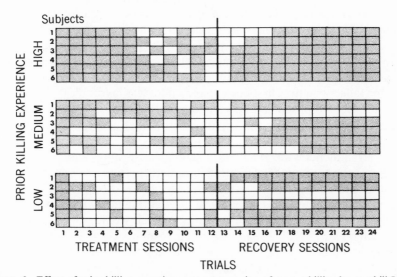

**Figure 2.** Effect of prior killing experience on suppression of mouse killing by postkill LiCl treatments. Kills are indicated by dark squares, while an open square indicates that the rat did not kill during the 45-min session. Over the treatment phase, LiCl was injected following every trial. During the recovery phase no injections were given.

*b. Selective Factor.* A selective bias is, of necessity, introduced into the design of all muricide experiments, as only a small percentage of rats normally become mouse killers. The method used in screening rats affects the proportion of rats which will eventually kill. When mice are introduced to naive Long Evans rats maintained on *ad libitum* food and water, approximately 10–20% of the rats will kill; a greater proportion will kill if the rats are screened while under food deprivation and the proportion will be even greater if the animals are previously maintained on a cyclic food deprivation schedule. While the importance of such selective factors is open to conjecture, there is reason to believe that they affect the suppression of killing.

As previously mentioned, Krames *et al.* (1973) found that for inexperienced "killer" rats an average of 4.4 injections of LiCl were necessary to suppress killing during a 45-min testing session. DeCastro and Balagura (1975), on the other hand, found that an average of 2.4 LiCl treatments were necessary to suppress killing during a 60-min testing session. Since the animals tested by DeCastro and Balagura were allowed three kills before conditioning was started, their animals ought to have required more conditioning trials than the animals tested by Krames *et al.* Selection factors may well account for the more rapid acquisition reported by DeCastro and Balagura. Their screening procedure was preceded by a cyclic food deprivation schedule and as a consequence all 20 of their subjects became killers. In contrast, the screening procedure used by Krames *et al.* simply involved the presentation of mice, a method which detected a small number of killers. It seems likely that this latter procedure selects only animals which have a high initial prepotency to kill. On the other hand, the method used by DeCastro and Balagura undoubtably led to the selection of many animals which had a low initial prepotency to kill and would not have become killers had they first been tested under less favorable conditions. It does not seem improbable that individual differences in initial killing prepotency would influence the rapidity with which animals learn to stop killing.

Pretreatments with some pharmacological agents is another means of modifying the percentage of mouse killers selected and this selective factor might also affect the acquisition of an aversion to killing. Gay, Leaf, and Arble (1974) induced mouse killing by pretreating rats with pilocarpine, a drug which releases mouse killing in rats which would not otherwise kill (Vogel and Leaf, 1972). The mouse killing response could be suppressed in pilocarpine-induced killers by postkill administration of *d*-amphetamine; but compared to nondrug killers, suppression was considerably weaker.

### 2.1.2. Properties of the Aversive Stimulus

As previously mentioned, injections of either lithium chloride or atropine methylnitrate can be used to inhibit muricide. In addition, postkill treatment with amphetamine or pilocarpine also effectively suppresses killing (Gay *et al.*, 1974). In each instance, it is probable that the suppression resulted from the response-contingent administration rather than proactive effects or toxic consequences of repeated drug injections. Proactive effects of multiple drug treatments can be ruled out for atropine methylnitrate (Vogel and Leaf, 1972) and LiCl (Krames *et al.*, 1973). It is also improbable that proactive consequences are important when pilocarpine is used since repeated administration of this drug can actually induce killing, as previously mentioned. Noncontingent administration of amphetamine, on the other hand, does suppress mouse killing but this effect appears to be a central consequence, independent of the suppressive effects of postkill administration of amphetamine: Gay *et al.* (1974) found that *l*-amphetamine, a centrally inactive isomer, suppressed mouse killing when administered within 5 min after a kill, whereas prekill administration of *l*-amphetamine had no effect on muricide. Furthermore, killing recovered spontaneously after the drug had worn off in animals suppressed by prekill treatments with amphetamine, but not in animals given postkill injections.

These findings indicate that it is the aversive consequences of the drugs which are responsible for the suppression of killing. However, there are no specific behavioral or pharmacological effects common to all of the agents used; to the contrary, some have opposite effects. Lithium chloride causes a general behavioral inhibition and has obvious aversive side effects such as nausea (e.g., Sheard, 1975). On the other hand, *d*-amphetamine is a stimulant with no obvious aversive effects and in other situations has been used as a positive reinforcer (see Cappell and LeBlanc, Chapter 4). The noncontingent suppression of mouse killing by *d*-amphetamine also contrasts with the release of muricide by pilocarpine.

The only effect which is common to all of the agents under discussion is that on the physiological state of organism. Gay *et al.* (1974) consequently suggest that it is the production of discriminable changes in physiological state (independently of anything else the drugs may do) which accounts for the punishing consequences. At this point further research is clearly needed before this conclusion can be accepted. What is clear, however, is that the range of potentially effective aversive stimuli is extensive. It is also probable that any agent which supports food aversion learning will also be effective in suppressing mouse killing.

### 2.1.3. Long-Delay Learning

Although the same aversive agents can be used to suppress mouse killing and to establish food aversions, there seem to be parametric differences. As we have seen, aversions to killing differ from aversions to food in that the former are not typically acquired after a single treatment. Another possible difference is in the efficacy of suppression when there is a delay between the presentation of conditioned stimulus and the administration of the aversive stimulus. As is now well-documented, one of the remarkable properties of food aversion learning is that conditioning can occur after long delays. In contrast, suppression of killing has not been established following long delays. In every report of successful suppression, the delay between killing and the injection of the toxic chemical was less than 5 min and attempts using longer intervals have been unsuccessful. Berg and Baenninger (1974) used a 15-min delay between killing and LiCl treatment, and found no decrement in latency to kill. Using the same dose of LiCl and the same conditioning interval in another group of rats, they were able to suppress the eating of dead mice. O'Boyle *et al.* (1973) used a 3-h delay and found neither suppression of killing, nor any increase in latency to kill. Gay *et al.* (1974) were able to suppress killing when amphetamine was injected immediately following killing but not when the drug was injected 30 min after a kill. This finding must be viewed cautiously, as the subjects were initially nonkillers which became killers only after extended pretreatment with pilocarpine (see section 2.1.2). Finally, Krames *et al.* (1973) administered LiCl to a group of killer rats 12 h following a kill on each of 12 consecutive days; no effect on muricide was observed in any of the animals.

It is, of course, clear that these data do not preclude the possibility that mouse killing could be suppressed following a long delay in the delivery of reinforcement; more conditioning sessions and possibly a stronger aversive stimulus may be necessary. This is an empirical problem which deserves further attention. We can conclude, however, that even if it were possible to establish an aversion to killing using long delays, the parameters required would differ substantially from those which are effective in producing food aversions.

### 2.1.4. Recovery of Killing

In most instances, the suppression produced by postkill injections is not permanent: killing is likely to reappear after punishment is discontinued (Krames *et al.,* 1973; O'Boyle *et al.,* 1973; DeCastro and Balagura, 1975). Killing typically reemerges after several presentations of mice in the absence of any aversive treatment. Recovery also occurs when the presentation of mice is followed by control injections of saline; however, it is delayed, presumably because the saline injections acquire secondary reinforcing properties (DeCastro and Balagura, 1975).

On the other hand, the reemergence of muricide can be observed over repeated testing during which LiCl injections are administered following every trial. This can be seen in the left-hand side of Figure 2. During the first 12 days of this experiment, posttrial LiCl injections were administered daily, whether or not the animal killed. Every animal resumed killing at least once after it had stopped killing during the "treatment sessions." This observation may simply reflect the lability of drug-induced inhibition of killing. It is also possible that extinction occurs when LiCl injections are dissociated from the killing response, that is, when LiCl is injected following exposure to mice in the absence of any sensory cues associated with a successful kill.

The recovery process can be divided into two phases. The first involves the reemergence of killing within the testing period, which can either occur after a single no-kill trial or may take considerably longer. The individual differences are striking. For example, Krames *et al.* (1973) did not observe any recovery of killing in 2 of 14 animals, while a third animal began killing following 18 no-kill trials. At the other extreme, killing reappeared in some animals following a single no-kill trial. Prior experience with killing is another factor which can influence this aspect of recovery (O'Boyle *et al.*, 1973; Krames and Milgram, in prep.). This can be seen in Figure 2: every high-experience animal started killing again after a single successful suppression test; medium-experience animals recovered after a mean of 2.5 no-kill trials; while the low-experience animals took even longer—a mean of 3.5 trials. Figure 2 also illustrates that the rate of recovery is inversely related to the number of trials in the acquisition phase; the more rapidly the aversion is acquired, the slower the reemergence of killing.

The second phase of recovery involves the reestablishment of normal killing. Unpunished killer rats kill almost immediately after mice are presented. In contrast, the latency to kill of previously suppressed rats is initially long, but gradually decreases to the preconditioning baseline after successive unpunished kills (Krames and Milgram, in prep.).

It is possible that the recovery of killing following suppression may depend on the choice of aversive agent. Clody and Vogel (1973) reported that even after 17 daily saline injections there was no substantial recovery in animals aversively conditioned using atropine methylnitrate. Recovery has occurred much more rapidly when LiCl has been used, but it is not clear that atropine methylnitrate is a more effective reinforcer. Inspection of the results presented by Clody and Vogel indicates that some animals were killing during each of the 17 sessions, and it is not unlikely that every animal killed during one or more of the sessions. Possibly the secondary-reinforcing properties of the saline injections served to reinstitute suppression in their animals over the course of the nondrug sessions.

## 2.2. Dissociation of Killing and Eating

In order to suppress muricide, it is necessary to remove the mouse carcass immediately following each kill. If the rats are allowed to eat a part of the mouse, subsequent LiCl treatments produce an aversion to the eating of mice but not to the killing of mice (Clody and Vogel, 1973; Krames *et al.*, 1973; Rusiniak, Gustavson, Hankins, and Garcia, 1976). There are two possible explanations for the occurrence of a selective suppression of eating in this situation. First, according to the principle of stimulus relevance (see Revusky, Chapter 1), it would be expected that an association between eating and LiCl would be established more readily than an association between killing and LiCl. This seems to be the case. As previously mentioned, Berg and Baenninger (1974) found that a single injection of LiCl was sufficient to suppress mouse eating but not mouse killing. Krames *et al.* (1973) reported that mouse eating was suppressed more rapidly and recovered more slowly than mouse killing. Secondly, the principle of contiguity might account for the selective suppression since eating is temporally more contiguous with the LiCl injections than is killing. From this perspective, it is necessary to assume that killing and eating are discrete and dissociable responses, a position supported by the following experiment (Krames and Milgram, in prep.). Killer rats were tested for mouse killing every other day. On the intervening days, each animal was tested for mouse eating by presenting it with mice freshly killed by "soldier" rats (killer rats which did not otherwise participate in the experiment). The rats were randomly divided into two groups: the first group, "KEK," received LiCl injections following each of the first ten successive killing tests, but not following any of the interpersed tests of mouse eating. The procedure was reversed for the other group, "EKE": LiCl was injected following each of the first six eating tests, but not following any of the killing tests. The results of this experiment are shown in Figures 3 and 4. Killing but not eating was suppressed when the LiCl injections followed only killing (group KEK). Just the opposite occurred when the LiCl followed only eating (group EKE): eating was readily suppressed but killing was not affected. The principle of stimulus relevance also received support from this experiment, as the aversion to eating developed more rapidly than did the aversion to killing.

It is not possible to determine from these findings whether contiguity or stimulus relevance is the more important; both predict that eating but not killing will be suppressed when LiCl is administered after ingestion of a previously killed mouse. In an attempt to dissociate these two factors, Krames (unpub.) presented a group of killer rats with a dead mouse and allowed them to eat for 30 min. He then introduced a live mouse and within 5 min after each successful kill injected the animals with LiCl. In this situation, taste, the cue most relevant to poisoning, is not contiguous with the aversive treatments: contiguity and stimulus relevance are therefore acting in opposition. The results did not differentiate stimulus relevance and contiguity. What was most striking was the inconsistency of the data: some animals stopped killing but continued to eat; some animals acquired

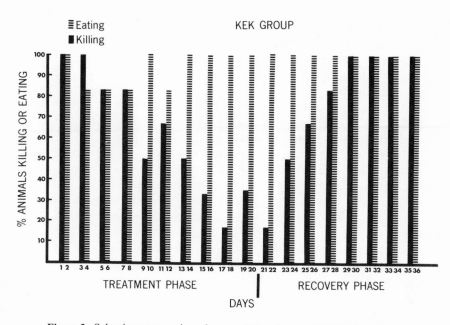

**Figure 3.** Selective suppression of mouse killing by postkill LiCl injections.

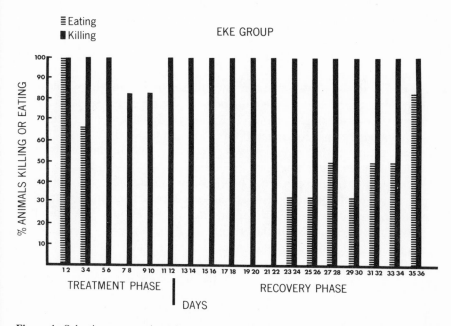

**Figure 4.** Selective suppression of mouse eating by LiCl injections following ingestion of freshly killed mice.

an aversion to eating but not to killing; finally, there were instances where both killing and eating were inhibited.

Given the history of the rats used in the experiments just described, it is not surprising that either mouse killing or eating could be selectively suppressed. Laboratory-bred rats are routinely raised on a diet of laboratory chow and water; they have never had the opportunity to kill mice or any other prey in order to obtain food; nor have they had the opportunity to eat flesh. It seems implausible that the initial kill by such naive rats should relate in any way to the rat's anticipation of a meal. By the same token, when rats do eat following an initial kill, it is likely to be a consequence of the adventitious availability of a highly preferred food (Karli, 1956). It remains possible, however, that the killing and eating could become associatively linked if the appropriate prior experience were provided. This hypothesis is indirectly supported by a recent study (Paul, 1975) which showed that mouse killing was more likely to occur in rats which were previously fed dead mice than in rats maintained on laboratory chow or fed another flesh diet.

Krames and Milgram (in prep.) attempted to establish an associative relationship between killing and eating by giving animals extensive experience with both. Killer rats were allowed both to kill and to eat twice a day for 10 days: half of the subjects were supplied with live mice prey as their only source of food; the other half were also given laboratory chow. The animals were subsequently tested for mouse killing on alternate days and mouse eating on the intervening days. Half of the animals received LiCl injections following killing but not following eating; the other half were poisoned following eating but not following a kill. The results provided no support for an associative-linkage hypothesis. Poisoning that followed eating alone produced an aversion only to eating in all subjects. The animals in the group poisoned only after killing either acquired an aversion to killing alone or else continued both to kill and to eat throughout the 20 testing sessions. The suppression was selective even in the animals which had had to kill in order to eat.

One goal of this research has been to determine whether or not muricide is a true predatory response. The answer depends on what is meant by predatory. If predation simply refers to interspecific killing, then muricide is predatory by definition. On the other hand, if the concept is used to refer to a goal-directed behavioral sequence, the aim of which is the ingestion of food, then the rats' mouse killing cannot be considered predatory; perhaps *capricious predation* is a more appropriate label. Anticipation of food is not essential for the initiation nor for the maintenance of mouse killing as rats will continue to kill mice which they will not eat. In addition, the eating of mice can be independent of the rats' tendency to kill: mouse eating is not disrupted in suppressed killers, even if killing has previously been linked with eating. Those events critical in the control of mouse eating must, therefore, be dissociable from those events critical in the control of mouse killing. Moreover, the aversion acquired by suppressed eaters must be different from that acquired by suppressed killers.

It is probable that conditioned gustatory aversions underlie the aversions to mouse eating established by LiCl injections. It has been convincingly demonstrated in most instances that food aversions are manifestations of conditioned taste aversions in the rat (see Chapter 3). Two additional lines of evidence suggest that gustatory cues are critical for the establishment of aversions to mouse eating. First, the fact that animals in which eating has been suppressed still kill suggests that olfactory or other exteroceptive characteristics of mice prey are not aversive, and by a process of elimination implicates taste. Second, gustatory cues are implicated by the pattern of recovery of mouse eating. Normal killer rats tend to feed on dead mice in a predictable manner, showing a marked preference for the brain and internal organs and generally leaving the skin, appendages, and the tail (Paul and Posner, 1973). In contrast, the recovery of feeding typically starts with rats' consuming those parts of the mice which they had previously avoided (Krames *et al.*, 1973); it may take considerable time before such rats start eating the brain and internal organs. A striking example of the unusual pattern of eating during recovery is illustrated in Figure 5, which shows a mouse that was completely skinned; such eating behavior has never been observed in the case of normal killer rats.

Since animals which have acquired an aversion to killing will nevertheless eat mice, it is unlikely that the acquired aversion is controlled by gustatory cues. Another possibility is that killers learn to inhibit the

**Figure 5.** Carcass of mouse prey skinned by rat during recovery from suppression of mouse eating.

specific responses associated with killing. Although this hypothesis cannot be ruled out, it seems unlikely because it has been demonstrated in other species that suppression of killing is specific to the prey associated with the poison (see Section 2.3). The more plausible alternative is that an aversion to mouse killing is a manifestation of an aversion to exteroceptive cues. This suggestion is consistent with the "freezing" behavior and avoidance of mice which is seen in suppressed killers. It can also account for the observation that suppressed killers will eat dead mice (presumably the taste of the mouse is not aversive). Finally, the parameters which are important for inhibiting killing are similar to those which are required for the establishment of aversions to specific exteroceptive stimuli. As discussed previously, conditioned aversions to killing require multiple trials and are difficult if not impossible to establish over long delays. Conditioned olfactory aversions are similar in both respects (Hankins, Garcia, and Rusiniak, 1973). On the other hand, conditioned taste aversions are typically acquired in a single trial and can be established over long delay intervals.

It is not clear which exteroceptive cues are used by rats in the acquisition of an aversion to mouse killing. The two most likely are olfactory and visual cues. The parallels between conditioned aversions to killing and conditioned olfactory aversions suggest that olfactory cues could serve as appropriate conditioned stimuli. This position is also consistent with evidence implicating odor in the initiation of mouse killing (e.g., Myer, 1964). On the other hand, it is difficult to reconcile this hypothesis with the occurrence of mouse eating in animals which show suppression of killing; it seems unlikely that the odor of a freshly killed mouse would differ significantly from that of a live mouse. Moreover, olfactory cues are not necessary for the maintenance of mouse killing, as killing persists even after the removal of the olfactory bulbs (e.g., Karli, 1961). Visual information may also be of importance, as it has been demonstrated that prey movement contributes to muricide (Van Hemel and Colucci, 1973), and it has been established that rats can acquire poison-induced aversions to visual cues (Best, Best, and Mickley, 1973). However, visual input is not essential for the maintenance of mouse killing as blinding does not abolish muricide (e.g., Karli, 1961).

Stanley and Milgram (unpub.) used sensory deafferentation in an attempt to determine the roles of olfactory and visual cues in the acquisition of an aversion to killing. Four groups of killer rats were used: the first was blinded, the second was made anosmic by removal of the olfactory bulbs, the third group was both blinded and bulbectomized, and the fourth group served as unoperated controls. Lithium chloride treatments were successfully used to establish aversions in every group. In addition, bulbectomy actually facilitated acquisition. This experiment indicates that neither olfaction nor vision is necessary in the establishment of an aversion to killing, but such negative evidence provides little indication of the sensory cues used by normal animals.

## 2.3. Comparison with an Exteroceptive Reinforcer—Foot Shock

In food aversion learning, the type of reinforcer used can be viewed as a constraint determining the nature of the aversion acquired and setting the limits under which learning can occur. If the reinforcer is an interoceptive stimulus, animals acquire an aversion to gustatory properties of the food, and such aversions can be established over long delays. On the other hand, if an exteroceptive stimulus such as foot shock follows the intake of food, rats learn to avoid exteroceptive, but not gustatory, properties of the food; moreover, it is very difficult to establish aversions over long delays. Such differences may be a consequence of the unique associative properties of interoceptive reinforcers. If so, suppression of mouse killing by interoceptive reinforcers should differ from aversions to killing produced by foot shock.

### 2.3.1. Effect of Foot Shock on Muricide

Myer and Baenninger (1966) discovered that mouse killing could be inhibited by response-contingent treatment with punishing foot shock. Using a criterion of no attack within a 5-min interval over three successive trials, they found that suppression of killing occurred within ten punishment trials (median, 6.5 trials). The suppression established with this procedure was transient: killing reappeared in every animal within 48 h. There were enduring effects of punishment, however, since it took fewer trials to reestablish suppression than it had to produce the initial suppression.

Myer and Baenninger's findings do not reveal any fundamental differences between foot shock and toxic injections: suppression, recovery following suppression, and facilitated reestablishment of suppression occur in either case. Nevertheless, the inhibition of killing produced by foot shock appeared to be weak, seemingly less robust than that resulting from the use of interoceptive reinforcers (Clody and Vogel, 1973; O'Boyle, 1974). In every published study, suppression of killing by aversive chemical treatments has required fewer than 6.5 trials. Moreover, it is likely that suppression would have developed even more slowly had Myer and Baenninger used testing sessions longer than 5 min. The apparently greater efficacy of toxicosis-induced suppression is consistent with the suggestion that aversive interoceptive treatments are more relevant to the killing response than are exteroceptive reinforcers; but this interpretation ignores a critically important procedural variable, that of previous experience with killing. Myer and Baenninger used animals which had had considerable prior killing experience. In a subsequent study, Myer (1967) found that it was far easier to inhibit killing using foot shock in inexperienced killers than it was in experienced killers; moreover, killing reappeared more rapidly in experienced killers than in inexperienced killers.

If prior killing experience is held constant, foot shock is, if anything, a more effective reinforcer than is LiCl. Caudarella et al. (in prep.) discovered that suppression of mouse killing was acquired more rapidly by animals punished with foot shock than by animals punished with LiCl. Rusiniak et al. (1976) were unable to inhibit the mouse killing response of ferrets when LiCl was injected following killing. Foot shock, on the other hand, was effective, although several trials were necessary. Such differences between foot shock and LiCl are, of course, difficult to evaluate because there is no a priori way of equating shock intensity with drug dosage. Consequently, we can conclude only that there are no obvious gounds at present for distinguishing the effects on killing of the two types of aversive stimuli.

## 2.3.2. Disinhibition

Myer and Baenninger (1966) discovered that killing which had been suppressed was reinstated by foot shock. This shock-induced killing can be attributed to disinhibition of a previously suppressed response since non-killer rats do not kill during the administration of foot shock (Baenninger, 1967). The disinhibition phenomenon provides another means of comparing the aversive consequences of foot shock and LiCl; if these reinforcers act differently, disinhibition might not occur following LiCl suppression. To investigate this possibility, Caudarella et al. (in prep.) injected rats with LiCl after each kill until the suppression criterion of no-kill during a half-hour interval was met and then delivered foot shock using the shock parameters described by Myer and Baenninger. Control rats which did not receive foot shock did not kill during the extended interval of time corresponding to the disinhibition (foot shock) interval. In contrast, mice were killed by four of the seven rats tested for shock-induced disinhibition. While this result appears to indicate some disinhibition of killing, in at least two cases there was no directed attack; the kill was a consequence of random bites from an agitated rat. Myer and Baenninger on the other hand reported that clearly directed attacks did occur during the delivery of foot shock in foot shock suppressed animals.

Caudarella et al. next attempted to obtain the disinhibition phenomenon using foot shock as the reinforcer as Myer and Baenninger had done. The procedure was a replication of the LiCl experiment with the exception that foot shock was used to suppress killing. Since only 5 of 11 animals showed disinhibition of killing, the experiment provided no evidence of a qualitative difference between the suppressive effects of LiCl and foot shock on killing.

Caudarella *et al.*'s findings differed from Myer and Baenninger's in that every animal tested by Myer and Baenninger showed disinhibition, while only about 50% of the animals tested by Caudarella *et al.* did. Experiential factors may account for this difference: Caudarella *et al.*'s animals were allowed five kills prior to the initial suppression training, whereas Myer and Baenninger used animals that had considerably more experience with killing. To examine the importance of prior experience with killing, Caudarella *et al.* examined disinhibition of killing in two groups of highly experienced killers (15 prior kills): LiCl was used to suppress killing in one group and foot shock was used in the other. Eighty percent of the animals in both groups showed directed attack and killing during the delivery of foot shock. While these results indicate the importance of experience with killing on the occurrence of disinhibition, they provide no basis for distinguishing LiCl from foot shock since disinhibition could be demonstrated with either aversive stimulus. In each instance, the only variable affecting disinhibition was prior experience: the larger the number of prior kills the more likely that the killing response would be triggered by foot shock.

## 2.4. Summary and Implications

The research summarized in this section indicates that muricide, the mouse killing response of rats, can be suppressed by postkill injections of toxic agents such as lithium chloride. Successful suppression is dependent on a sufficient number of conditioning trials, a lack of extensive prior experience with killing, and a relatively short interval between muricide and the presentation of the aversive stimulus. It is also important that ingestion of mice prey be prevented; toxicosis following ingestion inhibits the eating of mice, but does not affect muricide.

Of particular interest has been the question of the extent to which such aversions to killing are similar to aversions to feeding produced by toxicosis. The evidence indicates that muricide is more difficult to suppress, is more labile, and requires more immediate reinforcement. In addition, the importance of exteroceptive cues in the acquisition of an aversion to mouse killing contrasts with food aversion learning, which is generally a manifestation of a modification of gustatory preference.

A further topic, that of the suppressive effects of foot shock on muricide, was examined in order to compare the aversive properties of toxic reinforcers with foot shock. No marked differences were discovered.

The efficacy of both foot shock and LiCl is affected by prior experience with killing. In addition, foot shock has a similar disinhibiting effect on killing suppressed by LiCl and killing suppressed by foot shock. The apparent similarity in the suppressive effects on muricide of foot shock and LiCl contrasts with the differences between the aversive-conditioning consequences of foot shock and toxicosis when paired with ingestion. Apparently the properties of food aversion learning are not attributable simply to unique aversive consequences of toxicosis.

One striking property of food aversion learning is the rats' apparent predisposition to associate gustatory stimuli with toxic reinforcers. This is not the case when toxic stimuli are paired with killing in which the acquired aversions are to exteroceptive instead of gustatory cues. Since gustatory cues are present during both killing and eating, the difference may be due to the type of response preceding the presentation of the reinforcer (ingestion vs. killing). There is evidence that ingestion contributes to the acquisition of food aversion learning. Domjan and Wilson (1972) found that animals allowed to drink a flavored solution acquired a far more marked aversion to that solution than did animals which had the flavored solution perfused over their tongues. On the other hand, ingestion seems to be unimportant in the acquisition of an olfactory aversion (Domjan, 1973). The apparent differential action of ingestive activity in the acquisition of gustatory aversions suggests a possible explanation for the development of aversions to exteroceptive cues when muricide is paired with toxicosis. Attack and killing possibly facilitate the acquisition of aversions to exteroceptive cues just as ingestion facilitates the acquisition of aversions to interoceptive cues. Attentional processes could mediate these effects; just as the rat is likely to attend to taste while eating, it is likely that rats attend to exteroceptive aspects of prey during killing.

## 3. Some Species Differences: Suppression of Interspecific Aggression by Food Aversions in Predatory Species

As we have previously seen, prey killing and eating can occur independently in the rat. Such capricious predation is not a characteristic of all predators. There are at least two other types of predatory species in which the killing and ingestion are more closely related: species which capture and feed, and true predators.

### 3.1. The Relation between Killing and Eating in Organisms that Capture and Feed

In some species, killing and feeding can be considered to occur in a single behavioral sequence which is best described as the capture and ingestion of prey. Frogs, for example, capture prey by striking out with their tongues, pulling the prey into their mouths, and then injesting them. If the texture or flavor of the prey is made aversive, the frog's reaction is to "spit it out" and to reject the noxious prey in the future (Schaeffer, 1911). Moreover, there is a broad generalization gradient and after the initial conditioning, objects similar to the original stimulus are also rejected.

What is notable in the frog is that the occurrence of aversive events following ingestion is sufficient to suppress the attacking of prey. This contrast with the rat may be attributable to the fact that capturing and feeding are parts of the same response sequence for the frog.

## 3.2. Suppression of Predation in True Predators

True predators can be defined as organisms in which killing and feeding are distinct but closely related, since prey are an important source of food for them. In that their feeding and killing are closely related, true predators are like animals which capture and feed; the primary difference is that there is a longer delay between killing and ingestion in predators. The predatory response of true predators is similar to that of organisms which capture and feed in another respect: they rapidly learn to stop attacking prey which have been associated with aversive consequences.

### 3.2.1. Coyotes and Other Mammalian Predators

Two studies have convincingly demonstrated that coyotes learn to stop attacking prey when ingestion of the prey has been paired with toxicosis. In the first study, Gustavson, Garcia, Hankins, and Rusiniak (1974) fed coyotes either lamb or rabbit flesh which was adulterated with LiCl capsules and led to emesis. When the animals were subsequently tested with live prey, if they still killed they were allowed to consume the carcass and were then injected with LiCl. One or two treatments were sufficient to suppress both killing and eating of only the appropriate prey: the animals fed the adulterated lamb refused to attack lambs but would still attack rabbits; conversely, the animals fed rabbit meat stopped attacking rabbits though the response to lambs remained unchanged. Once killing of lambs had been suppressed, it was surprisingly resistant to extinction: one animal did not kill again during an 8-week period. Animals fed poisoned rabbit flesh, however, started killing again more rapidly.

In a second study, Gustavson, Kelly, Sweeney, and Garcia (1976) tested animals under more natural conditions in which killing was totally dissociated from eating; an even greater suppression of killing was observed. Coyotes were first fed baited rabbit flesh and then tested for killing. After a successful kill, they were allowed to eat the carcass, but they received no further LiCl treatments until 2 days later when they were again fed a baited meal. Thus, the LiCl treatments were never contingent on killing. One of the animals stopped killing after a single experience with baited rabbit meat and four other animals acquired an aversion to killing after two trials with treated bait. None of these animals recovered killing over the duration of the experiment. One animal tested in this experiment did not stop killing. The authors suggested that this failure was attributable to territorial defense as the animal did not kill when it was tested outside of its home cage.

Although this evidence indicates that prey killing by the coyote can be inhibited simply by producing an aversion to prey eating, the aversions to killing and to eating do not develop simultaneously. While some coyotes stop killing following a single trial, in the majority of cases, neither latency to attack nor the actual killing is disrupted following the first experience eating adulterated prey. An aversion to the eating of prey, however, is typically manifested following a single conditioning trial by either an increase in latency to eat or a total refusal to eat.

There are more limited data which indicate that the wolf's response to ingestion of adulterated prey is similar to that of the coyote. Gustavson *et al.* (1976) fed two wolves a LiCl-adulterated package of sheep flesh and subsequently tested the animals together with an adult sheep. Although the wolves initially charged the sheep, causing it to lose its balance, they did not complete the kill. To the contrary, the distance between the sheep and the wolves increased when, after a few minutes, the sheep began to make threatening charges, and eventually the sheep became dominant over the wolves.

The evidence that predation can be controlled with nonlethal bait may have practical implications (Gustavson *et al.*, 1974). Coyotes and other predators which kill domesticated species are usually controlled through the use of poison or by shooting; thus control is achieved by killing the predator. Gustavson *et al.* (1976) used field methods to study the possibility of controlling predation with nonlethal baits. The research was carried out over a 3,000-acre sheep ranch in which the rancher had estimates of losses due to predation over previous years. Bait, consisting either of sheep carcasses adulterated with lithium or of unsheared hides filled with dog food and lithium, was scattered over the range at specific stations and records were taken of bait consumption and of deaths to the sheep flock due to predation. Although it was difficult to establish with certainty that the losses were due to coyote predation, the most conservative estimate was that predation was 30% below that of the previous year, and it is likely that the actual figure was closer to 60%. Even this higher figure may have underestimated the effectiveness of scattering the bait: other indices of coyote activity suggested that the original population had left the ranch and were replaced by another population of coyotes which had had no prior experience with the baited meat.

## 3.2.2. Avian Species

Avian predators, like mammalian predators, can acquire an aversion to killing if they eat toxic prey. Brett, Hankins, and Garcia (1976) administered LiCl to Buteo hawks following ingestion of mice and were able to establish an aversion to both killing and eating. As in the coyote, an aversion to eating frequently developed before an aversion to killing. Brower (1969) showed that the bluejay can rapidly learn to avoid attacking and killing noxious prey. Captured bluejays were first trained to attack and eat monarch butterflies. The jays were then tested with monarchs which were toxic because they had consumed plants containing cardiac glycocides. After the birds attacked and ingested the prey, the glycocides caused emesis and the jays' subsequent behavior towards the butterflies was markedly different. They were likely to reject all monarchs on sight, although attacking was reinstated by deprivation of food. This study is of particular interest because it simulates what is likely to occur under natural conditions, and therefore indicates that food aversion learning may be important for natural predators.

## 3.3. A Two-Phase Hypothesis

Aversions to killing and to feeding established in predators, although closely related, can be dissociated. Evidence from the coyote, the hawk, and the bluejay indicates that the acquisition of food aversions precedes the acquisition of aversions to killing. Gustavson et al. (1974) therefore proposed a two-phase conditioning process. They proposed that the predatory sequence can be separated into two functionally distinct components: (1) an appetitive component including approaching, attacking, and killing, which is thought to be guided by the visual, auditory, and olfactory characteristics of the prey and (2) a consummatory component which involves the eating of the prey and is largely under the control of gustatory stimuli. The first phase of conditioning involves the suppression of the consummatory component, generally after a single trial; this results in an aversion to the taste of prey, but attack can still be triggered. The second phase occurs when the auditory, visual, and olfactory cues from the prey become associated with the aversive flavor, and results in the suppression of the appetitive component of the predatory sequence.

Brett et al. (1976) provide direct support for the two-phase hypothesis in the Buteo hawk. They first showed that a single LiCl treatment was sufficient to inhibit both attack and ingestion if paired with ingestion of both distinctively flavored and colored mice. Pairing of LiCl with prey which were distinctively flavored led to an initial suppression of eating, without inhibiting attack. On the other hand, when the hawks were poisoned following ingestion of distinctively colored mice, two and sometimes three LiCl treatments were necessary before either attack or ingestion was inhibited; moreover, there was evidence that the aversions established were to the taste rather than the color of the mice. These findings clearly implicate exteroceptive stimuli (visual) in the development of aversions to killing and suggest that gustatory cues are critical in the acquisition of food aversions.

## 3.4. The Origin of Species Differences

As we have previously seen, if a noxious interoceptive stimulus follows the ingestion of the prey for a capricious predator such as the rat, it does not lead to suppression of killing. Coyotes and other true predators are different: if they will not eat an organism, they will also not kill it. Rusiniak et al. (1976) attribute the generalization from feeding to killing that occurs in the coyote to a close relationship between the appetitive and consummatory phases of the predatory sequence; they further assume that the two phases are relatively independent in the rat. Such differences are thought to result from selection pressures. The behavioral repertoire of the laboratory rat has been selected over several generations. Selection pressures would be expected to favor traits contributing to ease in handling such as timidity and placidity, which disrupt the natural expression of the predatory sequence. In support of this argument, Rusiniak et al. (1976) found that the laboratory-bred ferret will also kill prey it has learned to avoid eating. The coyote is a wild species which must spend considerable time and energy foraging for food and water; it would seem maladaptive for such a species to waste its time and energy hunting and killing prey which are not subsequently consumed. This should also be true of other wild predators, and it is therefore not surprising that the wolf and the hawk are similar to the coyote in that predation in all these species can be suppressed by establishing an aversion to the taste of the prey.

Although such speculation is intuitively reasonable, it is not supported by empirical evidence. We cannot conclude that the association of the appetitive and consummatory responses has been lost in the laboratory rat until it has first been demonstrated to be present in the wild rat. This seems unlikely. While wild rats kill mice in laboratory environments (e.g., Galef, 1970), there is no evidence that they do so under natural conditions. Moreover, the wild rats' tendency to attack is inhibited by familiarization with mice, thus suggesting that mouse killing is more directly related to the stimulus properties (novelty) of mice than to a predator–prey relationship related to feeding (Galef, 1970). Even assuming that wild rats are predators, it does not follow that the predatory sequence would have been disrupted by selection for placidity and timidity. In rats, the predisposition to kill mice does not correlate with these behavioral traits or with other indices of nonpredatory aggression (e.g., Moyer, 1968); it is therefore not clear why the association between mouse killing and mouse eating should have been lost in laboratory breeding programs. It is, of course, obvious that phylogenetic history is of importance in the genesis of the differences between the rat and the coyote; what is not clear is the nature of the selective factors involved.

The problem of species differences can be approached from a different perspective. There are many obvious differences between the coyote and the rat which can account for the differing consequences of establishing food aversions to prey. Two in particular warrant further consideration: (1) differences in developmental history and (2) differences in the nature of acquired food aversions.

Developmental variables may be of particular importance in view of the barren ontogenetic experience of typical laboratory animals. Such organisms are rarely required to kill in order to eat; indeed, the opportunity to do so is generally not provided. In contrast, nearly all the true predators studied were captive animals, and it seems likely that prey killing and eating figured prominently in their past history. Whether or not laboratory-bred rats provided with appropriate prior experience will change their response to prey killing after establishing an aversion to mouse eating is still an empirical question. Prior adult experience with killing and eating is not sufficient to produce such a change in the case of the rat, but the effect of experience at a younger stage of development has not been investigated.

Another possible difference between the rat and the coyote is in the extent to which exteroceptive properties of food become aversive during the acquisition of a conditioned food aversion. Rats are known to rely primarily on taste; aversions to exteroceptive characteristics of food can be established, but with considerable difficulty and only if the taste is familiar. The coyote may be different: it may learn to avoid odor and sight as well as taste. If so, it would not be surprising for food aversions to generalize to the attacking of live prey which have olfactory and visual characteristics that are already aversive. This suggestion is speculative as virtually nothing is known about the nature of food aversions established in coyotes. There is evidence, however, that other species do not rely on taste to the same extent that the rat does. The guinea pig, for example, is similar to the rat in its preference for gustatory cues over visual cues, but can readily learn to use visual cues if taste is not a distinctive cue (Braveman, 1975). The Japanese quail, on the other hand, seems to rely on visual cues to a far greater extent than it relies on gustatory cues (Wilcoxon, Dragoin, and Kral, 1971).

## 4. Conclusions

The research reviewed in this chapter indicates that there are two ways in which toxicosis can be used to suppress interspecific killing: (1) the direct pairing of toxicosis with killing can be used to suppress the mouse-killing response of rats, and (2) killing can be suppressed by pairing ingestion of prey with toxicosis, a procedure which does not require killing. This second procedure has been used to suppress the prey-killing response of coyotes, wolves, hawks, and bluejays, but is not successful with rats. With either procedure, aversions to killing seem to be mediated by exteroceptive cues from prey, and develop either through the pairing of exteroceptive cues with toxicosis or through an association of exteroceptive cues with gustatory cues. Species differences in the development of aversions to killing when the eating of prey is paired with toxicosis are attributable to differences in the degree to which gustatory cues can become associated with exteroceptive cues. The origin of such differences is unresolved. Species differences are related to differences in the functional importance of predation, to differences in evolutionary development, and to differences in ontogenic development. However, the significance of such relations is not clear.

Evidence that rats do not acquire gustatory aversions when killing is paired with toxicosis (in spite of the presence of gustatory cues during killing) provides an apparent exception to the widely held belief that organisms (rats) are predisposed toward associating taste with illness. The associative properties of toxic reinforcing agents may depend on response characteristics as well as stimulus properties. Thus, while the pairing of ingestive activity with toxicosis is likely to produce gustatory aversions, the pairing of killing with toxicosis is likely to produce aversions to exteroceptive cues. Further research is required to test the applicability of this hypothesis to other types of behaviors.

The evidence that interspecific killing can be controlled by toxicosis clearly indicates that toxicosis can be used as an aversive stimulus for conditioning noningestive activities. However, toxicosis is more effective in suppressing ingestion or activities closely related to ingestion than in inhibiting noningestive activities. Indeed, in true predatory species, for which prey are an important dietary constituent, interspecific killing is far easier to suppress than it is in the rat, a capricious predator.

## 5. References

Baenninger, R. Contrasting effects of fear and pain. *Journal of Comparative and Physiological Psychology*, 1967, *63*, 298–303.
Barnett, S. A. *The rat: A study in behavior.* Chicago: Aldine, 1963.
Berg, D., and Baenninger, R. Predation: Separation of aggressive and hunger motivation by conditioned aversion. *Journal of Comparative and Physiological Psychology*, 1974, *86*, 601–606.
Best, P. J., Best, M. R., and Ahlers, R. H. Transfer of discriminated taste aversion to a lever pressing task. *Psychonomic Science*, 1971, *25*, 281–282.

Best, P. J., Best, M. R., and Mickley, G. A. Conditioned aversion to distinct environmental stimuli resulting from gastrointestinal distress. *Journal of Comparative and Physiological Psychology*, 1973, *85*, 250–257.

Braveman, N. S Relative salience of gustatory and visual cues in the formation of poison-based food aversions by guineas pigs *(Cavia porcellus)*. *Behavioral Biology*, 1975, *14*, 189–199.

Brett, L. P., Hankins, W. G., and Garcia, J. Prey–lithium aversions. III. Buteo hawks. *Behavioral Biology*, 1976, *17*, 87–98.

Brower, L. P. Ecological chemistry. *Scientific American*, 1969, *220*, 22–29.

Caudarella, M., Milgram, N. W., O'Dwyer, S., and Krames, L. Role of prior killing experience in the suppression of muricide in rats by either lithium chloride or foot shock. (In preparation.)

Clody, D. R., and Vogel, J. R. Drug induced conditioned aversion to mouse-killing rats. *Pharmacology, Biochemistry and Behavior*, 1973, *1*, 477–481.

DeCastro, J. M., and Balagura, S. Fornicotomy: Effect on the primary and secondary punishment of mouse killing by LiCl poisoning. *Behavioral Biology*, 1975, *13*, 438–489.

Domjan, M. Role of ingestion in odor-toxicosis learning the rat. *Journal of Comparative and Physiological Psychology*, 1973, *84*, 507–521.

Domjan, M., and Wilson, N. E. Contribution of ingestive behaviors to taste-aversion learning in the rat. *Journal of Comparative and Physiological Psychology*, 1972, *80*, 403–412.

Galef, B. G., Jr. Aggression and timidity: Responses to novelty in feral Norway rats. *Journal of Comparative and Physiological Psychology*, 1970, *70*, 370–381.

Garcia, J., Hankins, W. G., and Rusiniak, K. W. Behavioral regulation of the milieu interne in man and the rat. *Science*, 1974, *185*, 824–831.

Garcia, J., Kimeldorf, D. J., and Hunt, E. L. The use of ionizing radiation as a motivating stimulus. *Psychological Review*, 1961, *68*, 383–395.

Gay, P. E., Leaf, R. C., and Arble, F. B. Inhibitory effects of pre- and post-test drugs on mouse killing by rats. *Pharmacology, Biochemistry and Behavior*, 1974, *3*, 33–45.

Gustavson, C. R., Garcia, J., Hankins, W. G., and Rusiniak, K. I. Coyote predation: Control by aversive conditioning. *Science*, 1974, *184*, 581–583.

Gustavson, C. R., Kelly, D. J., Sweeney, M., and Garcia, J. Prey–lithium aversions. I. Coyotes and wolves. *Behavioral Biology*, 1976, *17*, 61–72.

Hankins, W. G., Garcia, J., and Rusiniak, K. W. Dissociation of odor and taste in bait shyness. *Behavioral Biology*, 1938, *8*, 407–419.

Karli, P. The Norway rats' killing response to the white mouse: An experimental analysis. *Behaviour*, 1956, *10*, 81–102.

Karli, P. Role des afférences sensorielles dans le déclenchement du comportement d'aggression interspécifique Rat-Souris. *Biologie. Comptes Rendus*. 1961, *155*, 644–646.

Krames, C., and Milgram, N. W. Differential suppression of muricide or mouse eating by contingent lithium chloride treatments. (In preparation.)

Krames, L., Milgram, N. W., and Christie, D. P. Predatory aggression: Differential suppression of killing and feeding. *Behavioral Biology*, 1973, *9*, 641–647.

Moyer, K. E. Kinds of aggression and their physiological basis. *Communications in Behavioral Biology*, 1968, *2*, 65–87.

Myer, J. S. Stimulus control of mouse killing rats. *Journal of Comparative and Physiological Psychology*, 1964, *58*, 112–127.

Myer, J. S. Prior killing experience and the effects of punishment on the killing of mice by rats. *Animal Behavior*, 1967, *15*, 59–61.

Myer, J. S., and Baenninger, R. Some effects of punishment and stress on mouse killing by rats. *Journal of Comparative and Physiological Psychology*, 1966, *62*, 292–297.

Myer, J. S., and White, R. T. Aggressive motivation in the rat. *Animal Behavior*, 1965, *13*, 540–433.

O'Boyle, M. Rats and mice together: The predatory nature of the rat's mouse-killing response. *Psychological Bulletin*, 1974, *81*, 261–269.

O'Boyle, M. The rat as a predator. *Psychological Bulletin*, 1975, *83*, 460–462.

O'Boyle, M., Looney, T. A., and Cohen, P. S. Suppression and recovery of mouse killing in rats following immediate lithium-chloride injections. *Bulletin Psychonomic Society*, 1973, *1*, 250–252.

Paul, L. Role of prior prey-eating experiences in the initiation of predation by rats. *Journal of Comparative Psychology*, 1975, *88*, 747–754.

Paul, L., Miley, W. M., and Baenninger, R. Mouse killing by rats: Roles of hunger and thirst in its initiation and maintenance. *Journal of Comparative and Physiological Psychology*, 1971, *16*, 242–249.

Paul, L., and Posner, I. Predation and feeding: Comparisons of feeding behavior of killer and non-killer rats. *Journal of Comparative and Physiological Psychology*, 1973, *84*, 258–264.

Rusiniak, K. W., Gustavson, C. R., Hankins, W. G., and Garcia, J. Prey–lithium aversions. II. Laboratory rats and ferrets. *Behavioral Biology*, 1976, *17*, 73–86.

Schaeffer, A. A. Habit formation in frogs. *Journal of Animal Behavior*, 1911, *1*, 309–335.

Sheard, M. H. Lithium in the treatment of aggression. *The Journal of Nervous and Mental Disease*, 1975, *160*, 108–118.

Stanley, L., and Milgram, N. W. Effects of blinding and bulbectomy on suppression of muricide by lithium chloride. (Unpublished manuscript.)

Van Hemel, P. E., and Colucci, V. M. Effects of target movement on mouse-killing attack by rats. *Journal of Comparative and Physiological Psychology*, 1973, *85*, 105–110.

Vogel, J. R., and Leaf, R. R. Initiation of mouse-killing in "non-killer" rats by repeated pilocarpine treatment. *Physiology and Behavior*, 1972, *8*, 421–424.

Wilcoxon, H., Dragoin, W., and Kral, P. Illness-induced aversions in rat and quail: Relative salience of visual and gustatory cues. *Science*, 1971, *171*, 826–828.

# Koalas, Men, and Other Conditioned Gastronomes

# 6

## John Garcia, Walter G. Hankins, and Janet D. Coil

## 1. Naturalistic and Anthropological Observations on Diet Selection

### 1.1. The Problem of the Infant Koala Bear

The vertebrate herbivore is a highly specialized consumer of vegetation, living in a precarious niche where probably one-quarter of all plants contain toxic glycosides and alkaloids (Garcia and Hankins, 1975). The plant eater, usually characterized as stupid compared to carnivores and omnivores, survives in this perilous niche by virtue of a remarkable learning capacity focused upon food selection by structural constraints resulting from natural selection. In our preoccupation with mnemonically coded information, we are apt to overlook the direction given to learning by the gross anatomical features of the body.

The koala bear (*Phascolarctos cinereus*) provides an exotic example of the consequences of inherited structure upon feeding behavior. It feeds almost exclusively on the pungent bitter leaves of about seven species of eucalyptus trees. Since the prussic acid in some eucalyptus reach fatal concentrations at times, the koala bear must be offered a variety of eu-

---

**John Garcia, Walter G. Hankins, and Janet D. Coil** • Departments of Psychiatry and Psychology, Mental Retardation Research Center, University of California, Los Angeles, California. This research was supported in part by United States Public Health Service Grants 1 R01 NS11618 and HD 05958.

calyptus species on which to feed selectively and thus survive (Martin, 1975). Consider the problem faced by the developing koala infant who is raised on mother's milk and presumably does not have the intestinal flora and fauna required to break down the bitter leaves into nutrients. The details of this process are not completely understood, but recent discoveries in gustatory–visceral conditioning research enable us to make some obvious guesses about this transition.

First, the powerful oil of eucalyptus permeates the tissues of the koala bear, making its flesh unpalatable to man and other predators; thus, eating the bitter diet enhances survival of the species. The mother's milk must also be flavored by eucalyptus—we know that in the rat the mother's diet flavors her milk and predisposes her pups to select her diet after weaning (Galef and Henderson, 1972; Capretta and Rawls, 1974). It is thus very likely that infantile nursing experience habituates the koala bear to eucalyptus.

Second, the koala is a marsupial that raises its infants in a pouch which opens caudally near the mother's anus. At weaning time, the normal feces of the mother are purged from her gastrointestinal tract and she eliminates half-digested masses of eucalyptus pulp. Infant koala bears have been observed to feed on this eucalyptus pulp while in the pouch. The first samplings provide an opportunity for the infant to acquire the intestinal flora and fauna required to produce nutrients from the eucalyptus pulp. We know that the palatability of any substance is increased when it is followed by nutritious aftereffects (Garcia, Hankins, and Rusiniak, 1974). Thus, by the time it emerges from its mother's pouch, the koala infant has probably been conditioned to eat bitter eucalyptus leaves in a controlled setting directed by inherited structures. These structural constraints program the behavior of the developing koala bear so closely that, no matter how plastic its feeding behavior may be, this animal appears to be irrevocably fixed to a eucalyptus diet.

Third, these speculations concerning the education of the koala palate are based on what we know about dietary choices of a wide variety of species, from caterpillars to rabbits. For example, caterpillars raised on a laboratory diet are fed a single bout (24 to 45 h) of one or another vegetable leaf which forms their diet under natural conditions; they are then returned to the laboratory diet. After they molt, the caterpillars are placed in an experimental cafeteria with several choices of leaves. During the molt, these caterpillars lose their external cuticle, their internal lining, and even the dendrites of their sensory cells. Despite this transformation, the adults exhibit both a food and oviposition preference for the leaf they had been previously exposed to (Jermy, Hanson, and Dethier, 1968; Hovanitz, 1969). Dethier (1976) then tested infant rabbits in the same way and found parallel results. While the infants were still nursing he allowed them to sample one or another vegetable leaf acceptable to wild rabbits. In many cases the infants chewed the leaves, dropped them, and returned to the mother's milk. After weaning them on commercial food, he gave the young rabbits choice tests and found that they preferred the vegetable leaf they had nibbled on in infancy. We cannot determine whether the similarities between the caterpillar and the rabbit are homologous or analogous, but we are certain that they share a common dietary niche.

In these examples it is also difficult to decide whether behavioral changes are due to simple habituation or to gustatory–visceral conditioning, in which the flavor preference is reinforced by the nutritive value of the leaf in the case of the caterpillar, or by subsequent nursing in the case of the infant rabbit. It is clear, however, that plastic conditioning and learning mechanisms, however constrained by inherited structure, play an important role in the dietary choice of a wide variety of vertebrate and invertebrate species (Garcia, Rusiniak, and Brett, 1977). In this chapter we will defend our speculations concerning the dietary education of the koala bear with a selective look at the history and research of food habits.

## 1.2. Historic Notes on Man's Feeding Habits

Patterns of food acquisition have been a dominant force underlying man's evolutionary development since he began to exist and have inevitably marked his culture. Bronowski (1973) has described the genetic evolution of wheat as the revolutionary factor that made civilization possible. Cultivation of grain allowed man to cease existence as a nomadic hunter and to begin life in a settled community. In addition to being a general cultural impetus, food habits have been among the most firmly imbedded traditions of differentiated ethnic groups. Adams (1960) points out that when a people are being absorbed into an alien culture they will forego their political ideas, their language, and their dress before they will alter their eating habits; when that fundamental change does occur it most likely signals that the conquered culture has been assimilated out of existence.

What is it that imparts such respect for traditional eating patterns? Surely, conservative and curious ethnic food habits are not mere coincidences. Adaptive utilization of available foodstuffs is overlaid by familiarity, bias, and, ultimately, habit, which William James (1890) called the "great flywheel of society." The Eskimo savors four delicacies: beaver tail, caribou jowl, loche liver, and moose nose—which may seem an unappetizing array to the foreigner! But to the Eskimo who faces the perpetual problem of a fat-deficient diet, these high-fat items become an important source of nutrition, as did the sheep tail to the Old Testament Hebrews who faced a similar crisis (Stefansson, 1960). Belgian Congo tribes use fried termites in their diets as an important source of protein and fat (Brothwell and Brothwell, 1969). The redundant significance of milk and honey in ancient folklores reflects their importance in the parent cultures. Neolithic man had learned to milk animals and Stone Age man is depicted robbing honey from hives in ancient cave paintings. In addition to the well-documented nutritional value of milk, honey is an excellent source of easily metabolized sugar, iron, calcium, phosphorus, and B vitamins. These two items were obviously important sources of nutrition available to the ancient Mediterranean societies. Historical food habits of cultures throughout the world time and again illustrate the fact that with no nutritional education except experience, primitive and modern man alike have found it possible to determine diet adaptively from available sources (Brothwell and Brothwell, 1969).

The development of new food habits arising out of food availability, nutritional need, and social interaction has been described in man's close relative, the baboon, by anthropologist Shirley Strum (1975a,b). When large lions, cheetahs, and hyenas are shot and trapped out by man, the density of cape hares, ground-nesting birds, and small antelope increases and the baboons are able to range far from the safety of the troop. First, the incidence of prey kills by dominant males increases as they are attracted to the prey species. Cooperative hunting tactics such as chasing young gazelle in relays develops out of this mutual interest. With increased kills, flesh becomes available to lower status members of the troop. Females with infants participate in the kill and then begin to hunt themselves. Strum noted that juveniles have only sporadic interest in the kills until they first eat flesh; thereafter they become persistent in attending every kill. Apparently gustatory–visceral conditioning is a powerful inducement to establish a hunting tradition in the baboon troop.

Once food habits become firmly established they may become a mark of social status which persist despite detrimental nutritional effects (Brothwell and Brothwell, 1969). For example, the South American and Mexican Indians discovered the value of the corn and bean diet, which continues to supply basic nutrition to the rural poor today. This staple diet has led to the paradoxical state of affairs that the poor in some areas actually have a diet superior to that of the wealthier Spanish-Americans, who are inclined toward the starchier, greasier European diet. The upper class avoids lower-class food and thus gustatory–visceral conditioning does not have the opportunity to regulate palatability. Fleshman (1973) reports cases in which Chinese aristocrats preferred to receive weekly $B_{12}$ injections rather than give up white rice for the more nutritional brown rice, the white being indicative of superior social class. Recently, food habits became a prominent badge of the revolutionary youth culture. Fleshman, as the director of a "free clinic" in San Francisco's Haight-Ashbury district, found that the "flower children" considered high-calorie sugar as well as food additives bad, while low-calorie herbs and tea found in folk medicines were considered good. She noted that the superstitions she found in the youth culture were not qualitatively different from many to which she had been exposed in nursing school, e.g., a low-protein diet causes obesity.

A curious combination of folk knowledge and prejudicial fantasy appears in the American narratives of 1830 to 1870 reviewed by Raymond Paredes (1976). It was said that chili flavor permeated the tissues of despised Mexicans much like eucalyptus flavor impregnates that of the koala bear. Not even coyotes and buzzards would eat the fallen Mexican soldiers at San Jacinto because of their peppery flavor. Their bodies lay unmolested and dried up under the hot sun. Later cows began to eat their bones (osteophagia), presumably to obtain calcium, and this imparted a chili flavor to the cows' milk which spoiled it for consumption by Texans. This legend represents the ultimate rejection.

If a person's nutritional needs and his food preferences are idiosyncratic, he is considered abnormal and may become an outcast, since common food habits are a primary group norm. Pica can be considered a conflict of individual need and cultural tradition in feeding behavior. Pica is the ingestion of substances not considered fit for food, e.g., plaster, clay, starch, ash. Textbooks and dictionaries generally equate the syndrome with such terms as perversion, psychosis, and appetite disorder. An historical example is found in the records of the early nineteenth century Italian physician Cesare Bressa. While practicing in Louisiana, he developed a treatment for an affliction which was affecting large numbers of slaves in the southern United States. The syndrome included anemia, melancholy, and ultimately heart failure; its most dramatic symptom, however, was compulsive dirt-eating. The curative treatment (which required 50–60 days) included rest and a diet of meat and vegetables together with an iron preparation. A modern analysis of Bressa's records (Mustacchi, 1971) suggests an etiology of nutritional deficiency, particularly thiamin, as well as hookworm infestation.

Pica has commonly been associated with, but certainly not limited to, pregnant women. Under the additional nutritional demands of pregnancy, women may consume clay or dirt (geophagia) and/or household starch (amyophagia), eating amounts ranging from 16 to 130 g and 15 to 21 g per day, respectively. A striking example of the intensity of this craving is found in the case of a young black woman in New Orleans who had managed to overcome racial and social barriers to acquire an education and become a teacher. Upon becoming pregnant she realized with horror that she was developing a craving for dirt as she had seen happen to pregnant women when she was a child. The craving became so intense that she found herself driving 100 miles each weekend to a particular site on the Mississippi riverbed where she collected her week's supply of clay which she consumed by the handful. The shame and guilt associated with her behavior finally drove her to seek psychiatric help; her symptoms were alleviated with iron and calcium pills (F. R. Ervin, personal communication). Most authors agree that these women have diets contributing to iron anemia as well as deficiency in energy foods, calcium, B vitamins, and zinc (Edwards, McDonald, Mitchell, Jones, Mason, Kemp, Laing, and Trigg, 1959; Edwards, McDonald, Mitchell, Jones, Mason, and Trigg, 1964). Administration of iron results in cessation of amyophagia and geophagia (Gleditsch, 1959) and, more surprisingly, caused women to discontinue cravings for ice—pagophagia (Coltman, 1969).

Recent studies in the United States have focused on the black population with research subjects usually selected from two groups, children and pregnant women from economically deprived circumstances. Literature from other countries, however, does not exclude adult males and is not limited to black subject populations, although economic deprivation continues to be a consistent factor. (See, for example, Say, Ozsoylu, and Berkel, 1969; Prasad, Halsted, and Nadimi, 1961; Cavdar and Arcasay, 1972.) The literature on children is consistent with the above, i.e., children exhibiting pica are characteristically malnourished and respond to treatment with iron (Cooper, 1957; Lanzowsky, 1959; Mohan, Agarwal, Bhutt, and Khandiya, 1968). Cooper (1957) has extensively reviewed the early literature on pica, with references dating to 1542 indicating that pica was documented in ancient times as well as during the medieval period. The practice has been reported by archaeologists and explorers in primitive and modern societies alike.

The physiological correlates of pica are disputed. Gutelius, Millican, Layman, Cohn, and Dublin (1962) have reported no correlation between blood hemoglobin and pica, although Baysu, Ersay, Camas, Kalaycioglu, and Kuleoglu (1973) in a study on lambs, have reported positive correlations between pica and blood iron and phosphorous levels. Further, Berkel, Say, and Kiran (1970) have reported that the jejunal histological investigation of iron-deficient, geophagic children showed mucosal abnormalities which were reversed after administration of iron and subsequent cessation of pica. While it is true that some investigators have reported that pica is not related to dietary deficiency (Posner, McCottry, and Posner, 1957; Gutelius *et al.*, 1962), by far the majority of studies have indicated that true pica, as distinguished from general mouthing and chewing of foreign objects, is initiated by a physiological need for a dietary constituent, often iron.

## 2. Experience and Taste Preference

### 2.1. Prenatal and Infant Influences

Gustatory–visceral conditioning does not record feeding experience upon an infantile *tabula rasa*. In many species, morphologically distinct taste buds appear early in fetal development. For example, in the human, the buds are clearly present at 12 weeks (Bradley and Stern, 1967). In the sheep, buds of comparable development are found at about 50 days (Bradley and Mistretta, 1973), and by 112 days, it is possible to record reliable electrophysiological data from the chorda tympani in response to chemical stimulation of the tongue (Bradley and Mistretta, 1971). The fetus swallows amniotic fluid, which contains a variety of nutrients including proteins that are digested by the developing infant (Gitlin, Kumant, Morales, Noriega, and Arevalo, 1972). The full-term human fetus has been found to drink 210–760 ml during a 24-h period (Pritchard, 1965), and the fetal sheep may drink over 400 ml per day (Bradley and Mistretta, 1973). Although it is not conclusive, there is evidence which suggests that fetal swallowing can be increased by injections of saccharin or sugar into the amniotic fluid and decreased by injections of quinine or other bitter tasting substances (Bradley and Mistretta, 1973; Liley, 1972; Pritchard, 1965). Thus, the developing infant, even in the uterine environment, has the opportunity to pair tastes with beneficial postingestinal consequences.

## 2.2. Neonatal Experience and Diet Selection

There is little doubt that newborn humans and other mammals enter the world predisposed to reject bitter or sour tastes, and to accept sweet or mildly salty tastes (Nowlis, 1973; Jensen, 1932). Taste tests conducted a few hours after birth produce characteristic facial expressions. Bitter elicits a grimace, sour evokes a pucker, while sugar is serenely accepted by both normal and brain-damaged (anencephalic and hydroencephalic) neonatal humans (Steiner, 1973).

Once the neonate begins to nurse, visceral feedback may rapidly increase the palatability of milk or sugar. The results of several experiments suggest that the human neonate, although relatively insensitive to variations in the caloric content of its diet, clearly prefers milk to dextrose solutions or corn syrup in water. Unfortunately, the first tests were conducted after the infants had received several experiences with the taste and nutritious effects of milk. Thus, the infants may have acquired a preference for the flavor of milk (Kron, Stein, Goddard, and Phoenix, 1967; Dubignon and Campbell, 1969). Similarly, Desor, Maller, and Turner (1973) report that newborn infants prefer sugar solutions to water. The infants in this experiment had prior experience with sucrose solutions, and thus had an opportunity to condition sweet tastes with nutritious aftereffects.

The food preferences of nursing young mammals is significantly affected by the specific diet the mothers consume during lactation. An exhaustive series of rat experiments eliminated prepartum maternal diet, the mother's diet up to 5 days postpartum, or food particles clinging to the fur of the mothers as having any effect. The flavor characteristics of the mother's diet is passed on through her milk to the nursing pups (Galef and Henderson, 1972; Bronstein, Levine, and Marcus, 1975). Moreover, rat pups nursing on one lactating female and poisoned after consumption of milk from a second female fed a different diet, will form an aversion for the diet consumed by the second mother (Galef and Sherry, 1973). Garlic in the lactating mother's water increases the garlic preference of juvenile rats in postweaning tests (Capretta and Rawls, 1974) and a preference for the fish-flavored diet of the mother is transferred to her nurslings in a similar way (Booth, Stoloff, and Nicholls, 1975).

The natural rejection of bitter has been pitted against early nutritional experience in the guinea pig. In one experiment, the nipples of lactating mothers were painted with a bitter solution and then the infants were allowed to nurse. In a second experiment newborn guinea pigs were raised with bitter-flavored water as their only source of fluid. At weaning, the young animals were tested for acceptance of bitter water. The nipple-painted weanlings reacted as adversely to bitter water as did normally reared controls, whereas the bitter-water-reared animals accepted the bitter solution equally with water. The effect was transient: when retested following 3 months of unflavored water, the latter group rejected the bitter water in a manner similar to controls (Warren and Pfaffman, 1959). However, young guinea pigs, which tend to nibble indiscriminately on any object available, whether edible or not, learn to prefer food objects as opposed to nonfood objects as a consequence of being reinforced for prior contact with food. For example, a single 10-min exposure to lettuce leaves produced a preference for lettuce a day later (Reisbeck, 1973).

Animals which do not nurse also exhibit the influence of early experience with flavor. Snapping turtles (*Chelydra serpentina*) fed one food immediately after hatching and a second food a week later chose the first fed food in choice tests conducted one week later (Burghardt, 1967). Newly hatched garter snakes (*Thamnophis sirtalis*) will initially strike at swabs dipped in either worm or guppy extract. When fed either of these foods for 8 days, the young snakes will strike at swabs dipped in extract of the prey they have been fed, but will refuse to strike at the alternative (Fuchs and Burghardt, 1971). With repeated feeding, gull chicks also choose the food on which they were reared, and parent gulls exhibit definite food preferences that also appear to be transmitted to the fledglings (Rabinowitch, 1968; Harris, 1965). Capretta (1969) has reported similar results for domestic chicks. In these bird studies visual aspects of the food may be critical determinants of choice. However, in Capretta's experiment, early consumption of less palatable food increased its appeal on subsequent exposure.

Although a critical developmental period for food imprinting has not been established, there does seem to be a strong primacy effect. This is particularly true in the case of the snapping turtle which develops a strong preference for the first food that it feeds on (Burghardt, 1967; Burghardt and Hess, 1966). It may also be true for many other species as well. Rats tend to eat what their lactating mother ate, but they soon learn to eat palatable or nutritious foods that were never experienced by their mothers. Furthermore, when rats are exposed to a variety of flavors at an early age, they are more accepting of novel flavors as adults than are either rats not exposed to novel flavors as juveniles or rats exposed to novel flavors as adults. Thus, variability experienced early in life exerts a more profound effect on adult food preference than does variability experienced later (Booth, Stoloff, and Nicholls, 1975; Capretta, Petersik, and Stewart, 1975).

Several points should be considered in interpreting the data from the infant feeding studies. First, in contrast to the human and sheep, the rat does not possess completely developed taste buds until several days after birth (Farbman, 1965; Torrey, 1940). This corresponds closely to the behavioral preference for saccharin which appears at 7–9 days of age (Jacobs, 1964). Thus, the failure of Galef and Henderson (1972) to demonstrate that rat pups prefer a diet to which they had been exposed only during the first 5 days of life may simply be due to the inability of the neonatal rat to taste anything for the first few days postpartum.

Second, there is little doubt that factors other than flavor–nutritional learning influence food selection. Social factors, such as the presence of adults or other pups feeding will encourage the acceptance of new foods in the young rat. Moreover, this effect can override early feeding experience. For example, rat pups who have eaten a diet in the nest which adults are avoiding will begin feeding on the diet the adults are eating. However, pups who are preexposed to the alternative begin feeding on the adult-avoided diet more rapidly than nonpreexposed pups (Galef and Clark, 1971, 1972).

## 2.3. Dietary Selection and the "Medicine" Effect

The extent to which the human infant can select an adequate diet of solid foods immediately after weaning may be influenced by predispositions and early flavor–nutrition experience. When a healthy newly weaned infant is presented with an array of foods and allowed to select its own meal, it chooses an adequate diet over a period of months, despite wide day-to-day fluctuations. The food available to the children was determined by the ethics of experimentation with humans and the cultural definition of what items are food. Thus, nonnutritious materials were not included, nor were refined sugars, custards, pies, cakes, termites, mealworms, or grubs. The only "sweet"-tasting foods offered to the children were fruit. These items were the overwhelming choice of the children, making up 50% of the total food consumed by weight over all, and as much as 70% and 75%, respectively, in two cases. Spinach and lettuce, which have a slightly bitter taste and are of low caloric density, were almost totally rejected (Davis, 1931). Although the results of these studies suggest that weanling humans can select a balanced diet from a restricted array of nutritious items, the evidence is not compelling.

The data from studies of diet selection by laboratory animals is much clearer. With these animals, we are free to produce imbalances and offer nonnutritional and even detrimental substances in the cafeteria. When healthy rats are presented with an array of foods and allowed to choose their diet, they, like the human weanling, select a balanced diet and grow at a rate similar to that of animals on a stock laboratory chow. When toxic substances are presented, the rats reject them. Moreover, when rats are subjected to imbalances, either by surgical procedures (e.g., para-thyroidectomy, pancreatectomy, adrenalectomy) or by restricting their intake of essential vitamins, they cope with the imbalances by altering their feeding habits in the cafeteria (Richter and Eckert, 1937; Richter and Hawkes, 1941; Richter, Schmidt, and Malone, 1945; Scott, Verney, and Morrisey, 1950).

Thiamine-deficient rats adopt an exaggerated sampling pattern when they are given an array of foods. They tend to sample a single food at each meal, and once a meal is taken from a food containing thiamine, a strong preference for that diet develops (Harris, Clay, Hargreaves, and Ward, 1933; Rozin, 1969). The healthy animal, normally suspicious of new foods, becomes neophillic when challenged with thiamine deficiency. A deficient animal given a choice between a familiar food, consumed during the deficient state, and a novel food, prefers the novel food. If the needed vitamin is not present in the novel food, but is added to the familiar food, the preference for the novel food declines and the animal returns to the familiar diet (Rodgers and Rozin, 1966).

Associative learning plays a major role in the coping behavior of the thiamine-deficient rat. For example, when a deficient animal is presented with a flavored food containing thiamine, his preference for that food is exhibited even after the thiamine is withdrawn and the symptoms of deficiency are again apparent (Harris *et al.*, 1933; Scott and Quint, 1946). Moreover, it is not necessary that the thiamine be present in the food. When thiamine-deficient rats drink nonnutritive saccharin-flavored water and are then injected with thiamine, they subsequently show an increased preference for saccharin relative to control animals (Garcia, Ervin, Yorke, and Koelling, 1967; Zahorik and Maier, 1969).

Aversions have been produced by pairing a distinctive flavor with a gastric load of unbalanced (histidine-free) amino acids (Simson and Booth, 1974). Thus, as Rozin and Kalat (1971) have pointed out, the depleted rat comes to the testing situation with a conditioned aversion to the familiar diet, due to its association with the malaise of deficiency. When the rat is offered a choice, he rejects the "poison" food and samples the available alternatives. The taste of the food consumed before repletion becomes more attractive, as its flavor is paired with the beneficial effects of recuperation, and the rat now prefers this "medicinal" food.

There is some evidence that the poison and medicine effects are symmetrical in opposing directions. The results of an experiment in which rats consumed one flavored fluid just before a bout of illness (produced by an injection of the emetic drug apomorphine) and a second fluid just before recuperation are shown in Figure 1. One group drank milk, then grape juice, while another group received the reverse order. Five acquisition trials were followed by extinction tests. The "poison" effect, i.e., the decrease in preference for flavors which precede illness, is symmetrical with the "medicine" effect, i.e., the increase in preference for flavors which precede recuperation from the same bout of illness. The initial preference for milk and its caloric superiority does not disrupt the symmetry; both the poison and medicine effects tend to return to baseline

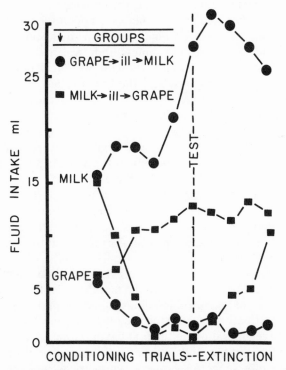

**Figure 1.** Symmetrical effects achieved when one flavor precedes illness and another flavor precedes recuperation from a noxious injection. The two-bottle "test" marks the end of acquisition. All other points are based on one-bottle intake. Note the tendency of high-calorie milk to return to baseline in extinction. (From Garcia, Hankins, and Rusiniak, 1974.)

levels. On the other hand, both poison and medicine effects remain stable in the low-calorie grape juice condition (Green and Garcia, 1971).

There are several important implications to be drawn from this study. First, oral placebos and folk remedies are given during malaise and prior to recuperation. Thus, the flavor of such medications may fortuitously gain hedonic value, though their effects may be unrelated to the recovery of health. Second, a drug which produces a brief intense bout of illness may not be the drug of choice in aversion studies, since the negative poison effect upon any flavor may be counteracted by the positive medicine effect which follows soon after. Since gustatory–visceral conditioning is relatively insensitive to delays up to an hour or so, the two effects may cancel each other. This may be the reason that the delay gradient for apomorphine is steeper than that for X-ray induced illness (see Figure 2). The ideal agent for aversive poison effects would be one that produces a rapid illness and a slow, almost imperceptible recovery. These agents are relatively easy to find. Conversely, agents which terminate a lingering malaise rapidly would be ideal to demonstrate the appetitive "medicine" effects. These latter agents are more difficult to find, and it is thus not surprising that there are more dramatic aversive studies than there are appetitive ones. Two such agents are thiamine, used to terminate thiamine-deficiency illness, and morphine, used to terminate morphine-withdrawal malaise. One other technique which shows promise involves the use of insulin. Insulin injections produce taste aversions, and the hyperinsulin state can be reversed quickly by giving dextrose. When insulin-injected rats are given sour water immediately before an intragastric intubation of dextrose, they show a marked preference for sour water when they are subsequently injected with insulin. When the sour taste is given 40 min before or 5 min after the gavage, no preference develops. If the animals are tested in their "normal" state, they show no marked preference for the sour water (Eldridge, 1971). The restricted conditions under which this effect occurs may be due to the quick onset, offset, and limited duration of the insulin shock state as compared to the thiamine-deficiency studies, where the onset of the illness state is slow, the relief is rapid, and the illness state is present for days.

Third, the reason that symmetrical effects were obtained in the Green and Garcia (1970) study may be due to the fact that two flavors were used. The aversive effects of apomorphine illness upon the first flavor may have been particularly effective because the second flavor may have blocked the counteraction of recuperation on the first flavor. Other factors aided symmetry. Initial intakes of the fluids were near the midrange of capacity, thus ceiling and floor effects were relatively symmetrical, and repeated trials produced slow effects in both directions. Finally, the slope of the prompt illness was matched by a steep recuperation from the malaise.

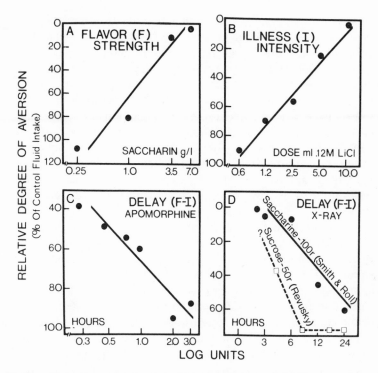

**Figure 2.** The effects of varying intensity and time parameters and also illness agents upon the strength of flavor aversions. (From Green and Garcia, 1971.)

## 3. Neural Structure and Feeding Function

### 3.1. Central Regulators and Gut Sensors

By the end of the nineteenth century, published medical case studies had made it apparent to physicians that trauma to the head could produce abnormal eating habits, including hyperphagia and ageusia (Paget, 1897; Rotch, 1878), but little else was known; the literature is replete with stories of persons kicked in the head by horses or hit in the head during fights and falls who were subsequently unable to taste or smell the most pungent stimuli and/or ate uncontrollably from morning to night. With the advent of stereotaxic surgery in the 1940s it was believed that the "appetite center" had been discovered when discrete lesions in specific hypothalamic nuclei in the rat brain led to dramatic changes in eating behavior (Heatherington and Ranson, 1942; Brobeck, Tepperman, and Long, 1943; Anand and Brobeck, 1951). A neural "appestat" was postulated in the interplay of two defined structures, the lateral hypothalamic nucleus stimulating appetite, and the ventromedial hypothalamic nucleus inhibiting appetite. More recent evidence suggests that these structures contain homeostats capable of responding to aspects of nutrient content in the blood and/or physiological factors of energy balance (Anand, 1961; Anand, Chhina, and Sharma, 1964). Analysis of behavioral reactions in patients afflicted with hypothalamic damage had indicated a striking correlation between animal studies and human case studies (Hashim and Van Itallie, 1965; Reeves and Plum, 1969; Bastrup-Madsen and Greisen, 1963). One should resist the temptation to oversimplify the feeding system, however. Tepperman has recently (1973) pointed out that the hypothalamic nuclei may be more properly regarded as integrating relay stations, as opposed to control centers.

The role of the peripheral nervous and visceral receptors was discounted while attention was focused on the brain. Regulation continued to be exhibited even after vagotomy (Grossman, Cummins, and Ivy, 1947; Grossman and Stein, 1948), gastrectomy (Wangensteen and Carlson, 1931), and sympathectomy (Grossman et al., 1947). Thus, many researchers concluded that the peripheral nervous system was an insignificant factor in nutrition regulation—a view that has more recently come under criticism. Visceral receptors do provide significant information on food intake, apparently sensing colligative, volumetric, and chemical properties of ingested material (Novin, 1976). Calories are important: a recent study demonstrated that rhesus monkeys inhibited their feeding in response to intragastric preloads so as to maintain a constant caloric intake. Regulation was dependent upon calorie intake and independent of volume, concentration, or the specific nature of the nutrient. X-ray examinations indicated that the monkeys stopped eating at the appropriate caloric count although a significant portion of the meal was still unabsorbed in the gut. Moreover, satiety was achieved while plasma glucose levels were falling as well as rising. The accuracy of this caloric regulation rivals that of the vital autonomic functions such as blood pressure and respiration (McHugh, Morgan, and Barton, 1975). These gut sensors appear to have an equipotential role in food regulation comparable to that of the homeostats in the area postrema and hypothalamus.

## 3.2. Palatability and Visceral Feedback

The link which binds the coping behavior of the hungry mammal to the food regulatory mechanisms is palatability. The pleasantness of food taste and odor properties is mediated by neural processes dependent on the internal regulating system. Palatability is not a rigid property of food but rather a plastic component which varies according to the experience and physiological state of the organism. Early data on human taste preference implicated blood glucose as a significant factor in taste preference (Mayer-Gross and Walker, 1946), but more recent evidence (Cabanac, Minaire, and Adair, 1968) indicates that the relationship between glucose and pleasantness of sweet taste is complex: ingested glucose, either drunk or intubated, causes progressive unpleasantness of the taste of glucose whereas glucose injected intravenously has no such effect. Studies on rats have shown that preference for glucose and/or saccharin is affected by several variables, including state of need (Vallenstein, 1967) and obscure developmental and hormonal factors (Wade and Zucker, 1969). Sanahuja and Harper (1962) and Adair, Miller, and Booth (1968) have demonstrated the importance of blood amino acid balance in food preference and general consummatory behavior. Adrenalectomized rats show immediate preference for salty flavors; since the temporal brevity precludes physiological feedback, modified taste perception has been postulated as the preference mechanism (Richter, 1942–1943; Nachman, 1962). Behaviorally, these gut receptors and homeostatic monitors appear to act as conduits for unconditioned stimuli, while the flavor of the food acts as the primary conditioned stimulus. Rats appear to be unable to directly use early gut stimuli to avoid drinking a toxic solution if flavor cues are eliminated or masked. The discrimination of equimolar lithium chloride (LiCl) and sodium chloride (NaCl) is a case in point.

First, the flavor stimuli of these two salts appear almost indistinguishable. They produce similar patterns of neural activity in the chorda typani and medulla (Fishman, 1957; Doetsch and Erikson, 1970) and an aversion to lithium generalizes without decrement to the sodium solution (Nachman, 1963; Garcia, McGowan, and Green, 1972). Furthermore, when rats are trained in a shuttlebox they can learn to shuttle adaptively when one flavor signals shock and another flavor signals no shock; but if 0.12 M LiCl and 0.12 M NaCl are the cues they cannot discriminate these two fluids in order to avoid shock (Rusiniak, unpub.).

Second, these two salts have markedly different postingestinal effects. Consumption of about 15 ml of 0.12 M LiCl will produce gastric upset and lethargy in rats while the equivalent dose of NaCl does not. Furthermore, rats accustomed to drinking safe salty water (0.12 M NaCl) will cease drinking toxic salty water (0.12 M LiCl) before drinking their normal fluid ration. With repeated trials they will progressively decrease their lithium intake while maintaining their sodium intake, as if they are learning to use early gastric feedback to escape the acute distress of lithium illness (Rusiniak, Garcia, and Hankins, 1976).

However, if rats obtain salty solution via an intragastric tube which bypasses the oral receptors, they cannot learn to progressively reduce their intake of the lithium chloride with repeated trials. This indicates that oral stimulation is required. Presumably there is a subtle taste difference between the sodium and the lithium solutions which can be discriminated when internal illness is the reinforcer, but not when external shock is the reinforcer. The effect of masking flavors supports this conclusion even when rats are allowed to drink both solutions. If a sweet flavor (saccharin) is added to both solutions, then the sodium–lithium discrimination becomes more difficult for rats, but it is still possible. If sweet, sour, and bitter are added to the two salty solutions, discrimination is virtually impossible (Rusiniak *et al.*, 1976). Thus, while rats can use a subtle flavor difference to avoid lithium illness they do not seem to be able to use early postingestional lithium effects to escape the severe malaise due to continued drinking.

The word "flavor" refers to a quality of a food that is a mixture of its characteristic taste and smell. Its archaic roots are probably *flaur* and *flator* which connote smell and puff, in keeping with the commonsense notion that the flavor of a food is mostly smell. Temporary anosmias due to colds seem to depress appetite by rendering food flavorless. But if we examine the central neuroanatomical projections we find that the fibers from the olfactory afferents project to the limbic system, primarily to the corticomedial amygdala and piriform and prepiriform cortex. On the other hand, taste fibers project directly to the nucleus solitarius, as do fibers from the internal monitors of the area postrema and nucleus of the vagus. Thus, there is rapid central convergence of taste and visceral information, but not of odor information.

Behavioral tests with rats reflect this anatomical convergence. First, it is relatively difficult to establish an aversion to a strong odor with delayed illness (Hankins, Garcia, and Rusiniak, 1973) unless the gaseous odor is blown directly into the mouth (Taukulis, 1974). Under these conditions, the gas can go into solution on the moist surface of the tongue and thus stimulate the taste receptors, producing a taste aversion. Second, when rats are rendered peripherally anosmic with zinc sulfate solution, they are not handicapped in the acquisition of an aversion for the flavor of apple juice paired with lithium illness. However, anosmia does reduce the neophobic response to apple juice on the first trial, indicating that olfactory projections to the limbic system are important in this finicky emotional response to a novel flavor. In contrast, when the flavor of apple juice is used to signal shock in a shuttlebox avoidance task, anosmic animals are severely handicapped compared to controls which can smell as well as taste (Hankins, Rusiniak, and Garcia, 1976). Figure 3 illustrates the differential effectiveness of odor cues in neophobia, internal regulation, and external defense. Whenever shock is used, the rat makes good use of the odor component of a flavored solution. He stretches his neck and sniffs the smelly spout. His behavior follows classic signal detection principles. If weak shock is used he may go ahead and lick; if strong shock is used he tends to avoid without licking. A conditioned suppression to odor can be mistaken for a taste aversion if licking is not observed when a strong shock is used (Krane and Wagner, 1975).

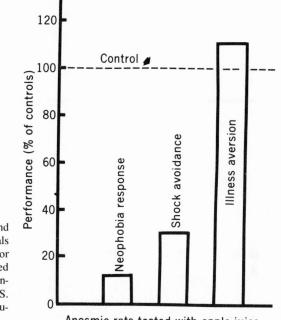

Figure 3. Differential odor and taste function. Anosmic animals display weak neophobia, poor shock avoidance, but unimpaired illness aversions compared to controls when apple juice is the CS. (From Garcia, Hankins and Rusiniak, 1974.)

The primary function of odor cues is to guide the appetitive phase of the food-seeking sequence. For example, mammalian predators are aroused by odor cues and use them instrumentally to seek their prey. The taste of the prey in the mouth reinforces and terminates this plastic coping phase and precedes the consummatory phase, which is a relatively fixed action pattern. The remarkable difference between wild animals and laboratory species in the functional integration of the appetitive and consummatory phases has been recently discussed (Garcia *et al.*, 1977). We will only summarize it here. When the consumption of the distinctive flavor of the prey is followed by an intense illness, both wild and laboratory species will in one or two trials acquire a taste aversion which effectively blocks consumption. Thereafter, wild-bred coyotes and wolves will avoid the living prey after one biting attack (Gustavson, Kelly, Sweeney, and Garcia, 1976). Most laboratory-bred ferrets and some laboratory rats will attack and eat mice. Moreover, if mouse eating is followed by lithium illness these laboratory species will be averted to mouse eating. However, this aversion will not block even the biting attack upon the prey, indicating the appetitive mechanisms are relatively independent of the consummatory process (Rusiniak, Gustavson, Hankins, and Garcia, 1976). Obviously motor activity and eating must be closely coordinated for survival in the natural niche of mammalian predators, but not for their survival in the breeding colony; thus, divergence in the behavioral patterns has been established by the differential breeding and rearing constraints in the two niches.

In most animals, it seems clear that the chemical property of the food in the mouth, i.e., its taste, is the most potent conditioned stimulus in the plastic gastronomic process. Visual, odorous, and other aspects of food appear to be less potent signals, except in the case of quail and perhaps other seed-eating birds who prefer visual cues rather than taste (Wilcoxon, Dragoin, and Kral, 1971). For the carnivorous hawk, taste is the primary cue which guides consumption, although it can visually avoid a poisoned prey after one taste–illness trial (Brett, Hankins, and Garcia, 1976).

## 4. Summary: The Prototypical Gastronome

The oral cavity of the prototypical gastronome is the port of entry at the border between the external physical environment and the internal homeostatic environment. At this point in history, these two domains appear to be governed by different behavioral laws. The external domain is ruled by information about objects in time and space. The prototypical gastronome gathers this information primarily via the telereceptors mounted in tandem on a head perched on a swiveling neck. It stores the information in a cognitive representation which preserves its awareness of the temporal and spatial relationships between food objects and other objects. Driven by tissue need, the gastronome uses the information to find objects which taste good and to avoid objects which taste bad.

The internal domain is ruled by utility of ingested material. Shape, size, and color, vital information in the external world, are of no importance. Even time loses its urgency. Chemical analysis is of paramount importance. The gastronome is fitted with two sets of chemical analyzers; a peripheral set in the oral cavity samples the incoming food and records its hedonic scaling and its flavor quality at an and-gate in the midbrain. If the hedonic rating is positive, the food is swallowed. The second set of analyzers in the gastric sac are backed up by internal sensors which monitor the humors of the *milieu interne*. Together, these receptors assess the utility of the ingested material for the needs of the internal economy. If the material is useful to repair tissue deficits, signals are sent to the and-gate in the midbrain and the palatability of the food is automatically increased. If the ingested material proves harmful, its palatability is decreased dramatically. The gastronome need not be aware of either the causal relationship of flavor to illness or of the palatability adjustment. On the next encounter, the food may look and even smell attractive, but the gastronome may be surprised to find that it tastes bad. In this conflict the oral receptors prevail, blocking consumption. The gastronome retreats from the food showing signs of disgust and confusion.

Nature and nurture combine to make the prototypical gastronome a food expert. It comes into the world with an innate preference for the sweet taste of natural foods and an innate aversion for the bitter taste of natural toxins. During development, it constantly explores objects with its oral sensors and samples them empirically. If the samples prove useful internally, their hedonic scale is adjusted accordingly, and even bitter flavors may thus become more pleasant. The look, the sound, and the smell of food become associated with the taste of food. Of the three external telereceptive sensors, the olfactory sense is most intimately related to taste because the nose, strategically placed above the mouth, sniffs the food just before it is tasted. But olfaction has no inherent neurological advantage over vision and audition. Like the eyes and the ears, the nose learns about food from the mouth. Thus the taste receptors reinforce the final event in the appetitive sequence and signal the initial event in the consummatory sequence. Once a suitable feeding repertoire is established the prototypical gastronome is very conservative and stays with his habitual diet. However, if the habitual diet fails the internal economy at any time, the gastronome begins to sample objects anew.

The prototypical gastronome is a theoretical organism and some details will have to be adjusted as it is applied to one species or another, but in its main features, it fits a broad phylogenetic array from man to mollusc and beyond.

## 5. References

Adair, E. R., Miller, N. E., and Booth, D. A. Effects of continuous intravenous infusion of nutritive substances on consummatory behavior in rats. *Communications in Behavioral Biology,* 1968, *2,* 25–37.

Adams, R. N. Food habits in Latin America: A preliminary historical survey. In I. Galdstone (Ed.), *Human nutrition historic and scientific.* New York: International Universities Press, 1960.

Anand, B. K. Nervous regulation of food intake. *Physiological Review,* 1961, *41,* 677–708.

Anand, B. K., and Brobeck, J. R. Hypothalamic control of food intake in rats and cats. *Yale Journal of Biology and Medicine,* 1951, *24,* 123–132.

Anand, B. K., Chhina, G. S., and Sharma, K. N. Activity of single neurons in the hypothalamic feeding centers: Effect of glucose. *American Journal of Physiology,* 1964, *207,* 1146–1154.

Bastrup-Madsen, P., and Greisen, O. Hypothalamic obesity in acute leukemia. *Acta Haematologia,* 1963, *29,* 109–116.

Baysu, N., Ersay, E., Camas, H., Kalaycioglu, L., and Kuleoglu, R. Some minerals in the blood of lambs with pica. *Ankara Universitesi Veteriner Fakultesi Dergisi,* 1973, *20,* 9–13.

Berkel, I., Say, B., and Kiran, O. Intestinal mucosa in children with geophagia and iron-deficiency anaemia. *Scandinavian Journal of Haematology,* 1970, *7,* 18–25.

Booth, D. A., Stoloff, R., and Nicholls, J. Dietary flavor acceptance in infant rats established by association with effects of nutrient composition. *Physiological Psychology,* 1974, *3,* 119–126.

Bradley, R. M., and Mistretta, C. M. The morphological and functional development of fetal gustatory receptors. In N. Emmlin and Y. Zotterman (Eds.), *Oral physiology.* New York: Pergamon Press, 239–253, 1971.

Bradley, R. M., and Mistretta, C. M. Investigations of taste function and swallowing in fetal sheep. In J. F. Bosma (Ed.), *Fourth symposium on oral sensation and perception.* U. S. Department of Health, Education and Welfare, Bethesda, 1973, 185–205.

Bradley, R. M., and Stern, I. B. The development of the human taste bud during the foetal period. *Journal of Anatomy,* 1967, *101,* 743–752.

Brett, L. P., Hankins, W. G., and Garcia, J. Prey–lithium aversions III: Buteo hawks. *Behavioral Biology,* 1976, *17,* 87–98.

Brobeck, J. R., Tepperman, J., and Long, C. Experimental hypothalamic hyperphagia in the albino rat. *Yale Journal of Biology and Medicine,* 1943, *15,* 831–838.

Bronowski, J. *The ascent of man.* Boston: Little Brown and Co., 1973.

Bronstein, P. M., Levine, M. J., and Marcus, M. A rat's first bite: The nongenetic cross-generational transfer of information. *Journal of Comparative and Physiological Psychology,* 1975, *89,* 295–298.

Brothwell, P., and Brothwell, D. *Food in antiquity.* London: Thames and Hudson Press, 1969.

Burghardt, G. M. The primacy effect of the first feeding experience in the snapping turtle. *Psychonomic Science,* 1967, *7,* 383–384.

Burghardt, G. M., and Hess, E. H. Food imprinting in the snapping turtle. *Science,* 1966, *151,* 108–109.

Cabanac, M., Minaire, Y., and Adair, E. R. Influence of internal factors on the pleasantness of a gustative sweet sensation. *Communications in Behavioral Biology,* 1968, *1,* 77–82.

Capretta, P. J. The establishment of food preferences in chicks *Gallus gallus. Animal Behaviour,* 1969, *17,* 229–231.

Capretta, P. J., Petersik, T. J., and Stewart, D. J. Acceptance of novel flavours is increased after early experience of diverse tastes. *Nature,* 1975, *254,* 689–691.

Capretta, P. J., and Rawls, L. H. Establishment of a flavor preference in rats: Importance of nursing and weaning experience. *Journal of Comparative and Physiological Psychology,* 1974, *86,* 670–673.

Cavdar, A. O., and Arcasay, A. Trace metals in children with pica. *Acta Medica Turcica,* 1972, *9,* 33–47.

Coltman, C. A. Pagophagia and iron lack. *Journal of the American Medical Association,* 1969, *207,* 513–516.

Cooper, M. *Pica.* Springfield, Illinois: Charles C Thomas Press, 1957.

Davis, C. M. Self-selection of diets. An experiment with infants. *Trained Nurse and Hospital Review,* 1931, *86,* 629–634.

Desor, J. A., Maller, O., and Turner, R. E. Taste acceptance of sugars by human infants. *Journal of Comparative and Physiological Psychology,* 1973, *84,* 496–501.

Dethier, V. G. Tiny brains. Paper presented at the *Ninth Annual Winter Conference on Brain Research,* Keystone, Colorado, January 1976.

Doetsch, G., and Erickson, R. Synaptic processing of taste-quality information in the nucleus solitarius of the rat. *Journal of Neurophysiology,* 1970, *33,* 490–507.

Dubignon, J., and Campbell, D. Discrimination between nutriments by the human neonate. *Psychonomic Science*, 1969, *16*, 186–187.

Edwards, C. H., McDonald, S., Mitchell, J. R., Jones, L., Mason, L., Kemp, A. M., Laing, D., and Trigg, L. Clay and cornstarch-eating women. *Journal of the American Dietetic Association*, 1959, *35*, 810–815.

Edwards, C. H., McDonald, S., Mitchell, J. R., Jones, L., Mason, L., and Trigg, L. Effect of clay and cornstarch intake on women and their infants. *Journal of the American Dietetic Association*, 1964, *44*, 109–115.

Eldridge, L. Appetitive conditioning with insulin and gustatory cues. Unpublished Ph.D. thesis, Yale University, New Haven, Connecticut, 1971.

Farbman, A. I. Electron microscope study of the developing taste bud in rat fungiform papilla. *Developmental Biology*, 1965, *11*, 110–135.

Fishman, I. Single fiber gustatory inpulses in rat and hamster. *Journal of Cellular and Comparative Physiology*, 1957, *49*, 319–334.

Fleshman, R. P. Eating rituals and realities. *The Nursing Clinics of North America*, 1973, *8*, 91–104.

Fuchs, J. L., and Burghardt, G. M. Effects of early feeding experience on the responses of garter snakes to food chemicals. *Learning and Motivation*, 1971, *2*, 271–279.

Galef, B. G., and Clark, M. M. Social factors in the poison avoidance and feeding behavior of wild and domesticated rat pups. *Journal of Comparative and Physiological Psychology*, 1971, *75*, 341–357.

Galef, B. G., and Clark, M. M. Mother's milk and adult presence: Two factors determining initial dietary selection by weanling rats. *Journal of Comparative and Physiological Psychology*, 1972, *78*, 220–225.

Galef, B. G., and Henderson, P. W. Mother's milk: A determinant of the feeding preferences of weaning rat pups. *Journal of Comparative and Physiological Psychology*, 1972, *78*, 213–219.

Galef, B. G., and Sherry, D. F. Mother's milk: A medium for transmission of cues reflecting the flavor of mother's diet. *Journal of Comparative and Physiological Psychology*, 1973, *83*, 374–378.

Garcia, J., Ervin, F., Yorke, C. and Koelling, R. Conditioning with delayed vitamin injections. *Science*, 1967, *155*, 716–718.

Garcia, J., and Hankins, W. G. The evolution of bitter and the acquisition of toxiphobia. In D. A. Denton and J. P. Coghlan (Eds.), *Olfaction and taste V*. New York: Academic Press, 1975, pp. 39–45.

Garcia, J., Hankins, W., and Rusiniak, K. Behavioral regulation of the *milieu interne* in man and rat. *Science*, 1974, *185*, 824–831.

Garcia, J., McGowan, B., and Green, K. Biological constraints on conditioning. In A. Black and W. Prokasy (Eds.), *Classical conditioning II: Current research and theory*. Appleton-Century-Crofts, New York, 1972, 3–27.

Garcia, J., Rusiniak, K. W., and Brett, L. P. Conditioning food-illness aversions in wild animals: *Caveant canonici*. In H. Davis and H. M. B. Hurwitz (Eds.), *Operant-Pavlovian interactions*. New Jersey: Lawrence Erlbaum Associates, 1977, 273–316.

Gitlin, D., Kumate, J., Morales, C., Noriega, L., and Arevalo, N. The turnover of amniotic fluid protein in the human conceptus. *American Journal of Obstetrics and Gynecology*, 1972, *113*, 632–645.

Gleditsch, E. Pica in iron deficiency. *Tidsskr Norske Laegeforening*, 1959, *79*, 398–399.

Green, K., and Garcia, J. Recuperation from illness: Flavor enhancement for rats. *Science*, 1970, *173*, 749–751.

Grossman, M. E., Cummins, G. A., and Ivy, A. C. The effect of insulin on food intake after vagotomy and sympathectomy. *American Journal of Physiology*, 1947, *149*, 100–102.

Grossman, M. E., and Stein, I. F. Vagotomy and the hunger-producing action of insulin in man. *Journal of Applied Physiology*, 1948, *1*, 263–269.

Gustavson, C. R., Kelly, D. J., Sweeney, M., and Garcia, J. Prey–lithium aversions I: Coyotes and wolves. *Behavioral Biology*, 1976, *17*, 61–72.

Gutelius, M. F., Millican, F. K., Layman, E. M., Cohn, G. J., and Dublin, C. C. Nutritional studies of children with pica. *Pediatrics*, 1962, *29*, 1012–1017.

Hankins, W. G., Garcia, J., and Rusiniak, K. Dissociation of odor and taste in baitshyness. *Behavioral Biology*, 1973, *8*, 407–419.

Hankins, W. G., Rusiniak, K. W., and Garcia, J. Dissociation of odor and taste in shock avoidance learning. *Behavioral Biology*, 1976, *18*, 345–358.

Harris, M. P. The food of some Larus gulls. *Ibis*, 1965, *107*, 43–53.

Harris, L. J., Clay, J., Hargreaves, F. J., and Ward, A. Appetite and choice of diet. The ability of the vitamin B deficient rat to discriminate between diets containing and lacking the vitamin. *Proceedings of the Royal Society of London (b)*, 1933, *63*, 161–190.

Hashim, S. A., and Van Itallie, T. B. Clinical and physiologic aspects of obesity. *Journal of the American Dietary Association*, 1965, *46*, 15–19.

Heatherington, A. W., and Ranson, S. W. Effect of early hypophysectomy on hypothalamic obesity. *Endocrinology*, 1942, *31*, 30.

Hovanitz, W. Inherited and/or conditioned changes in host-plant preferences in pieris. *Entomologia Experimentalis et Applicata*, 1969, *12*, 729–735.

Jacobs, H. L. Observations on the ontogeny of saccharine preference in the neonate rat. *Psychonomic Science*, 1964, *1*, 105–106.

James, W. *Principles of psychology, Volume I.* New York: Holt, 1890, p. 121.

Jensen, K. Differential reactions to taste and temperature stimuli in newborn infants. *Genetic Psychology Monographs*, 1932, *12*, 361–479.

Jermy, T., Hanson, F., and Dethier, V. Induction of specific food preference in lepidopterous larvae. *Entomologia Experimentalis et Applicata*, 1968, *11*, 211–230.

Krane, R. V., and Wagner, A. R. Taste aversion learning with a delayed shock US: Implications for the generality of the laws of learning. *Journal of Comparative and Physiological Psychology*, 1975, *88*, 882–889.

Kron, R. E., Stein, M., Goddard, K. E., and Phoenix, M. D. Effect of nutrient upon sucking behavior of newborn infants. *Psychosomatic Medicine*, 1967, *29*, 24–32.

Lanzowsky, P. Investigation into the aetiology and treatment of pica. *Archives of Diseases of Childhood*, 1959, *34*, 140–148.

Liley, A. W. Disorders of amniotic fluid. In N. S. Assali (Ed.), *Pathophysiology of gestation, Volume II.* New York: Academic Press, 1972.

Martin, L. Tough and cuddly. *International Wildlife*, Nov.–Dec. 1975, 15–17.

Mayer-Gross, W., and Walker, J. W. Taste and selection of food in hypoglycemia. *Experimental Pathology*, 1946, *27*, 297–305.

McHugh, P. R., Morgan, T. H., and Barton, G. N. Satiety: A graded behavioral phenomenon regulating caloric intake. *Science*, 1975, *190*, 167–169.

Mohan, M., Agarwal, K. N., Bhutt, I., and Khandiya, P. C. Iron therapy in pica. *Journal of the Indian Medical Association*, 1968, *51*, 16–18.

Mustacchi, P. Cesare Bressa (1785–1836) on dirt eating in Louisiana. A critical analysis of his unpublished manuscript "De la dissolution scorbutique." *Journal of the American Medical Association*, 1971, *218*, 229–232.

Nachman, M. Taste preferences for sodium salts by adrenalectomized rats. *Journal of Comparative and Physiological Psychology*, 1962, *55*, 1124–1129.

Nachman, M. Learned aversions to the taste of lithium chloride and generalization to other salts. *Journal of Comparative and Physiological Psychology*, 1963, *56*, 343–349.

Novin, D. Visceral mechanisms in the control of food intake. In D. Novin, W. Wyrwicka, and G. A. Bray (Eds.), *Hunger: Basic mechanisms and clinical applications.* New York: Ravin Press, 1976.

Nowlis, G. H. Taste-elicited tongue movements in human newborn infants: An approach to palatability. In J.F. Bosma (Ed.), *Fourth Symposium on Oral Sensation and Perception.* Bethesda, Maryland: U.S. Department of Health, Education and Welfare, 1973, pp. 292–310.

Paget, S. On cases of voracious hunger and thirst from injury or disease of the brain. *The Clinical Society of London,* 1897, *13,* 8–119.

Paredes, R. A. The Mexican image in American travel literature, 1831–1869. Unpublished manuscript, Department of English, University of California, Los Angeles, 1976.

Posner, L. B., McCottry, C. M., and Posner, A. C. Pregnancy craving and pica. *Obstetrical Gynecology,* 1957, *9,* 270–272.

Prasad, A. S., Halsted, J. A., and Nadimi, M. Syndrome of iron deficiency anemia, hepatosplenomegaly, hypogonadism, dwarfism and geophagia. *American Journal of Medicine,* 1961, *31,* 532–546.

Pritchard, J. A. Deglutition by normal and anencephalic fetuses. *Obstetrics and Gynecology,* 1965, *25,* 289–297, 1965.

Rabinowitch, V. E. The role of experience in the development of food preferences in gull chicks. *Animal Behavior,* 1968, *16,* 425–428.

Reeves, A. G., and Plum, F. Hyperphagia, rage and dementia accompanying a ventromedial hypothalamic neoplasm. *Archives of Neurology,* 1969, *20,* 616–624.

Reisbeck, S. H. Development of food preferences in newborn guinea pigs. *Journal of Comparative and Physiological Psychology,* 1973, *85,* 427–442.

Richter, C. P. Total self-regulatory functions in animals and human beings. *The Harvey Lectures,* 1942–1943, *38,* 63–103.

Richter, C. P., and Eckert, J. F. Increased calcium appetite of parathyroidectomized rats. *Endocrinology,* 1937, *21,* 50–54.

Richter, C. P., and Hawkes, C. D. The dependence of the carbohydrate, fat and protein appetite of rats on the various components of the vitamin B complex. *American Journal of Physiology,* 1941, *131,* 639–649.

Richter, C. P., Schmidt, E. C. H., and Malone, P. D. Further observations on the self-regulatory dietary selections of rats made diabetic by pancreatectomy. *Johns Hopkins Hospital Bulletin,* 1945, *76,* 192–219.

Rodgers, W., and Rozin, P. Novel food preferences in thiamine-deficient rats. *Journal of Comparative and Physiological Psychology,* 1966, *61,* 1–4.

Rotch, T. A case of traumatic anosmia and ageusia, with partial loss of hearing and sight; recovery in six weeks. *Boston Medical and Surgical Journal,* 1878, *49,* 130–132.

Rozin, P. Adaptive food sampling patterns in vitamin deficient rats. *Journal of Comparative and Physiological Psychology,* 1969, *69,* 126–132.

Rozin, P., and Kalat, J. Specific hungers and poison avoidance as adaptive specializations of learning. *Psychological Review,* 1971, *78,* 459–486.

Rusiniak, K. W. Unpublished data, Department of Psychology, University of California, Los Angeles, 1975.

Rusiniak, K. W., Garcia, J. and Hankins, W. G. Baitshyness: Avoidance of the taste without escape from the illness. *Journal of Comparative and Physiological Psychology,* 1976a, *90,* 460–467.

Rusiniak, K. W., Gustavson, C. R., Hankins, W. G., and Garcia, J. Prey–lithium aversions II: Laboratory rats and ferrets. *Behavioral Biology,* 1976b, *17,* 73–85.

Sanahuja, J. C., and Harper, A. E. Effect of amino acid imbalance on food intake and preference. *American Journal of Physiology,* 1962, *202,* 165–170.

Say, B., Ozsoylu, S., and Berkel, I. Geophagia associated with iron-deficiency anemia, hepatosplenomegaly, hypogonadism, and dwarfism. *Clinical Pediatrics,* 1969, *8,* 661–668.

Scott, E. M., and Quint, E. Self selection of diet, III. Appetites for B vitamins. *Journal of Nutrition,* 1946, *32,* 285–291.

Scott, E. M., Verney, E. L., and Morissey, P. D. Self selection of diet, XII. Effects of B vitamin deficiencies on selection of food components. *Journal of Nutrition*, 1950, *41*, 373–381.

Simson, P., and Booth, D. The rejection of a diet which has been associated with a single administration of an histidine-free amino acid mixture. *British Journal of Nutrition*, 1974, *31*, 285–296.

Stefansson, V. Food and food habits in Alaska and Northern Canada. In I. Galdston (Ed.), *Human nutrition historic and scientific*. New York: International Universities Press, Inc., 1960.

Steiner, J. E. The gustofacial response: Observation on normal and anencephalic newborn infants. In J. F. Bosma (Ed.), *Fourth Symposium on Oral Sensation and Perception*. Bethesda, Maryland: U.S. Department of Health, Education and Welfare, 1973, pp. 254–278.

Strum, S. L. Primate predation: Interim report on the development of a tradition in a troop of olive baboons. *Science*, 1975a, *187*, 755–757.

Strum, S. L. Baboon predation and human evolution. Paper presented at the Symposium "The Evolutionary Biology of Primates," Neuropsychiatric Institue, University of California, Los Angeles, 1975b.

Taukulis, H. Odor aversions produced over long CS–US delays. *Behavioral Biology*, 1974, *10*, 505–510.

Tepperman, J. *Metabolic and endocrine physiology*. Chicago: Year Book Medical Publishers, 1973.

Torrey, T. W. The influence of nerve fibers upon taste buds during embryonic development. *Proceedings of the National Academy of Sciences*, 1940, *26*, 627–634.

Vallenstein, E. S. Selections of nutritive and non-nutritive solutions under different conditions of need. *Journal of Comparative and Physiological Psychology*, 1967, *63*, 429–433.

Wade, G. N., and Zucker, I. Hormonal and developmental influences on rat saccharin preferences. *Journal of Comparative and Physiological Psychology*, 1969, *69*, 291–300.

Wangensteen, O. H., and Carlson, A. J. Hunger sensation in a patient after total gastrectomy. *Proceedings of the Society of Experimental Biology and Medicine*, 1931, *28*, 545–547.

Warren, R., and Pfaffman, C. Early experience and taste aversion. *Journal of Comparative and Physiological Psychology*, 1959, *52*, 263–266.

Wilcoxon, H., Dragoin, W., and Kral, P. Illness-induced aversions in rat and quail: Relative salience of visual and gustatory cues. *Science*, 1971, *171*, 826–828.

Zahorik, D., and Maier, S. Appetitive conditioning with recovery from thiamine deficiency as the unconditioned stimulus. *Psychonomic Science*, 1969, *17*, 309–310.

# Physiological Mechanisms    7
# of Conditioned Food
# Aversion

## J. Bureš and O. Burešová

### 1. Introduction

The remarkable properties of conditioned taste aversions (CTA), or of the more general phenomena of conditioned food aversions (CFA) reviewed in other chapters of this volume, have stimulated growing interest in the underlying neural mechanisms. A recent bibliography of CFA (Riley and Baril, 1976) lists 403 articles, about 15% of which are concerned with the physiological analysis of the phenomenon. One-trial acquisition, high reliability, reproducibility, and easy quantification of retention make CFA and particularly CTA well-suited for analytic investigations. Not only is CTA a convenient model for studying short-term and long-term memory, but also it is a special case of neural regulation of food intake. It can be expected that lesion, stimulation, and pharmacological studies, which have predominated up to the present, will soon be supplemented by electrophysiological and neurochemical experiments and that CTA will become an important paradigm for research on neural plasticity.

**J. Bureš and O. Burešová**  •  Institute of Physiology, Czechoslovak Academy of Sciences, Prague, Czechoslovakia.

For the purposes of a physiological analysis, CTA can be divided into several distinct phases which are mediated by different mechanisms.

1. Processing of the gustatory signal
2. Formation of the short-term gustatory trace
3. Retention of the short-term gustatory trace
4. Association of the short-term gustatory trace with poisoning
5. Formation of the long-term CTA engram
6. Retention of the long-term CTA engram
7. Retrieval of the long-term CTA engram
8. Extinction of CTA

Unfortunately, it is rather difficult to devise methods that allow isolated examination of these phases. As in other types of memory experiments, effects arising during the earlier phases can only be inferred from the results of retrieval testing. Careful planning of experiments and the use of appropriate control groups is a necessary prerequisite for a meaningful analysis. Comparison of various experiments is complicated by procedural differences which often account for conflicting results. Attempts to localize neural centers and pathways involved in CTA use either lesions made before CTA acquisition in naive animals or lesions made in CTA-trained animals prior to retention testing. Comparison of both approaches can indicate the significance of the damaged structure for acquisition as opposed to retrieval of CTA.

## 2. Functional Organization of CFA Circuits

### 2.1. CS and UCS Processing

#### 2.1.1. Gustatory System

The first stage of CTA learning consists of the processing of gustatory signals entering the brain through sensory fibers of the facial, glossopharyngeal, and vagal nerves which together form the tractus solitarius with the nucleus tracti solitarii, nucleus parasolitarius, and nucleus intercalatus (Zeman and Innes, 1963). Although taste is often classified as a special visceral afferent, it was believed until recently that its central connections parallel the somatosensory system (Crosby, Humphrey, and Lauer, 1962). According to the classical view, the secondary projection reaches the contralateral ventrobasal thalamus, where it forms a circumscribed nucleus (Benjamin and Akert, 1959; Ables and Benjamin, 1960) sending tertiary fibers to the orbital cortex (Benjamin and Pfaffman, 1955). This scheme has been substantially changed by recent anatomical and electrophysiological findings (Norgren and Leonard, 1973; Norgren, 1974; Norgren and Pfaffman, 1975) which show that the second-order neurons of the nucleus of the solitary tract project to a group of neurons in the ipsilateral brachium conjunctivum, dorsomedial to the principal trigeminal nucleus. The third-order neurons of this pontine taste area form a bilateral projection to the thalamic taste relay and also send collaterals that pass through the subthalamus and terminate in the substantia innominata. These direct collateral connections of the pontine taste area with the ventral forebrain provide an extracortical link between the gustatory system and the brain centers that regulate ingestive behavior.

The importance of food-related signals is indicated by the high redundancy of gustatory afferentation. Attempts to produce ageusia by interrupting peripheral gustatory fibers (chorda tympani, glossopharyngeal and vagal nerves) caused only minor interference with taste functions (Oakley and Benjamin, 1966; Vance, 1967). These findings indicate the presence of other gustatory inputs (e.g., trigeminal innervation of the taste buds around the nasoincisor ducts or esophageal and gastric afferentation) which might participate in CTA learning.

## 2.1.2. Nongustatory Food Aversions

Flavor stimuli are usually accompanied by olfactory stimuli and it is possible to produce conditioned odor aversions which are independent of gustatory cues. According to some reports, conditioned odor aversions are considerably weaker than CTA (Garcia and Koelling, 1967) and do not develop with CS–UCS delays exceeding 10 min (Hankins, Garcia, and Rusiniak, 1973). However, other studies stress the similarity between gustatory and olfactory learning of food aversion (Lorden, Kenfield, and Braun, 1970; Supak, Macrides, and Chorover, 1971; Domjan, 1973). Taukulis (1974) produced conditioned odor aversion in rats by pairing amyl acetate vapors streaming around the drinking tube with lithium chloride (0.15, 2% body weight) administered 0 to 12 h later. Significant aversion was obtained even with a 4-h odor–poisoning delay. Visually guided, poison-based avoidance learning with 30-min CS–UCS delays was demonstrated in birds (Capretta and Moore, 1970; Wilcoxon, Dragoin, and Kral, 1971; Ionescu, Burešová, and Bureš, 1975), guinea pigs (Braveman, 1974, 1975) and monkeys (Johnson, Beaton, and Hall, 1975). The possibility of forming a conditioned aversion to the temperature of water (43°C) was demonstrated by Nachman (1970a).

Although gustatory cues appear to be prepotent in most species, the significance of nongustatory cues depends upon evolutionary factors and may become crucial in the absence of taste cues. An important implication of these findings is that learning with long CS–UCS delays is not limited to gustatory–visceral associations but can be extended to other sensory modalities. Contrary to the suggestion that the plastic changes underlying CTA take place in the nucleus of the solitary tract receiving both gustatory and visceral afferents (Garcia and Ervin, 1968), the evidence reviewed above indicates that conditioned food aversions are mediated by higher centers which integrate complex information about the sensory properties of food.

### 2.1.3. Projection of the UCS

The projection of the UCS is less clear. If it elicits peripheral gastrointentinal distress (e.g., poisoning with lithium chloride), the information reaches the medulla through the thinly myelinated axons of the dorsobasal cell columns of the spinal cord which reach the reticular formation and the nucleus of the solitary tract through multisynaptic connections. Further projections of this system are unknown. CTA can also be produced by a UCS that causes nausea by central action (e.g., apomorphine), by activation of other sensory inputs (vestibular stimulation—Hutchison, 1973; Braun and McIntosh, 1973; Green and Rachlin, 1973) or by anorexogenic drugs (amphetamine). It seems that all these influences converge to a common link in the central representation of visceral systems.

Experimental analysis of the UCS is even more limited. Early CTA studies which used ionizing radiation as the UCS indicated that the arousal induced by irradiation of the body is blocked by transsection of the spinal cord (Cooper and Kimeldorf, 1964). Since experiments with ophthalmectomized rats eliminated any possible role of radiation effect on the retina as the source of CTA (Garcia and Kimeldorf, 1957), it was suggested that the onset of radiation sickness is accompanied by gastrointestinal disturbances which stimulate the brain through spinal pathways rather than through the vagal nerves. Transport of toxic substances through the circulatory system becomes more important in the later phases of radiation sickness and in many types of poisoning. Toxic agents present in the blood can be detected by chemoreceptive regions of the brain such as the area postrema (Borison and Wang, 1953) which is an emetic trigger zone. Berger, Wise, and Stein (1973) found that thermocoagulation of the area postrema in rats prevented CTA learning when the CS (5 ml of flavored milk) was paired with scopolamine methylnitrate (1 mg/kg) but that CTA developed in lesioned animals when amphetamine sulphate (2 mg/kg) was employed as the UCS. Since methylscopolamine does not penetrate the blood–brain barrier, it may act as a peripheral blood-borne toxin. Unfortunately it is not clear whether the area postrema plays a similar role in other poisonings (lithium chloride). On the other hand, the occurrence of strong amphetamine-induced CTA in rats with total ablation of the area postrema suggests that centrally acting drugs may bypass this region and directly enter the higher levels of the CTA mechanisms.

' Although the above evidence shows that neither gustatory nor visceral afferents are indispensable for CFA learning, association of these two inputs is essential for most experimental and real-life instances of bait-shyness. This is the reason why the analysis of the CS-processing mechanisms is almost exclusively limited to CTA and to the gustatory projection.

## 2.2. Cortical Level

### 2.2.1. Surgical Ablations

Emmers and Nocenti (1967) allowed parathyrectomized rats to select dietary substances from two dry and seven liquid sources. The rats learned within 3 to 8 days after operation to compensate for calcium losses by increasing consumption of calcium gluconate. Subsequent lateral lesions of the gustatory thalamus abolished these acquired preferences for various dietary items and thus reduced the increased calcium intake to levels that were inadequate for survival. These experiments indicate that adjustment of the diet to match the needs of the organism depends on the thalamocortical gustatory projection. This conclusion can be extended to CTA, which represents a special case of self-selection of diet (Rozin and Kalat, 1971).

Braun, Slick, and Lorden (1972) studied CTA acquisition in rats with large lesions of the gustatory neocortex (25% cortical damage). Association of 0.1% sodium saccharin with cyclophosphamide (100 mg/kg) reduced subsequent saccharin intake to 25% of the control values in intact rats but failed to produce CTA in lesioned animals. Control lesions of the same size which spared the gustatory projection area had no effect. Ablation of the gustatory cortex neither changed the animals' preference for saccharin nor prevented CTA induced by association of quinine ($10^{-4}$ M quinine HCl) with poisoning. Hankins, Garcia, and Rusiniak (1974) reported that rats with bilateral ablation of the gustatory cortex did not learn a conditioned saccharin aversion (0.1% saccharin, 5 ml of 0.15 M LiCl) with a 30-min CS–UCS delay. However, the lesioned animals did acquire a CTA when a stronger saccharin (0.35%) was used as the CS and when LiCl was injected immediately following ingestion of the CS. These effects were not specific to the gustatory projection area. Lesions of the nongustatory frontal cortex produced similar deficits; posterior neocortical lesions, however, had no effect. The suggestion that the anterior cortical lesions may affect other links of the CTA mechanism, particularly at the level of limbic system and hypothalamus, was not confirmed by Divac, Gade, and Wik-mark (1975). These authors made bilateral ablations of the anteromedial cortex, the dorsal bank of the rhinal sulcus, or the anteromedial caudate nucleus 80 days before CTA training (CS, 0.1% sodium saccharin; UCS, 0.15 M LiCl, 1.5% body weight). None of the three lesions interfered with CTA acquisition.

### 2.2.2. Functional Decortication

*a. Acquisition.* Several investigators have used cortical spreading depression to examine the role of the cerebral cortex in CTA acquisition. Best and Zuckerman (1971) reported that rats with bilaterally depressed cortices acquired CTA to saccharin in the same way as normal animals. Functional decortication was probably incomplete in these experiments, however, since bilateral application of 25% KCl onto the exposed dura did not cause the reduction of water intake described by other authors (Schneider, 1965; Levitt and Krikstone, 1968; Lehr and Nachman, 1973; Bureš, Burešová, and Křivanek, 1974). The results of Best and Zuckerman (1971) are probably due to deterioration of the exposed cortex during the long interval (4 days) between surgery and the first KCl application. Cortical damage in the KCl focus reduces the rate of CSD waves (Freedman and Bureš, 1972) and makes the functional decortication incomplete (Bureš *et al.,* 1974). With a more adequate CSD technique spontaneous water intake is diminished to the extent that rats must be force-fed. Burešová and Bureš (1973) showed that functionally decorticated rats force-fed with 0.1% saccharin dropped on the base of the tongue with a pipette immediately followed by LiCl poisoning (0.15 M LiCl, 2% body weight) did not develop CTA to the sweet taste, although a similar procedure lead to significant CTA in intact animals (Figure 1).

*b. Short-Term Memory.* On the other hand, bilateral CSD produced after presentation of the gustatory stimulus (0.1% saccharin) but before or immediately after poisoning (0.15 M LiCl, 2% body weight) did not prevent CTA acquisition or consolidation (Figure 1, Burešová and Bureš, 1973, 1974). Functional decortication that was maintained during the whole CS–UCS interval decreased the lifetime of the short-term gustatory trace from 5 h to 1 h (Burešová and Bureš, 1974). The more rapid decline of the short-term trace under CSD indicates either that a duplicate cortical engram was eliminated or that the subcortical trace was deprived of a supporting cortical influence. A series of CSD waves lasting for about 1 h interfered with CTA acquisition most strikingly when it was introduced in the middle of a 5-h CS–UCS interval (Davis and Bureš, 1972). The aver-

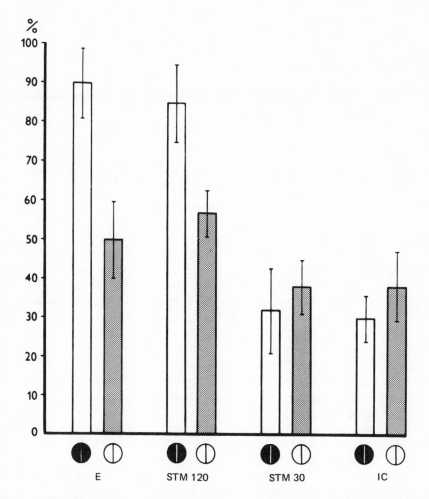

**Figure 1.** The effect of bilateral functional decortication, elicited before saccharin ingestion (E), at the beginning of the CS–UCS interval (STM 120, STM 30) and immediately before UCS application (IC) on the saccharin consumption during retention testing. Ordinate: saccharin intake on Day 4 (retrieval) expressed in percentages of saccharin consumption on Day 3 (acquisition). E, exteroceptive phase; STM 120, STM 30, short-term memory with the CS–UCS delays 120 and 30 min, respectively; IC, interoceptive phase and consolidation of the permanent engram. White columns, control animals; shaded columns, experimental animals. The brain schemes below the columns indicate the condition of cerebral cortex in the corresponding phase of the experiment. Functional decortication denoted by black color. The vertical bars indicate SEM values.

sive effect tested by a two-bottle, saccharin–water preference test was much less pronounced when the CSD episode was introduced shortly after saccharin ingestion or before LiCl injection. These results indicate that the association of the short-term gustatory trace with poisoning as well as the subsequent consolidation of the CTA trace can proceed without cortical participation. This is easily understandable since the biological significance of CTA requires that the association be formed even during severe poisoning which may impair cortical activity. The short-term gustatory trace is also subcortical, but its decay depends on an interaction with the intact neocortex.

   *c. Lateralization.* The obligatory participation of the cerebral cortex in the formation of the short-term gustatory trace suggested that CTA could be lateralized using a reversible split-brain technique. Lehr and Nachman (1973) allowed thirsty rats with unilateral CSD in the right hemisphere to drink 0.15 M LiCl for 10 min. During a retention test performed with CSD in the same hemisphere, LiCl consumption dropped by 80%, but almost no CTA was observed with CSD in the opposite hemisphere. The lateralization was less pronounced after two acquisition trials with CSD in the right hemisphere. During subsequent CSD in the right hemisphere, LiCl ingestion decreased by one-third. No lateralization of CTA acquired during unilateral CSD was found by Burešová and Bureš (1973), who used 0.1% saccharin as the CS and intraperitoneal injections of LiCl (0.15 M, 2% body weight) as the UCS. During retrieval of the unilaterally acquired CTA, saccharin intake was decreased by 80% with ipsilateral and 65% contralateral CSD. It must be stressed that in the above experiments CSD affects both the acquisition and the retrieval processes. Lateralization indicates that the hemisphere used during CTA acquisition is also indispensable for retrieval of the subcortical engram. Although this may be the case under certain conditions, usually the memory readout can also be accomplished through the untrained hemisphere. This fact may indicate either that the memory trace is bilaterally represented or that a lateralized trace is accessible through both hemispheres.

   CTA established under unilateral CSD is not weaker than CTA acquired with the intact brain (Burešová and Bureš, 1973; Lehr and Nachman, 1973), but the subcortical short-term trace produced by the gustatory stimulus applied with one hemisphere depressed decays more rapidly under bilateral CSD than the trace established with the brain intact (Burešová and Bureš, 1974). This finding suggests that the strength of the short-term trace is proportional to the volume of the neocortical tissue participating in the processing of the gustatory signal.

   *d. Retrieval and Extinction.* The adipsia produced in bilateral CSD prevents testing for retention of CTA in functionally decorticated rats by measuring spontaneous consumption of the aversive fluid; but force-feeding makes it possible to observe the immediate reaction of the animal to the CS. Intact, CTA-trained rats vigorously resist swallowing an aversive fluid introduced into their mouths and succeed in spilling most of it. On the contrary, functionally decorticate rats readily swallow a force-fed saccharin solution and obviously do not recognize its aversive qualities (Brozek, Burešová, and Bureš, 1974). When these rats are subsequently offered saccharin with the brain intact, they show a significantly weaker CTA (Figure 2), a fact which indicates that force-feeding saccharin under bilateral CSD caused partial extinction of the CTA. Functional decortication prevents the CTA readout that would cause active rejection of the aversive stimulus; but CTA extinction suggests that the gustatory stimulus was nevertheless correctly recognized and interpreted as safe.

This distinction between cortical function in retrieval and recognition was still more strikingly demonstrated in experiments in which the force-feeding of saccharin to CTA-trained rats was followed by reinforcement with another LiCl poisoning. In normal rats CTA was not only not extinguished, but further increased by this treatment. In contrast, functionally decorticate rats manifested extinction in the same way as if they had not been poisoned at all (Burešová and Bureš, 1975a,b). The above

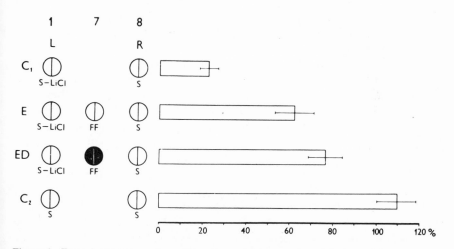

**Figure 2.** Forced extinction of conditioned saccharin aversion. Diagrams represent the experimental conditions during Days 1, 7, and 8; S, saccharin; LiCl, i.p. injection of lithium chloride; FF, forced feeding. Functional decortication is shown by black color in the scheme of the cerebral hemispheres. The horizontal columns indicate average saccharin consumption on Day 8 expressed in percentages of saccharin intake on Day 1. The horizontal bars denote SEM values. On Days 2 to 6 the animals had free access to water in the home cage.

CSD experiments indicate that the cerebral cortex is indispensable for CTA acquisition and active CTA retrieval, but that the passive retrieval which underlies CTA extinction occurs even in functionally decorticate rats. The implications of these and related findings will be discussed later.

## 2.3. Subcortical Centers

### 2.3.1. Septum and Hippocampus

The incomplete elimination of CTA acquisition and retrieval by destruction of gustatory cortex as well as the results of experiments which demonstrated subcortical storage of the short-term gustatory trace and subcortical consolidation of the long-term CTA engram prompted a search for the relevant brain centers. The close relationship of CTA to motivation and feeding behavior directed attention to the limbic structures which are believed to evaluate the biological significance of gustatory and visceral stimuli (MacLean, 1958) and to mediate the inhibition of innate or acquired behaviors.

Septal and hippocampal lesions did not disrupt CTA consistently. McGowan, Garcia, Ervin, and Schwartz (1969) showed that lesions of the medial or lateral septal nuclei not only failed to interfere with the acquisition of CTA (CS, 20-min access to 0.15% saccharin; UCS, 50 R X-irradiation, single-bottle technique) but even facilitated CTA acquisition. With CS (0.025% saccharin) and UCS (25 R) intensities subthreshold for CTA learning in control animals, CTA extinction was clearly retarded. Rats with lesions in the medial septum displayed little CTA attenuation after nine nonreinforced presentations of saccharin. On the other hand, septal lesions prevented acquisition of conditioned suppression of drinking induced by pairing an auditory stimulus (buzzer) with painful shock. These results suggest that flavor–illness and noise–shock associations are mediated by different neural circuits and that lesions which interfere with the processing of external events make the animal more sensitive to oral–visceral consequences. In a later study, McGowan, Hankins, and Garcia (1972) demonstrated that septal lesions do not interfere with CTA when lithium chloride poisoning (0.12 M LiCl, 1.5% body weight) is used instead of radiation as the UCS. Septal animals developed a stronger aversion than control rats after four saccharin–LiCl associations. In contrast, Hobbs, Elkins, and Peacock (1974) found that septal lesions had no effect upon acquisition of a CTA when a two-bottle preference technique was employed and radiation was used as the UCS. The lack of enhanced aversion in septal animals can perhaps be accounted for by a reduction in motivational conflict in a testing situation with water freely available. Increased intake of saccharin in rats with lesions in the ventral medial part of septum (Carey, 1971) must also be considered when interpreting the effect of septal lesions on CTA.

McGowan *et al.* (1972) also reported a significant enhancement of radiation-induced CTA in rats with lesions in the ventral hippocampus. Lesions of dorsal hippocampus were without effect. Nachman and Ashe (1974) found that posterior hippocampal lesions did not interfere with retrieval of a preoperatively acquired CTA (CS, 15% sucrose; UCS, 0.15 M LiCl, 2% body weight). The lesioned rats displayed normal CTA acquisition to 15% sucrose and 0.001% quinine hydrochloride. On the other hand, Miller, Elkins, and Peacock (1971) found that rats with large aspiration lesions of the whole hippocampus continued to exhibit a preference for a familiar saccharin solution even after it had been paired with radiation illness (73 R), which caused a slight transient decrease of saccharin preference (from 95% to 75% in a two-bottle test) in intact controls. According to Best and Orr (1973) dorsal, but not ventral, hippocampal lesions interfered with a weak CTA learning in which a novel taste (0.15% saccharin) was followed by a familiar anise solution before poisoning with apomorphine (15 mg/kg). Since a two-bottle preference technique was used in the last two studies, the fact that the results did not agree with those affirmed by McGowan *et al.* (1972) can perhaps be attributed to differences in motivational level during retention testing.

DeCastro and Balagura (1975) studied the effect of fornicotomy on the inhibition of mouse killing in rats. Response suppression was induced by pairing killing with LiCl poisoning, a paradigm which resembles aversions learned under natural conditions. The lesion impaired neither learning nor subsequent extinction of this type of CTA. Fornicotomy eliminated the secondary punishing effect of somesthetic stimuli associated with intraperitoneal injection of LiCl. Needle insertion caused an increase in kill latencies in trained controls, but not in lesioned rats.

### 2.3.2. Amygdala

More consistent results have been obtained with amygdala lesions. McGowan *et al.* (1972) showed that rats with bilateral lesions in the basolateral and corticomedial amygdala did not develop any appreciable CTA after four pairings of 0.025% saccharin with lithium chloride (0.12 M, 1.5% body weight), a treatment that reduced saccharin intake by 70% in control animals. The lesion also impaired acquisition of a conditioned emotional response induced by pairing noise with painful foot shock, so that the auditory CS did not elicit suppression of drinking. Rolls and Rolls (1973a,b) studied the effect of amygdalectomy (primarily basolateral lesions) on food selection in rats. Although normal rats preferred the familiar chow over palatable novel foods during a 10-min preference test, amygdalectomized animals selected the food according to palatability alone. With repeated testing, the normal rats' preferences approached those of amygdalectomized animals. The overall food and water intake was not affected by the lesion which significantly impaired acquisition of CTA induced by LiCl drinking. Whereas normal rats offered 0.12 M LiCl during acquisition avoided the similar-tasting NaCl during retention testing, NaCl intake in amygdalectomized rats was influenced by previous experience only when large quantities of the poisonous LiCl were consumed (three times the amount effective in control animals). The authors concluded that the basolateral amygdala plays an important role in the experience-dependent regulation of eating and drinking, the most important manifestations of which are neophobia and CTA. They suggested that the modulating influences are mediated by amygdalohypothalamic pathways.

The results described above were supported and extended by Nachman and Ashe (1974) in a study employing over 300 rats. Lesions of the basolateral amygdala impaired, but did not completely prevent, CTA acquisition (CS 15% sucrose, UCS, 0.15 M LiCl, 2% body weight). The impairment was more pronounced 10 days after lesioning than 25 days postoperatively, but was not further diminished by longer recovery times (50 and 100 days). Amygdala lesions following CTA acquisition caused a complete loss of aversion. The operated animals showed a diminished neophobia to novel sucrose or saccharin solutions, generalized aversion to water after the sucrose–sickness trial, and less sodium appetite than normal rats in response to repeated injections of desoxycorticosterone acetate. The lesioned animals did not differ from the controls in rejection of 0.01% or 0.001% quinine hydrochloride, but they formed a weaker CTA than the controls when the latter solution was used as the CS. When control rats were exposed to sucrose for 3 days prior to poisoning, CTA to the familiar taste was weak and comparable to that found in amygdala-lesioned animals. The last finding indicates that rats with lesions in the amygdala do not show a learning deficit. Instead they are unable to recognize the biological significance of stimuli. Whereas a normal rat is alerted to the potential risks of a new taste and inhibits ingestion of the novel substance, lesioned rats treat all tastes as familiar and accept or reject them only according to their palatability. This hypothesis applies not only to the recognition of significance based on previous experience but also to the recognition of innate needs such as the need for sodium.

Although CTA impairment caused by amygdalectomy is clear-cut, the lesion does not completely prevent CTA learning. The fact that retrieval of CTA acquired prior to the lesion is affected more that acquisition of a new aversion indicates that the amygdala mediates CTA acquisition and retrieval in the intact brain. However, after lesions to the amygdala, weaker CTA can be formed by other circuits.

Less clear effects were obtained in experiments with electrical stimulation of the amygdala. Kesner *et al.* (1975) stimulated rats with bilaterally implanted amygdala electrodes using 30-s trains of 25-$\mu$A, 30-Hz, 0.1-ms biphasic pulses. Four such trains separated by 30-s intervals were applied either immediately after the CS (fruit juice) or at various intervals after the UCS (15 mg/kg apomorphine). Such subconvulsive stimulation applied 1 min or 30 min after the UCS disrupted CTA acquisition. There was no effect if the stimulation was administered 12 h following the UCS or if the stimulus was administered after the CS but before the UCS. Arthur (1975) used much stronger bilateral stimulation of amygdala (115-$\mu$A, 60-Hz sine waves for 10 s) to disrupt CTA (20-min exposure to 0.1% saccharin followed 30 min later by 0.4 M LiCl, 1% body weight). Contrary to the results of Kesner *et al.* (1975) disruption was more pronounced when the electrical stimulation was applied at the midpoint of the 30-min CS–UCS interval; but CTA was unaffected by stimulation applied 15 min after LiCl injection. The different results of the two studies are probably due to procedural variables (strength of the UCS, intensity of the electrical stimulus), but are compatible with the role ascribed to the amygdala in CTA acquisition.

### 2.3.3. Hypothalamus

*a. VMH Lesions.* Since CTA can be considered a special case of regulation of food intake, considerable attention has been paid to the role of hypothalamic centers. Three studies concerned with the effects of ventromedial hypothalamus (VMH) lesions on CTA led to inconsistent results. Gold and Proulx (1973) used a very weak CTA paradigm (CS, 0.1% saccharin; UCS, 24 mg/kg apomorphine; CS–UCS pairings every third day). In intact rats, this procedure resulted in a 50% reduction of saccharin intake after five trials when saccharin was novel and after 8 days when it was familiar at the onset of learning. Rats with VMH lesions required 17 trials to decrease the intake of familiar saccharin to 50% but did not differ from controls in acquisition of CTA when saccharin was novel. VMH lesions administered after CTA acquisition did not disrupt the establishment or the extinction of the aversion.

Weisman and Hamilton (1972) used a stronger CTA paradigm (CS, condensed sweetened milk; UCS, 1 mg/kg methylatropine). After a single acquisition trial CTA was more pronounced and more resistant to extinction in rats with VMH lesions than in controls. Although this finding differs from that of Gold and Proulx (1973), the results of both papers were interpreted as being due to increased responsivity of VMH animals to environmental stimuli, a factor which was believed either to interfere with the formation of the gustatory–visceral associations (Gold and Proulx, 1973) or to produce a stronger CTA (Weisman and Hamilton, 1972).

Peters and Reich (1973) used sucrose pellets as the CS and lithium choloride (0.15 M, 2% body weight) as the UCS. VMH-lesioned rats maintained at 95% body weight acquired a CTA of the same intensity after a single CS–UCS pairing as unoperated controls maintained at 80% body weight. In both groups the CTA was less pronounced than in control animals maintained at 90% body weight. The authors argued that CTA learning is unimpaired in VMH-lesioned rats but that increased hunger motivation decreases CTA retrieval.

A common denominator in the above studies, which are so different in techniques and results, is the ability of VMH rats to establish CTA. It can be concluded, therefore, that the VMH is not an indispensable link of the CTA mechanism.

*b. LH Lesions.* It is more difficult to examine the effect of lateral hypothalamic (LH) lesions on CTA, since the ensuing aphagia interferes with the usual testing. Roth, Schwartz, and Teitelbaum (1973) studied CTA in six rats following the recovery of spontaneous feeding 1.5 to 6.5 months after damage of the lateral hypothalamus. Repeated association of a normally preferred flavored diet with LiCl poisoning gradually decreased intake of this diet and resulted in an almost complete avoidance of the flavor that had been paired with poison in control rats, but it had no influence on the preferences of recovered LH rats. Even after four poisonings, these animals continued to eat with gusto the diet that had been associated with poisoning. The ability of LH rats to acquire CTA improved with prolonged periods of recovery (in two rats CTA was absent 5 months after surgery but normal 3 months later). The lesioned animals were also impaired in acquisition of a shock-induced taste aversion in which ingestion of a flavored substance was punished by electrical stimulation of the tongue. Control experiments ruled out gustatory deficits, weaker poisoning, or general hypoactivity as an explanation of the effects of LH lesions.

The failure of LH rats to learn a CTA is also not due to a general impairment of inhibition. This was demonstrated in another series of experiments (Schwartz and Teitelbaum, 1974) in which a CTA was established prior to the production of LH lesions. The animals were subsequently tested after the recovery of normal eating 3 to 4 weeks after surgery. The preference for the CS dropped after training from the original 68% to 5% in the controls and 9.9% in LH rats tested 3 to 4 weeks after the lesion. In two LH rats retrieval was poor when they were first tested but it improved on a second test performed after another 2 to 4 weeks. LH rats that showed normal CTA retrieval were unable to acquire a new CTA, however. Detailed histologic analysis of the lesions indicated that the critical damage included not only the dorsolateral tip of lateral hypothalamus but also the zona incerta and Forel's field $H^2$. The authors concluded that LH lesions do not interfere with fear or with the anticipation of the consequences of environmental stimuli, but rather that they cause a learning deficit which is probably not restricted to the CTA paradigm. Retrieval of previously learned CTA and dietary selection based on past experience is not affected.

*c. Chemical and Electrical Stimulation.* A possible mechanism of CTA may be activation of the satiety centers in the VMH and/or inhibition of the feeding center in the LH. Although there is ample evidence for a reciprocal relationship between these hypothalamic centers (Kawamura, Lasahara, and Funakoshi, 1970; Khanna, Nayar, and Anand, 1972) the LH appears to be more important for CTA mediation. According to Margules (1970a) the suppressant effects of taste cues on the lateral hypothalamic feeding system are mediated by beta-adrenergic receptors. To test this hypothesis, Margules (1970b) implanted cannulae into the medial forebrain of rats and administered either a beta-adrenergic agonist ($d,l$-isoproterenol) or a beta-adrenergic antagonist (LB 46: $d,l$-4-[2hydroxy-3-isopropyl-amino-propoxy]-indole). The first drug enhanced the aversion to milk adulterated with quinine without affecting intake of sweet milk. The second drug had the opposite effect; it reduced the aversion induced by quinine and hastened satiation. Margules's (1970b) suggestion that beta-adrenergic receptors mediate CTA retrieval was tested by Kral and Omer (1972), who used 10-min access to saccharin as a CS followed 4 h later by lithium chloride poisoning (0.4 M, 1% body weight). During retention tests performed 3 days later, animals received an intraventricular injection of saline, isoproterenol, or LB 46, 30 min prior to drinking. Saccharin consumption was decreased (i.e., CTA was enhanced) by the first drug and increased (i.e., CTA was reduced) by the second drug. Unfortunately these findings cannot be interpreted as an unequivocal confirmation of Margules's hypothesis because similar changes in saccharin intake were also obtained in naive control animals and seem to be independent of learned behaviors.

Another question raised by the lesion experiments is whether the lateral hypothalamus responds to inhibitory signals produced elsewhere, or whether it has the capacity to form new associations which change the interpretation of food-related cues. The latter possibility is supported by the recent demonstration that electrical stimulation of LH (50 Hz, 10–20 $\mu$A, 0.5 s, 30–60/min) which overlaps with the first 15 to 20 min of lithium chloride sickness (0.15 M, 2% body weight) almost eliminates CTA for flavored substances (salt, coffee) administered prior to poisoning (Lett and Harley, 1974). Since LH stimulation delivered either during the CS–UCS interval or 10 min after LiCl injection had no effect, it seems that the stimulation interferes with formation of the long-term engram. An analogous procedure was employed by Balagura, Ralph, and Gold (1972) and Ralph and Balagura (1974) who reported that 6 h of stimulation of the lateral hypothalamus which occurred during the noxious postingestional effects of LiCl drinking attenuated subsequent aversion to NaCl. No difference was found between electrode placements yielding self-stimulation and neutral hypothalamic sites. Generalization of CTA to NaCl was also prevented by stimulation of the mesencephalic reticular formation and the somatosensory cortex. Interpretation of the above experiments is complicated by the fact that prolonged intracranial stimulation did not reduce CTA to LiCl, the taste of which was employed as the gustatory CS. The stimulation not only failed to interfere with learning but even appeared to improve the animals' capability to distinguish between LiCl and NaCl.

The effect of hypothalamic stimulation on CTA retrieval was examined in a different context by Wise and Albin (1973). Rats with electrodes in the lateral hypothalamus were first tested for stimulation-induced eating. CTA elicited by pairing canned cat food with poisoning (0.15 M LiCl, 2% of body weight) did not affect stimulation-induced eating of standard pellets, but cat food was not eaten even with current three times the original threshold. After several days the rats started to eat cat food again but at higher thresholds than before the poisoning. Since spontaneous and stimulation-induced eating was similarly influenced by CTA, retrieval of the CTA trace seems to be unaffected by LH stimulation which produces strong feeding motivation. This important finding suggests that CTA retrieval does not reduce motivation (hunger, thirst) but that the inhibition of the consummatory behavior occurs at other levels of the central nervous system which integrate the hypothalamic output with synaptic influences originating elsewhere.

## 3. ECS Studies

### 3.1. Short-Term Memory and Consolidation

The stimulation experiments are closely related to ECS studies which examined the possibility of interfering with CTA by nonspecific brain stimulation administered during the CS–UCS interval or after the UCS.

Riege (1969) was the first to attempt to disrupt CTA by ECS. After establishing a saccharin (0.1%) preference score (about 95%) against water, this author paired saccharin with 82-R X-irradiation applied during 4 h. ECS (35 mA, 0.5 s) administered immediately after irradiation significantly reduced the decline of saccharin preference in comparison to that observed over the next 7 days in control animals. Similar CTA disruption was also obtained when ECS was applied after 1 h of irradiation before saccharin drinking (trace conditioning). The dynamics of the ECS effect in this study are unfortunately obscured by the slow onset of radiation illness.

Nachman (1970b) administered ECS (50 mA, 0.2 s) immediately after a brief exposure (5, 10, or 30 s) to 0.25% sodium saccharin CS. LiCl (0.15 M, 2% body weight) was injected 5 min later. There was a partial disruption of CTA in the 5-s and 10-s, but not in the 30-s groups. It must be stressed that this study examined effect of ECS on the short-term gustatory trace rather than on the consolidation of long-term CTA engram. This second problem was systematically examined by Kral (1971a,b, 1972).

In the first study (Kral, 1971b), a 60-mA ECS of variable duration (0.4, 0.8, 1.6, 3.2 s) was applied through electrodes implanted over the cerebellum. ECS followed immediately after a 10-min exposure to the CS (sour water, 0.7% volume/volume of 37% HCl) and preceded the UCS (0.4 M LiCl, 1% of body weight) by 30 min. All ECS durations caused significant disruptions of CTA but only the longest ECS (3.2 s) eliminated the memory completely. Increasing the intensity of a 1.0-s shock had a similar effect. A 12-mA ECS failed to interfere with CTA formation, whereas a 60-mA ECS had a marked disrupting effect but did not prevent learning completely. Kral (1971b) points out that an ECS interpolated between the CS and the UCS might produce retrograde amnesia for the CS, trigger proactive interference with the UCS, and/or prevent CS–UCS association. The latter possibility (so-called disassociation) is supported by experiments (Kral, 1971a) in which ECS (60 mA, 0.7 s, ear electrodes) administered immediately after a 10-min exposure to a novel taste (sour, 0.7% volume/volume of 37% HCl; sweet, 0.35% sodium saccharin) did not prevent habituation to these stimuli, an effect manifested by increased drinking of the flavored fluid on the next exposure. Since habituation implies retrieval of the previous experience, retention seems to be unaffected by ECS. In another experiment (Kral, 1971a), ECS was applied at the onset, in the middle, or at the end of a 4-h CS–UCS interval (0.1% saccharin, 0.4 M LiCl, 1% of body weight). During retention testing, saccharin consumption of the shocked animals was intermediate between that of nonshocked poisoned controls and shocked nonpoisoned controls, but the intensity of the disruptive effect was unrelated to the CS–UCS delay. These findings are inconsistent with the active interference explanation of the ECS effect. A weak point of the disassociation hypothesis proposed by Kral (1970) is that no associations are formed at the time of ECS administration. It seems that ECS decreases the associability of the short-term gustatory trace with the subsequent poisoning without affecting long-term storage of the primary gustatory experience.

ECS (80 mA, 1 s) applied 5 min or later after UCS administration (Kral and Beggarly, 1973) did not disrupt CTA (CS, 0.1% saccharin; UCS, 0.4 M LiCl, 1% body weight). Only ECS administered immediately after LiCl injection (and thus still before the onset of illness) had an interfering effect comparable to that caused by ECS in the CS–UCS interval. A 2.5-min UCS–ECS delay caused only a moderate interference with CTA learning. The authors argue that the permanent CTA engram becomes resistant to the interfering effect of ECS within 5 min of LiCl effect.

The ECS effect depends on the path of the electric current through the brain. Kral (1972) applied ECS across a pair of screw electrodes implanted 4 mm apart either 2 mm anterior to bregma or 4 mm posterior to lambda. Ten-min access to 0.1% sodium saccharin was followed 30 min later by an intraperitoneal injection of LiCl (0.4 M, 1% body weight). A 1.0-s ECS was applied in the midpoint of the CS–UCS interval. CTA strength was inversely related to current intensity (20, 40, and 80 mA), but anterior ECS was always less disruptive than posterior ECS of the same intensity. Some CTA remained even after an 80-mA posterior ECS.

## 3.2. Metrazol

Seizures elicited by metrazol seem to be more disruptive than those elicited by ECS. Ahlers and Best (1972) produced CTA by pairing a novel saccharin solution (0.15%) followed by familiar anise with apomorphine (15 mg/kg) applied 15 min later. The conditioning trial was repeated after a 6-h interval. Metrazol (40 mg/kg) was injected either at the beginning of the CS–UCS interval or 2 h after UCS administration. Whereas the proportion of saccharin consumed by poisoned control animals was only 20% during a two-bottle retention test performed 24 h later, metrazol treatment increased the proportion of saccharin in the total fluid intake to the 60–70% level typical for unpoisoned controls. Association of metrazol alone with the gustatory stimulus did not elicit significant CTA. Post-UCS injection of metrazol seems to be slightly more disruptive than pre-UCS injection of metrazol.

The stronger disruption of CTA by metrazol than by ECS could be due to the week learning procedure used by Ahlers and Best (1972). Millner and Palfai (1975) produced CTA by pairing a 15-min access to sodium saccharin (0.2%) with LiCl poisoning (2 M, 0.1% body weight) administered 10 min later. Metrazol (40 mg/kg) applied 10 min after LiCl injection did not weaken the subsequent CTA. When the CS–UCS interval was prolonged to 20 min, metrazol applied in the middle of this interval did not prevent acquisition. Only metrazol injections administered 2 min before, simultaneously with, or 3 min after LiCl injection (10-min CS–UCS delay) blocked CTA formation. The steep temporal gradient of the metrazol effect in this experiment indicates that onset of the UCS is the most vulnerable link in the engram-forming process.

## 3.3. Repeated ECS Treatment

The effect of repeated ECS treatments on well-established CTA was examined by Vogel (1974). Using the procedure introduced by Hunt and Brady (1951), this author gave rats a series of 21 ECSs (60 mA, 0.25 s, three ECS per day) beginning 4 days after CTA acquisition (CS, sweetened condensed milk; UCS, 0.25 mg/kg methylatropine). During retention testing, in contrast to sham-ECS controls, ECS-treated animals drank sweetened milk. Since CTA spontaneously reappeared 14 to 21 days after the treatment, chronic administration of ECS did not wipe out the CTA engram, but rather it either prevented the engram's retrieval or released responding from conditioned suppression. In this respect, CTA resembles effects of other types of punishment which are also attenuated by repeated administration of ECS (Brady, 1951).

## 4. Drug Effects

## 4.1. Drugs as UCS

The discovery that CTA can be evoked not only by toxic substances which cause obvious signs of sickness, but also by nontoxic concentrations of a wide spectrum of drugs (including cholinergic drugs, hypnotics, chlordiazepoxide, amphetamine, mescaline, hashish, alcohol, and many others) stimulated extensive pharmacological research, which has been covered by Vogel (1975) and in this volume by Cappell and LeBlanc (Chapter 5). Since most of these studies are oriented toward pharmacological and clinical problems and are therefore beyond the scope of this chapter, only experiments directly relevant to the mechanism of CTA will be discussed here.

The first fact to be noted is that some obviously toxic drugs do not induce CTA when employed as a UCS. This was demonstrated for metrazol in the previously mentioned experiments by Ahlers and Best (1972) and Millner and Palfai (1975) as well as for strychnine (Berger, 1972; Vogel, 1975). It remains to be established whether these failures to induce CTA are restricted to convulsants. This line of research may contribute not only to the understanding of the nature of the UCS necessary for CTA induction but also shed light on the mechanisms of the association of the short-term gustatory trace with poisoning and of the subsequent formation of the long-term CTA engram

## 4.2. Effects on CTA Acquisition

More important are pharmacological studies in which drugs were used not to induce CTA but rather to influence a definite phase of its acquisition or retrieval. Rozin and Ree (1972) anesthetized rats after exposure to a gustatory CS with halothane or equithesine and maintained the anesthesia for about 9 h. After awakening, the animal was poisoned (0.15 M LiCl, 2% of body weight). In a two-bottle preference test administered 2 days later, the animals anesthetized during the CS–UCS interval showed a significantly stronger aversion than control animals that had been only poisoned or only anesthetized. The authors suggested that anesthesia during the CS–UCS interval protects the short-term gustatory trace against potential interfering stimuli and/or prevents acquisition of "learned safety" (Rozin and Kalat, 1971) which opposes subsequent aversion learning proportionally to the duration of the illness-free postingestional interval. Since anesthesia alone also elicited a weak CTA, the results may also be due to mutual potentiation of the two aversive treatments.

In a replication of this study, Burešová and Bureš (1975b) found that allobarbital anesthesia during a 5-h CS–UCS interval significantly increased CTA to saccharin (0.1% sodium saccharin, 0.15 M LiCl, 4% of body weight). Since mild CTA was caused by pairing saccharin drinking with subsequent anesthesia alone, CTA facilitation would again be explained by summation of the aversive effects which persisted even when LiCl was applied to anesthetized animals.

The effectiveness of poisoning under anesthesia was convincingly demonstrated by Roll and Smith (1972) who anesthetized rats after presentation of a gustatory CS and administered X-irradiation under anesthesia maintained for a period allowing for dissipation of the major signs of poisoning. In spite of anesthesia, the animals developed strong CTA. Similar results were reported by Millner and Palfai (1975). Ten minutes after exposure to the CS (0.2% sodium saccharin) rats received either Nembutal (60 mg/kg) alone or in combination with LiCl (2 M, 0.1% of body weight). Although anesthesia developed within 3 min of injection and preceded the earliest symptoms of poisoning, the resulting CTA was as strong as in rats poisoned while awake. Saccharin intake was unaffected in rats exposed to anesthesia alone. Although it is possible that learning in the above experiments is due to association of the traces of the CS and UCS after awakening, it seems more likely that the long-term CTA engram is formed under anesthesia. A similar failure to interfere with CTA acquisition was demonstrated for bilateral cortical spreading depression induced after presentation of a gustatory CS but before and during poisoning (Burešová and Bureš, 1973, 1975a; Davis and Bureš, 1972).

Blocking cholinergic synapses by administration of the anti-cholinergics atropine and scopolamine before the CS–UCS interval also does not impair CTA acquisition (Smith and Morris, 1964; Kral, 1971c).

## 4.3. Effects on CTA Retrieval

Gadusek and Kalat (1975) administered up to 10 mg/kg of scopolamine to CTA-trained rats 30 min before a 30-min preference test. CTA retention was not markedly affected. Vogel (1975) showed that chlordiazepoxide blocks retrieval of CTA induced by pairing sweetened condensed milk (100 licks) with methylatropine (1 mg/kg) or *d*-amphetamine sulfate (2 mg/kg). Six days after the acquisition session, rats received distilled water or 5, 10, or 15 mg/kg of chlordiazepoxide. When exposed to the CS 15 min later, control rats showed a marked hesitancy to drink the milk. However, CTA was significantly decreased in animals which received 10 or 15 mg/kg of chlordiazepoxide prior to testing. The author explains the CTA attenuation as being due to the release of suppressed responding analogous to the effect of chlordiazepoxide in other conflict situations (Geller and Seifter, 1960).

Vogel's (1975) results are consistent with the observation by Cappell, LeBlanc, and Endrenyi (1972) that chlordiazepoxide facilitates extinction of CTA (CS, 0.1% saccharin; UCS, 0.15 M LiCl, 2% of body weight). Every third day after the acquisition session, rats were exposed to saccharin which was presented 30 min after intraperitoneal injection of either saline, chlordiazepoxide (3 to 6.75 mg/kg), or ethanol (600 to 1200 mg/kg). After five extinction sessions, rats pretreated with chlordiazepoxide drank more saccharin than the saline-treated controls, which extinguished significantly faster than the ethanol-treated animals. This result was attributed to the antipunishment effect of chlordiazepoxide.

The effects of prior exposure to the UCS on subsequent conditioning were described by Cappell, LeBlanc, and Herling (1975) and are discussed by Cappell and LeBlanc in Chapter 5 of this volume.

## 4.4. Experiments with Intravascular Taste

Possibilities for pharmacological analysis were considerably extended by evidence indicating that a gustatory stimulus can reach the taste receptors after parenteral injections. Bradley and Mistretta (1971) demonstrated that injection of 1 ml of 0.05, 0.15, or 0.5 M sodium saccharin into the tail vein, when paired with irradiation (100 to 200 R) produced marked CTA as manifested by significant aversion to saccharin in a subsequent saccharin–water preference test. Since intravascular administration of gustatory stimuli elicits electrophysiological responses in the chorda tympani, taste receptors in the tongue are obviously responsible for detection of the stimulus. This is confirmed by the subjective experience of humans who perceive a sweet taste which rapidly passes from the base to the tip of the tongue after intravenous injection of saccharin (Fishberg, Hitzig, and King, 1933).

Even intraperitoneal injections can stimulate taste receptors. Scarborough and McLaurin (1961) failed to elicit CTA to intraperitoneally injected sodium saccharin, but Baum, Foidart, and Lapointe (1974) demonstrated that intraperitoneal application of more concentrated sweeteners (2.286% sodium cyclamate with 0.228% sodium saccharin, 1% of body weight) induced extinction of CTA established 18 h earlier by administering LiCl (0.15 M LiCl, 1% of body weight) following drinking of a much weaker sweet solution (20 times lower concentration). Burešová (1976) used an intraperitoneal injection of 2% sodium saccharin (1% of body weight) as the CS followed 30 min later by lithium chloride (0.15 M, 4% of body weight). Retention testing revealed a marked saccharin aversion. No CTA developed, however, when Nembutal anesthesia (40 mg/kg) was induced 5 to 10 min before the intraperitoneal saccharin injection and maintained throughout the poisoning. The conditioned saccharin aversion could be extinguished by an intraperitoneal injection of saccharin 24 h after CTA acquisition in the same way as in the experiments performed by Baum *et al.* (1974). Extinction was not prevented when Nembutal anesthesia (40 mg/kg) was induced 10 min before the saccharin injection. Since Nembutal anesthesia alone did not influence CTA retention, the above results indicate that processing of gustatory signals which continue during anesthesia can modify the stored information. In this respect, anesthesia resembles bilateral CSD (see p. 227) which blocks the formation of the short-term gustatory trace but does not prevent the transformation of the already present short-term trace into the permanent CTA engram or the modification of the latter by extinction.

## 5. Developmental Studies

In some respects, the brains of young animals are similar to those of adults which have been lesioned. Teitelbaum (1971) pointed out that recovery of food intake after bilateral CSD recapitulates on a condensed time scale the development of feeding during the weaning period. Although many electrophysiological (Scherrer, 1968; Deza and Eidelberg, 1967; Bureš, Fifkova, and Mares, 1964) and metabolic (Himwich, 1970) functions of the cerebral cortex mature between 14 and 18 days of age in rats, cortical myelinization culminates between 30 and 40 days of age (Bass, Netsky, and Young, 1969). Also the formation of cortical synapses and dendritic arborization proceeds until 30 days of age (Aghajanian and Bloom, 1967). Neurological immaturity is accompanied by moderate impairment of learning and by strikingly accelerated forgetting of behaviors acquired early in life. This has been demonstrated for active and passive avoidance responses (Feigley and Spear, 1970; Campbell, Misanin, White, and Lytle, 1974), for light–dark discriminations (Campbell, Jaynes, and Misanin, 1968), as well as for simple escape responding (Smith, 1968).

The ontogenetic analysis of CTA may not only reveal similarities and dissimilarities between CTA and other learned behaviors but may also indicate which structures are indispensable for various phases of CTA learning.

A methodological problem in the developmental analysis of the CTA is the need to test retrieval in weaned animals that are capable of spontaneously selecting different diets. In an impressive series of experiments, Galef and Clark (1971, 1972) and Galef and Henderson (1972) demonstrated that weanling rats are influenced in their choice of diet not only by imitation of the adult members of the colony but also by gustatory and olfactory cues contained in the milk of the lactating mother and correlated with the mother's diet. When pups were tested in the absence of adult rats, they started to eat solid food at the age of 25 days and consistently preferred the diet fed to their mother in a two-choice situation. The preference persisted for more than 10 days. Similar results were obtained by Capretta and Rawls (1974) who gave lactating females garlic-flavored water. Pups weaned at 22 days showed a marked preference for garlic water in a two-bottle test 7 days or 1 month later. These experiments indicate that early gustatory experience and young–adult interaction are important for the establishment of food preferences which enable the weanling to discriminate safe foods.

Less clear results were obtained with CTA learning. Strong CTA can be acquired by neonate guinea pigs which are precocial (Coulon, 1971). Kalat (1975) hand-fed guinea pigs aged 0–11 days 1 ml of 10% sucrose and poisoned them either immediately or after 30 min with lithium chloride (0.15 M, 2% of body weight). A two-bottle, water–sucrose test performed 1–2 months later revealed significant sucrose aversion in all groups, but the difference between experimental and control animals was greatest in animals exposed to sucrose at 7–11 days. This result was due to decreased neophobia to sucrose in the corresponding controls. The author suggested that young guinea pigs can acquire CTA immediately after birth, but that they are deficient in the formation of long-term appetitive traces. Grote and Brown (1971) put 20-day-old rats on a restricted fluid regimen and offered them a 0.12-M LiCl solution on day 23. During a 1-h test, the weanling rats drank only slightly less lithium chloride than water. Three days later the drinking tubes were again filled with LiCl, and the animals' consumption of LiCl was recorded after 1 h. It was considerably lower than the animals' water consumption on the preceding day. Although the interpretation of this result is complicated by the identity of the CS and UCS and by the long testing time, it suggests that weanling rats can acquire a CTA.

Galef and Sherry (1973) fed two groups of lactating females different diets (A and B). At 21 days of age, pups whose mother was eating diet A (B) were fed with a syringe 0.5 ml of milk expressed from a female eating diet B (A). Immediately afterwards they were intraperitoneally injected with 0.12 M LiCl (2% of body weight) and returned to their mothers. The next day each pup was given a 24-h preference test for diets A and B. Pups poisoned after ingesting milk from a lactating female eating diet B avoided that diet and increased their preference for diet A, which had been eaten by their own mother. The permanence of this effect was not tested.

Klein, Barter, Murphy, and Richardson (1974) fed adult and young (25 days) rats a daily dose of 10 mg/kg mercuric chloride in a 2% sucrose solution. After 7 days, adult males drank significantly less sugar solution than the control rats given no mercury. No CTA developed in the young rats after 7 days. A weak aversion which was obtained using a 20 mg/kg mercuric chloride solution over 13 days of treatment was unstable in young rats.

Bureš and Burešová (1977) tested CTA acquisition in young rats aged 20, 30, and 50 days. The animals of the youngest group were prematurely weaned at the age of 18 days by replacing their mothers with adult males. After 2 days' exposure to water in the testing chamber, the animals were offered saccharin for 30 min and poisoned 5 min later with LiCl (0.15 M, 4% of body weight). Control animals received the same amount of NaCl. Retention testing was performed after 7 days of free access to food and water in the home cage. The animals were put on a 24-h water deprivation schedule and offered water only during a 30-min single-bottle test. Saccharin was presented on the third day of testing. Saccharin–LiCl pairing in 40- and 50-day-old rats yielded CTA of almost the same intensity as in adult animals. The same experience in 20-day-old rats did not result in a CTA that was detectable 10 days later. Weak but significant CTA was obtained in 30-day-old rats.

The above results do not contradict the findings of Grote and Brown (1971) and Galef and Sherry (1973) but rather indicate that the CTA demonstrated by the above authors is either short-lived or so weak that it cannot be demonstrated against a background of increased motivational level. Other procedural differences may also account for the different results (preference testing versus single bottle testing, eating solid food versus drinking, 24-h versus 10-min duration of the retention test).

The available experimental evidence indicates that early gustatory experiences transmitted by the mother's milk provide for acquisition of appetitive habits which influence dietary selection in weanling animals. Since poisoning by mother's milk is extremely unlikely, CTA appears only around the time of weaning and is probably related to maturation of neocortical connections with subcortical regions, including the limbic system and hypothalamus. Similar mechanisms akin to imprinting lead to subcortical recognition of maternal odors which serve in species identification in adult animals (Salas, Schapiro, and Guzman-Flores, 1970).

## 6. Electrophysiological Analysis

### 6.1. Gustatory Control of Licking

Despite intensive research into the electrical correlates of gustation (for a review, see Pfaffman, 1969), electrophysiological methods have not yet contributed to the analysis of CTA. Most of the electrophysiological taste studies were performed in anesthetized or curarized animals and employed prolonged washing of the tongue as the gustatory stimulus. Such experimental conditions permit indirect comparisons of the quality and intensity of stimuli eliciting behavioral and electrophysiological responses. However, they are not suited for a more detailed analysis of the electrical concomitants of taste-elicited behavior. Also the belief that taste responses are slow to develop, and therefore unlikely to trigger detectable evoked responses, discouraged attempts to employ in taste studies the techniques which are used in the electrophysiology of vision and audition.

A promising line of electrophysiological investigation of CTA has been started by Halpern and Tapper (1971) who analyzed the licking behavior of CTA-trained rats (300 mM NaCl followed by radiation sickness). During retention testing, rats were exposed to twelve 10-s presentations of 300 mM NaCl alternating with water, and their licking behavior was recorded. Whereas water was freely consumed (50 to 60 licks per the 10-s test), the aversive stimulus elicited only a few licks (4 or less) followed by prolonged cessation of licking. With continuing practice, a single lick was often sufficient for recognition of the aversive stimulus and for its discrimination from other gustatory stimuli (e.g., 500 mM sucrose).

Similar results were obtained in a two-choice situation in which rats were simultaneously offered water and 0.15 M NaCl or LiCl from two drinking spouts placed 20 mm apart (Bureš and Burešová, 1976). The position of the gustatory stimuli was automatically alternated at 4- to 8-s intervals. The change of the fluid did not affect drinking in control rats, which continued to lick at the same spout. When rats with CTA to NaCl and LiCl were drinking water before the switching of the fluids, they made 1–3 licks at the salt solution and then shifted to the other tube which now contained water. Recognition and rejection of the aversive stimulus was completed after approximately 200 ms; licking at the tube which contained water started 500 ms after switching.

A cinematographic analysis of licking movements (Marowitz and Halpern, 1971) showed that 54 ms elapsed from the initiation of the jaw movement to the tongue-to-liquid contact. Since the average lick duration was 40–80 ms and the average licking rate was 6 Hz, about one-third of the interlick interval (168 ms) was occupied by the approach movement. If drinking is suppressed by a single lick, the decision not to make the next lick must occur in the first two-thirds of the interlick interval. Recording of chorda tympani responses to brief (55 ms) artificial licks produced by a fluidic logic-operated stimulus system (Halpern and Marowitz, 1973) indicated that the neural response starts after a 30-ms latency. Thus, stimulus recognition must occur in the 80-ms interval starting 30 ms after the first tongue-lick contact. This interval overlaps with the early premaximum portion of the chorda tympani response and precedes the maximum response (110 ms). The authors suggested that the initial phasic response may trigger simple behavior decisions, whereas late components of the phasic response and the tonic responses are required for the more difficult discriminations. Their work provides important information about the dynamics of the neural mechanisms of the CTA retrieval and delineates the time intervals critical for stimulus recognition and response inhibition. Evoked responses elicited by pulsed gustatory stimuli and recorded in the gustatory cortex of anesthetized rats (Yamamoto and Kawamura, 1972) suggest the possibility of detecting lick- and taste-dependent EEG activity along the gustatory pathways.

## 6.2. EEG Correlates of CTA

Two electrophysiological studies employed hippocampal and cortical EEG as an index of CS recognition. Brozek *et al.* (1974) established a strong saccharin aversion in rats with implanted oral cannulae and hippocampal recording electrodes. Thirty-second perfusion of the oral cavity with a 0.1% saccharin (CS) increased hippocampal theta activity in CTA-trained animals but had little effect in naive rats. Hippocampal activation in CTA-trained animals was suppressed by bilateral functional decortication. Hippocampal reactions accompanied the attempts of the animal to remove the aversive solution by spitting, head shaking, and mouth wiping. Such attempts were absent in functionally decorticate rats.

Burešová and Bureš (unpub.) used the cortical arousal reaction to determine whether CTA retrieval is possible under anesthesia. Animals with a strong conditioned saccharin aversion were anesthetized with urethane (0.9 g/kg). Intraperitoneal injection of 2% sodium saccharin (1% of body weight) caused marked EEG desynchronization in CTA-trained rats but was ineffective in naive animals. This result confirms reports about EEG conditioning under urethane (Sinz, 1971), shows that stimulus recognition is not prevented by anesthesia, and explains CTA extinction induced by the administration of a CS to anesthetized animals (see page 240). Extinction can proceed, however, even in absence of electrocortical arousal (e.g., in functionally decorticate rats).

## 6.3. Unit Activity Correlates of CTA

Unit activity recording in curarized rats was used to determine which neural regions are responsible for the readout of the gustatory information (Aleksanyan, Burešová, Dolbakyan, and Bureš, 1974; Aleksanyan, Burešová, and Bureš, 1976). Naive and CTA-trained rats were immobilized with gallamine iodide. The effect of perfusion of the mouth with a 0.1% saccharin solution was studied by recording unit activity in the reticular formation, the gustatory thalamus, and the lateral and ventromedial hypothalamus. Analysis of computer-plotted, poststimulus histograms showed that the number of responsive units and the types of responses in the reticular formation and the thalamus were similar in naive and CTA-trained rats (Fig. 3). Reactivity of hypothalamic neurons was significantly modified by CTA training. In naive animals saccharin elicited responses in 70% of the neurons in the lateral hypothalamus and in only 30% of the neurons in the ventromedial hypothalamus. This proportion was almost reversed in CTA-trained rats. Taking into account the fact that increased activity of the lateral hypothalamus accompanies feeding and the fact that activation of the ventromedial hypothalamus corresponds to satiety (Oomura, 1969; Kawamura, Lasahara, and Funakoshi, 1970), these results indicate that saccharin stimulates feeding in naive animals and inhibits it in CTA-trained rats. The fact that thalamic responses are not changed by CTA training suggests that the readout occurs at suprathalamic levels that control the hypothalamic mechanisms. Gustatory afferents to the substantia innominata in the ventral forebrain (Norgren, 1974) represent an alternative pathway which may account for the gustatory functions spared by decortication.

## 7. Conclusions

The experimental evidence does not permit a satisfactory description of the physiological mechanisms of CTA. The locus of short-term and

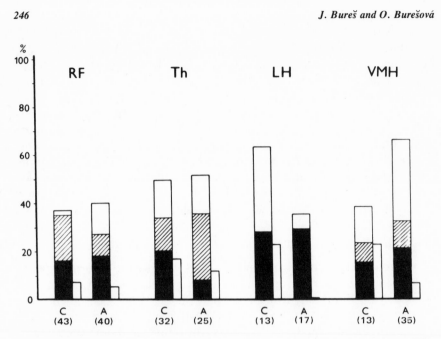

**Figure 3.** Reaction of single units in the reticular formation (RF), gustatory thalamus (Th), lateral hypothalamus (LH), and ventromedial hypothalamus (VMH) to 10-s perfusion of the mouth with 0.1% saccharin in naive (C) and CTA-trained (A) rats. Ordinate: percentage of reacting units. Wide columns: on-reactions (inhibition, black; excitation, white; excitation/inhibition, shaded). Narrow columns: all off-reactions. The numbers below the columns indicate the size of the examined population.

long-term CTA storage remains unknown. Nor is it known where CTA readout causes inhibition of feeding.

Garcia and Ervin (1968) suggested that convergence of gustatory and visceral afferents to the nucleus of the solitary tract provides for formation of the CTA engram in this region and in the adjacent reticular formation. The universal validity of this hypothesis is questionable since CTA can also be established to nongustatory properties of food (smell, color) (the sensory signals of which do not reach the lower brainstem) and to centrally acting stimuli which bypass the visceral input. CTA impairment due to cortical, amygdalar, and hypothalamic lesions indicates that the critical CTA circuits must be sought in the higher centers that mediate the sensory control of feeding. Results of surgical and functional ablation studies and of developmental research suggest that the neural mechanisms of CTA use a complex memory file equipped with two independent inputs.

1. There is a cortical input which is activated by both voluntary eating and unconditioned swallowing, which is associated with the subcortical buffer memory, and which mediates the long CS–UCS delays typical of gustatory visceral learning. This input, which is prevalent in adult animals,

is used for anticipatory evaluation of the visceral consequences of feeding and is essential for acquisition and retrieval of appetitive and aversive feeding habits.

2. There is a subcortical input which corresponds to the preweaning control of food intake and which is activated by innate consummatory behaviors such as sucking and swallowing. Since adverse consequences of sucking are highly improbable, this input has no provisions for delayed learning and is only used for the evaluation of the immediate palatability of gustatory stimuli. A similar limitation applies to the formation of the long-term traces.

During postnatal development the subcortical input gradually becomes less important relative to the cortical input, which becomes vital after weaning, when the animal has to select from a large variety of novel, potentially noxious foods. Evaluation of the anticipated consequences of the ingestion of food which has been associated with poisoning overrides the immediate palatability and inhibits consummatory behavior. The cortical input suppresses the influence of the subcortical input in intact animals; but in functionally decorticate rats, the gustatory memories can only be accessed through the subcortex. Under these conditions gustatory stimuli do not trigger aversive behavior. This failure is due to the impairment of food-rejection mechanisms rather than to nonrecognition of the gustatory trace. In fact, the experience received under CSD is connected with the proper trace, the aversiveness of which is reduced on subsequent testing with the brain intact. The appetitive interpretation of palatable gustatory stimuli presented under bilateral CSD cannot be reversed by poisoning, probably because the cortically accessed short-term memory file contains no gustatory information and the brain has no other means of connecting the gustatory experience with the sickness. The hypothetical cortical and subcortical mechanisms of CTA are schematically illustrated in Figure 4.

This hypothesis, which is derived from experiments on functional decortication, is also supported by the following types of evidence: ablation studies which demonstrate dissociation of the acquisition and the retrieval mechanisms (LH lesions: Schwartz and Teitelbaum, 1974), ablations which produced changes in the immediate palatability and the anticipation of the consequences of food intake (amygdala lesions: Rolls and Rolls, 1973b; Nachman and Ashe, 1974), studies showing the differential effect of ECS on the the short-term memory and consolidation phases of CTA (Kral, 1971a, 1972), studies showing differential effects of anesthesia on the formation and retention of the short-term gustatory trace, and on the acquisition and extinction of CTA.

The interpretation of the experimental data is complicated by the redundancy of the CTA circuits, which can be restored by compensatory processes even after extensive lesions. It appears that the gustatory cortex and the amygdala form important links in the anticipatory regulation of feeding, whereas the hypothalamic centers are sufficient for control of food intake based on palatability alone. The hypothalamus probably participates in CTA acquisition (Roth *et al.*, 1973) and mediation (Alesksanyan *et al.*, 1976); but readout of CTA engrams can proceed even after LH lesions (Schwartz and Teitelbaum, 1974) or during LH stimulation (Wise and Albin, 1973). Thus, it appears that the extrahypothalamic centers which participate in the regulation of feeding (for review, see Grossman, 1975) contribute to the CTA mechanism.

Although the above picture of CTA mechanisms is incomplete and controversial it can serve as a departure point for further research which will be aimed at more specific aspects of the problem and which will use more sophisticated methods (e.g., electrophysiology and neurochemistry).

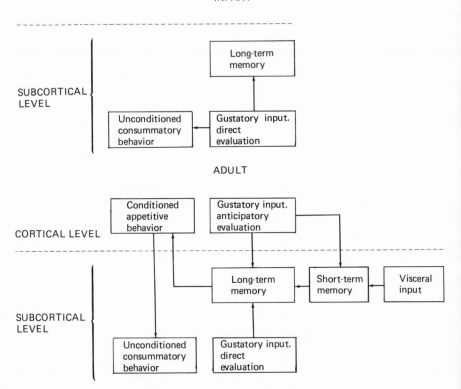

**Figure 4.** Schematic illustration of the hypothetical cortical and subcortical mechanisms of acquisition and extinction of CTA. For details see text.

# 8. References

Ables, M. F., and Benjamin, R. M. Thalamic relay nucleus for taste in albino rats. *Journal of Neurophysiology*, 1960, *23*, 376–382.

Aghajanian, G. K., and Bloom, F. W. The formation of synaptic junctions in developing rat brain: A quantitative electron microscopic study. *Brain Research*, 1967, *6*, 716–727.

Ahlers, R. H., and Best, P. J. Retrograde amnesia for discriminated taste aversions: A memory deficit. *Journal of Comparative and Physiological Psychology*, 1972, *79*, 371–376.

Aleksanyan, Z. A., and Burešová, O., Dolbakyan, E., and Bureš, J. Unit activity changes induced by taste aversion conditioning in rats. *Physiologia Bohemoslovaca*, 1974, *23*, 341.

Aleksanyan, Z. A., Burešová, O., and Bureš, J. Modification of unit responses to gustatory stimuli by conditioned taste aversion in rats. *Physiology and Behavior*, 1976, *17*, 173–179.

Arthur, J. B. Taste aversion learning is impaired by interpolated amygdaloid stimulation but not by posttraining amygdaloid stimulation. *Behavioral Biology*, 1975, *13*, 369–376.

Balagura, S., Ralph, T. L., and Gold, R. Effect of electrical brain stimulation of diencephalic and mesencephalic structures on the generalized NaCl aversion after LiCl poisoning. *Physiologist*, 1972, *15*, 77.

Bass, N. H., Netsky, M. G., and Young, E. Microchemical studies of postnatal development in rat cerebrum: 2. Formation of myelin. *Neurology*, 1969, *19*, 405–414.

Baum, N., Foidart, D. S., and Lapointe, A. Rapid extinction of a conditioned taste aversion following unreinforced intraperitoneal injection of the fluid CS. *Physiology and Behavior*, 1974, *12*, 871–873.

Benjamin, R. M., and Akert, K. Cortical and thalamic areas involved in taste discrimination in the albino rat. *Journal of Comparative Neurology*, 1959, *111*, 231–260.

Benjamin, R. M., and Pfaffman, C. Cortical localization of taste in the albino rat. *Journal of Neurophysiology*, 1955, *18*, 56–64.

Berger, B. D. Conditioning of food aversions by injections of psychoactive drugs. *Journal of Comparative and Physiological Psychology*, 1972, *81*, 21–26.

Berger, B. D., Wise, C. D., and Stein, L. Area postrema damage and bait shyness. *Journal of Comparative and Physiological Psychology*, 1973, *82*, 475–479.

Best, P. J., and Orr, J., Jr. Effects of hippocampal lesions on passive avoidance and taste aversion conditioning. *Physiology and Behavior*, 1973, *10*, 193–196.

Best, P. J., and Zuckerman, K. Subcortical mediation of learned taste aversion. *Physiology and Behavior*, 1971, *7*, 317–320.

Borison, H. L., and Wang, S. C. Physiology and pharmacology of vomiting. *Pharmacological Review*, 1953, *5*, 193–230.

Bradley, R. M., and Mistretta, C. M. Intravascular taste in rats as demonstrated by conditioned aversion to sodium saccharin. *Journal of Comparative and Physiological Psychology*, 1971, *75*, 186–189.

Brady, J. V. The effect of electro-convulsive shock on a conditioned emotional response: The permanence of the effect. *Journal of Comparative and Physiological Psychology*, 1951, *44*, 507–511.

Braun, J. J., Slick, T. B., and Lorden, J. F. Involvement of gustatory neocortex in the learning of taste aversions. *Physiology and Behavior*, 1972, *9*, 637–641.

Braun, J. J., and McIntosh, H., Jr. Learned taste aversions induced by rotational stimulation. *Physiological Psychology*, 1973, *1*, 301–304.

Braveman, N. S. Poison-based avoidance learning with flavored or colored water in guinea pigs. *Learning and Motivation*, 1974, *5*, 182–194.

Braveman, N. S. Relative salience of gustatory and visual cues in the formation of poison-based food aversions by guinea pigs (*Cavia porcellus*). *Behavioral Biology*, 1975, *14*, 189–199.

Brozek, G., Burešová, O., and Bureš, J. Effect of bilateral cortical spreading depression on the hippocampal theta activity induced by oral infusion of aversive gustatory stimulus. *Experimental Neurology*, 1974, *42*, 661–668.

Bureš, J., and Burešová, O. Gustatory recognition time in rats with conditioned taste aversion. *Physiologia Bohemoslovaca*, 1976, *25*, 257.

Bureš, J., and Burešová, O. Behavioral and electrophysiological analysis of the conditioned taste aversion in rats. In E. M. Kreps (Ed.), *Modern trends in neurophysiology* (in Russian), Leningrad: Nanka, 1977, pp. 60–67.

Bureš, J., Burešová, O., and Křivanek, J. *The mechanism and applications of Leao's spreading depression of electroencephalographic activity*. New York, London: Academic Press, 1974.

Bureš, J., Fifková, E., and Mares, P. Spreading depression and maturation of some forebrain structures in rats. In P. Kellaway, and I. Petersen (Eds.), *Neurological and electroencephalographic correlative studies in infancy*, New York: Grune and Stratton, 1964, pp. 27–36.

Burešová, O. Differential role of cerebral cortex and subcortical centers in the acquisition and extinction of conditioned taste aversion. *Activitas Nervosa Superior*. 1976, *18*, 118–119.

Burešová, O., and Bureš, J. Cortical and subcortical components of the conditioned saccharin aversion. *Physiology and Behavior*, 1973, *11*, 435–439.

Burešová, O., and Bureš, J. Functional decortication in the CS–US interval decreases efficiency of taste aversion learning. *Behavioral Biology*, 1974, *12*, 357–364.

Burešová, O., and Bureš, J. Functional decortication by cortical spreading depression does not prevent forced extinction of conditioned saccharin aversion in rats. *Journal of Comparative and Physiological Psychology*, 1975a, *88*, 47–52.

Burešová, O., and Bureš, J. The antagonistic influence of anesthesia and functional decortication on conditioned taste aversion. *Activitas Nervosa Superior* (Praha), 1975b, *17*, 58.

Campbell, B. A., Jaynes, J., and Misanin, J. Retention of a light–dark discrimination in rats of different ages. *Journal of Comparative and Physiological Psychology*, 1968, *66*, 467–472.

Campbell, B. A., Misanin, J. R., White, B. C., and Lytle, L. D. Species differences in ontogeny of memory: Indirect support for neural maturation as a determinant of forgetting. *Journal of Comparative and Physiological Psychology*, 1974, *87*, 193–202.

Cappell, H. D., LeBlanc, A. E., and Endrenyi, L. Effects of chlordiazepoxide and ethanol on the extinction of a conditioned taste aversion. *Physiology and Behavior*, 1972, *9*, 167–169.

Cappell, H., LeBlanc, A. E., and Herling S. Modification of the punishing effects of psychoactive drugs in rats by previous drug experience. *Journal of Comparative and Physiological Psychology*, 1975, *89*, 347–356.

Capretta, P. J., and Moore, M. J. Appropriateness of reinforcement to cue in the conditioning of food aversion in chickens (*Gallus gallus*). *Journal of Comparative and Physiological Psychology*, 1970, *72*, 85–89.

Capretta, P. J., Rawls, L. H. Establishment of a flavor preference in rats: Importance of nursing and weaning experience. *Journal of Comparative and Physiological Psychology*, 1974, *86*, 670–673.

Carey, R. J. Quinine and saccharin preference-aversion threshold determinations in rats with septal ablations. *Journal of Comparative and Physiological Psychology,* 1971, *76,* 316–326.

Cooper, G. P., and Kimeldorf, D. J. Electroencephalographic desynchronization in irradiated rats with transected spinal cords. *Science,* 1964, *143,* 1040–1041.

Coulon, J. Influence de l'isolement social sur le comportment du cobaye. *Behaviour,* 1971, *38,* 93–120.

Crosby, E. C., Humphrey, T., and Lauer, E. W. *Correlative anatomy of the nervous system,* New York: Macmillan, 1962.

Davis, J. L., and Bureš, J. Disruption of saccharin-aversion learning in rats by cortical spreading depression in the CS–US interval. *Journal of Comparative and Physiological Psychology,* 1972, *80,* 398–402.

DeCastro, J. M., and Balagura, S. Fornicotomy: Effect on the primary and secondary punishment of mouse killing by LiCl poisoning. *Behavioral Biology,* 1975, *13,* 483–489.

Deza, L., and Eidelberg, E. Development of cortical electrical activity in the rat. *Experimental Neurology,* 1967, *17,* 425–438.

Divac, I., Gade, A., and Wikmark, R. E. G. Taste aversion in rats with lesions in the frontal lobes: No evidence for interoceptive agnosia. *Physiological Psychology,* 1975, *8,* 43–48.

Domjan, M. Role of ingestion in odor-toxicosis learning in the rat. *Journal of Comparative and Physiological Psychology,* 1973, *84,* 507–521.

Emmers, R., and Nocenti, M. R. Role of thalamic gustatory nucleus in diet selection by normal and parathyroidectomized rats. *Proceedings of the Society for Experimental Biology and Medicine,* 1967, *125,* 1264–1270.

Feigley, D. A., and Spear, N. E. Effect of age and punishment condition on long-term retention by the rat of active and passive-avoidance learning. *Journal of Comparative and Physiological Psychology,* 1970, *73,* 515–526.

Fishberg, A. M., Hitzig, W. M., and King, R. H. Measurement of the circulation time with saccharin. *Proceedings of the Society for Experimental Biology and Medicine,* 1933, *30,* 651–652.

Freedman, N. L., and Bureš, J. Conditions of phasic impairment of avoidance responding during bilateral spreading depression. *Journal of Comparative and Physiological Psychology,* 1972, *78,* 433–441.

Gadusek, F. J., and Kalat, J. W. Effects of scopolamine on retention of taste-aversion learning in rats. *Physiological Psychology,* 1975, *3,* 130–132.

Galef, B. G., Jr., and Clark, M. M. Social factors in the poison avoidance and feeding behavior of wild and domesticated rat pups. *Journal of Comparative and Physiological Psychology,* 1971, *75,* 341–357.

Galef, B. G., Jr., and Clark, M. M. Mother's milk and adult presence: Two factors determining initial dietary selection by weanling rats. *Journal of Comparative and Physiological Psychology,* 1972, *78,* 220–225.

Galef, B. G., Jr., and Henderson, P. W. Mother's milk: A determinant of the feeding preferences of weaning rat pups. *Journal of Comparative and Physiological Psychology,* 1972, *78,* 213–219.

Galef, B. G., Jr., and Sherry, D. F. Mother's milk: A medium for the transmission of cues reflecting the flavor of mother's diet. *Journal of Comparative and Physiological Psychology,* 1973, *83,* 374–378.

Garcia, J., and Ervin, F. R. Gustatory–visceral and telereceptor cutaneous conditioning: Adaptation in internal and external milieus. *Communications in Behavioral Biology,* 1968, *1,* 389–415.

Garcia, J., and Kimeldorf, D. J. Temporal relationships within the conditioning of a saccharin aversion through radiation exposure. *Journal of Comparative and Physiological Psychology,* 1957, *50,* 180–183.

Garcia, J., and Koelling, R. A. A comparison of aversions induced by X-rays, toxins, and drugs in the rat. *Radiation Research Supplement,* 1967, *7,* 439–450.

Geller, I., and Seifter, J. The effects of meprobamate, barbiturates, *d*-amphetamine and promazine on experimentally induced conflict in the rat. *Psychopharmacologia,* 1960, *1,* 482–492.

Gold, R. M., and Proulx, D. M. Bait-shyness acquisition is impaired by VMH lesion that produce obesity. *Journal of Comparative and Physiological Psychology,* 1973, *84,* 488–495.

Green, L., and Rachlin, H. The effect of rotation on the learning of taste aversions. *Bulletin of the Psychonomic Society,* 1973, *1,* 137–138.

Grossman, S. P. Role of the hypothalamus in the regulation of food and water intake. *Psychological Review,* 1975, *82,* 200–224.

Grote, F. W., Jr., and Brown, R. T. Rapid learning of passive avoidance by weanling rats: Conditioned taste aversion. *Psychonomic Science,* 1971, *25,* 163–164.

Halpern, B. P., and Marowitz, L. A. Taste responses to lick-duration stimuli. *Brain Research,* 1973, *57,* 473–478.

Halpern, B. P., and Tapper, D. M. Taste stimuli: Quality coding time. *Science,* 1971, *171,* 1256–1258.

Hankins, W. G., Garcia, J., and Rusiniak, K. W. Dissociation of odor and taste in bait shyness. *Behavioral Biology,* 1973, *8,* 407–419.

Hankins, W. G., Garcia, J., and Rusiniak, K. W. Cortical lesions: Flavor-illness and noise–shock conditioning. *Behavioral Biology,* 1974, *10,* 173–181.

Himwich, W. A. (Ed.), *Developmental neurobiology.* Springfield, Ill.: Charles C Thomas, 1970.

Hobbs, S. H., Elkins, R. L., and Peacock, L. J. Taste-aversion conditioning in rats with septal lesions. *Behavioral Biology,* 1974, *11,* 239–245.

Hunt, H. F., and Brady, J. V. Some effects of electroconvulsive shock on a conditioned emotional response ("anxiety"). *Journal of Comparative and Physiological Psychology.* 1951. *44,* 88–98.

Hutchison, S. L., Jr. Taste aversion in albino rats using centrifugal spin as an unconditioned stimulus. *Psychological Reports,* 1973, *33,* 467–470.

Ionescu, B., Burešová, O., and Bureš, J. The significance of gustatory and visual cues for conditioned food aversion in rats and chickens. *Physiologia Bohemoslovaca,* 1975, *24,* 58.

Johnson, C., Beaton, R., and Hall, K. Poison-based avoidance learning in nonhuman primates: Use of visual cues. *Physiology and Behavior,* 1975, *14,* 403–407.

Kalat, J. W. Taste-aversion learning in infant guinea pigs. *Developmental Psychobiology,* 1975, *8*(5), 383–387.

Kawamura, Y., Lasahara, Y., and Funakoshi, M. A possible mechanism for rejection behavior to strong salt solution. *Physiology and Behavior,* 1970, *5,* 67–74.

Kesner, R. P., Berman, R. F., Burton, B., and Hankins, W. G. Effects of electrical stimulation of amygdala upon neophobia and taste aversion. *Behavioral Biology,* 1975, *13,* 349–358.

Khanna, Y., Nayar, U., Anand, B. K. Effect of fenfluramine on the single neuron activities of the hypothalamic feeding center. *Physiology and Behavior,* 1972, *8,* 453–456.

Klein, S. B., Barter, M. J., Murphy, A. L., and Richardson, J. H. Aversion to low doses of mercuric chloride in rats. *Physiological Psychology,* 1974, *2,*(3A), 397–400.

Kral, P. A. Interpolation of electroconvulsive shock during CS–US interval as an impediment to the conditioning of taste aversion. *Psychonomic Science,* 1970, *19,* 36–37.

Kral, P. A. Electroconvulsive shock during the taste–illness interval: Evidence for induced disassociation. *Physiology and Behavior,* 1971a, *7,* 667–670.

Kral, P. A. ECS between tasting and illness: Effects of current parameters on a taste aversion. *Physiology and Behavior*, 1971b, *7*, 779–782.

Kral, P. A. Effects of scopolamine injection during CS–US interval on conditioning. *Psychological Reports*, 1971c, *28*, 690.

Kral, P. A. Localized ECS impedes taste aversion learning. *Behavioral Biology*, 1972, *7*, 761–765.

Kral, P. A., and Beggarly, H. D. Electroconvulsive shock impedes association formation: Conditioned taste aversion paradigm. *Physiology and Behavior*, 1973, *10*, 145–147.

Kral, P. A., and St. Omer, V. V. Beta-adrenergic receptor involvement in the mediation of learned taste aversions. *Psychopharmacologia*, 1972, *26*, 79–83.

Lehr, P. P., and Nachman, M. Lateralization of learned taste aversion by cortical spreading depression. *Physiology and Behavior*, 1973, *10*, 79–83.

Lett, B. T., and Harley, C. W. Stimulation of lateral hypothalamus during a sickness attenuates learned flavor aversion. *Physiology and Behavior*, 1974, *12*, 79–83.

Levitt, R. A., and Krikstone, B. J. Cortical spreading depression and thirst. *Physiology and Behavior*, 1968, *3*, 421–423.

Lorden, J. F., Kenfield, M., and Braun, J. J. Response suppression to odors paired with toxicosis. *Learning and Motivation*, 1970, *1*, 391–400.

Margules, D. L. Alpha-adrenergic receptors in hypothalamus for the suppression of feeding behavior by satiety. *Journal of Comparative and Physiological Psychology*, 1970a, *73*, 1–12.

Margules, D. L. Beta-adrenergic receptors in the hypothalamus for learned and unlearned taste aversions. *Journal of Comparative and Physiological Psychology*, 1970b, *73*, 13–21.

Marowitz, L. A., and Halpern, B. P. The effects of behavioral constraints upon licking pattern. *Physiology and Behavior*, 1971, *11*, 259–263.

McGowan, B. K., Garcia, J., Ervin, F. R., and Schwartz, J. Effects of septal lesions on bait-shyness in the rat. *Physiology and Behavior*, 1969, *4*, 907–909.

McGowan, B. K., Hankins, W. G., and Garcia, J. Limbic lesions and control of the internal and external environment. *Behavioral Biology*, 1972, *7*, 841–852.

MacLean, P. D. The limbic system with respect to self-preservation and preservation of the species. *Journal of Nervous and Mental Diseases*, 1958, *127*, 1–11.

Miller, C. R., Elkins, R. L., and Peacock, L. J. Disruption of a radiation-induced preference shift by hippocampal lesions. *Physiology and Behavior*, 1971, *6*, 283–285.

Millner, J. R., and Palfai, T. Metrazol impairs conditioned aversion produced by LiCl: A time dependent effect. *Pharmacology, Biochemistry and Behavior*, 1975, *3*, 201–204.

Nachman, M. Learned taste and temperature aversions due to lithium chloride sickness after temporal delays. *Journal of Comparative and Physiological Psychology*, 1970a, *73*, 22–30.

Nachman, M. Limited effects of electroconvulsive shock on memory of taste stimulation. *Journal of Comparative and Physiological Psychology*, 1970b, *73*, 31–37.

Nachman, M., and Ashe, J. H. Effects of basolateral amygdala lesions on neophobia, learned taste aversions, and sodium appetite in rats. *Journal of Comparative and Physiological Psychology*, 1974, *87*, 622–643.

Norgren, R. Gustatory afferents to ventral forebrain. *Brain Research*, 1974, *81*, 285–295.

Norgren, R., and Leonard, C. M. Ascending central gustatory connections. *Journal of Comparative Neurology*, 1973, *150*, 217–238.

Norgren, R., and Pfaffmann, C. The pontine taste area in the rat. *Brain Research*, 1975, *91*, 99–117.

Oakley, B., and Benjamin, R. M. Neural mechanisms of taste. *Physiological Review*, 1966, *46*, 173–211.

Oomura, Y., Ooyama, H., Naka, F., Yamamoto, T., Ono, T., and Kobayashi, N. Some stochastical patterns of single unit discharge in the cat hypothalamus under chronic conditions. *Annals of the New York Academy of Sciences,* 1969, *157,* 666–689.

Peters, R. H., and Reich, M. J. Effects of ventromedial hypothalamic lesions on conditioned sucrose aversions in rats. *Journal of Comparative and Physiological Psychology,* 1973, *84,* 502–506.

Pfaffman, C. *Olfaction and taste.* New York: Rockefeller University Press, 1969.

Ralph, T. L., and Balagura, S. Effect of intracranial electrical stimulation on the primary learned aversion to LiCl and the generalized aversion to NaCl. *Journal of Comparative and Physiological Psychology,* 1974, *86,* 664–669.

Riege, W. H. Disruption of radiation-induced aversion to saccharin by electroconvulsive shock. *Physiology and Behavior,* 1969, *4,* 157–161.

Riley, A. L., and Baril, L. L. Conditioned aversions: A bibliography. *Animal Learning and Behavior,* 1976, *4,* 15–135.

Roll, D. L., and Smith, J. C. Conditioned taste aversion in anesthetized rats. In M. E. P. Seligman and J. L. Hager (Eds.), *Biological boundaries of learning.* New York: Appleton-Century-Crofts, 1972, pp. 98–102.

Rolls, B. J., and Rolls, E. T. Effects of lesions in the basolateral amygdala on fluid intake in the rat. *Journal of Comparative and Physiological Psychology,* 1973a, *83,* 240–247.

Rolls, E. T., and Rolls, B. J. Altered food preferences after lesions in the basolateral region of the amygdala in the rat. *Journal of Comparative and Physiological Psychology,* 1973b, *83,* 248–259.

Roth, S. R., Schwartz, M., and Teitelbaum, P. Failure of recovered lateral hypothalamic rats to learn specific food aversions. *Journal of Comparative and Physiological Psychology,* 1973, *83,* 184–197.

Rozin, P., and Kalat, J. W. Specific hungers and poison avoidance as adaptive specializations of learning. *Psychological Review,* 1971, *78,* 459–486.

Rozin, P., and Ree, P. Long extension of effective CS–US interval by anesthesia between CS and US. *Journal of Comparative and Physiological Psychology,* 1972, *80,* 43–48.

Salas, M., Schapiro, S., and Guzman-Flores, C. Development of olfactory bulb discrimination between maternal and food odors. *Physiology and Behavior,* 1970, *5,* 1261–1264.

Sarborough, B. B., and McLaurin, W. A. The effect of intraperitoneal injection on aversive behavior conditioning with X-irradiation. *Radiation Research,* 1961, *15,* 829–839.

Scherrer, J. Electrophysiological aspects of cortical development *Progress in Brain Research,* 1968, *22,* 480–489.

Schneider, A. M. Effects of unilateral and bilateral spreading depression on water intake. *Psychonomic Science,* 1965, *3,* 287–288.

Schwartz and Teitelbaum, P. Dissociation between learning and remembering in rats with lesions in the lateral hypothalamus. *Journal of Comparative and Physiological Psychology,* 1974, *87,* 384–398.

Sinz, R. Ausbildung bedingter Reaktionen bei Ratten in Urethannarkose und ihre Prüfung im Wachzustand. *Acta Biologica et Medica Germanica,* 1971, *26,* 733–746.

Smith, J. C., and Morris, D. D. The effects of atropine sulfate and physostigmine on the conditioned aversion to saccharin solution with X-rays as the unconditioned stimulus. In T. J. Haley and R. S. Snider (Eds.), *Response of the nervous system to ionizing radiation.* New York: Little, Brown, and Company, 1964, 662–672.

Smith, N. F. Effects of interpolated learning on the retention of an escape response in rats as a function of age. *Journal of Comparative and Physiological Psychology,* 1968, *65,* 422–426.

Supak, T. D., Macrides, F., and Chorover, S. L. The bait-shyness effect extended to olfactory discrimination. *Communications in Behavioral Biology,* 1971, *5,* 321–324.

Teitelbaum, P. The encephalization of hunger. *Progress in Physiological Psychology*, 1971, *4*, 319–350.

Taukulis, H. K. Odor aversions produced over long CS–US delays. *Behavioral Biology*, 1974, *10*, 505–510.

Vance, W. B. Hypogeusia and taste preference behavior in the rat. *Life Sciences*, 1967, *6*, 743–748.

Vogel, J. R. Antagonism of a learned taste aversion following repeated administrations of electroconvulsive shock. *Physiological Psychology*, 1974, *2*, 493–496.

Vogel, J. R. Conditioning of taste aversion by drugs of abuse. In H. Lal and J. Singh (Eds.), *Neurobiology of drug dependence, Volume 1, Behavioral analysis of drug dependence*. New York: Futura, 1975.

Weisman, R. N., and Hamilton, L. W. Increased conditioned gustatory aversion following VMH lesions in rats. *Physiology and Behavior*, 1972, *9*, 801–804.

Wilcoxon, H. C., Dragoin, W. B., and Kral, P. A. Illness-induced aversions in rats and quail: Relative salience of visual and gustatory cues. *Science*, 1971, *171*, 826–828.

Wise, R. A., and Albin, J. Stimulation-induced eating disrupted by a conditioned taste aversion. *Behavioral Biology*, 1973, *9*, 289–297.

Yamamoto, T., and Kawamura, Y. Summated cerebral responses to taste stimuli in rat. *Physiology and Behavior*, 1972, *9*, 789–793.

Zeman, W., and Innes, J. R. M. *Craigie's neuroanatomy of the rat*. New York, London: Academic Press, 1963.

# Index